BIBLE KEY WORDS

BIBLE KEY WORDS

from GERHARD KITTEL'S

THEOLOGISCHES WÖRTERBUCH
ZUM NEUEN TESTAMENT

TRANSLATED AND EDITED BY

J. R. COATES

A ONE-VOLUME EDITION CONTAINING

FOUR BOOKS:

I. LOVE

by Gottfried Quell *and* Ethelbert Stauffer

II. THE CHURCH

by Karl Ludwig Schmidt

III. SIN

by Gottfried Quell, Georg Bertram,
Gustav Stählin *and* Walter Grundmann

IV. RIGHTEOUSNESS

by Gottfried Quell *and* Gottlob Schrenk

Harper & Brothers, Publishers, New York

BIBLE KEY WORDS
Volume III, *Sin*, and Volume IV, *Righteousness*,
Copyright, 1951, by Harper & Brothers
Printed in the United States of America
All rights in this book are reserved.
No part of the book may be used or
reproduced in any manner whatsoever with-
out written permission except in the case
of brief quotations embodied in critical
articles and reviews. For information address
Harper & Brothers, 49 East 33rd Street,
New York 16, N. Y.

PREFACE

THE most important happening of our time is the maturing of the catholic consciousness of the world-wide Christian Church. This miracle of the Holy Spirit is being wrought largely through the re-emergence of Biblical theology, which not only brings the Word of God again to bear livingly upon the tragic need of individuals, but also challenges the ideologies that are widely destroying human freedom, and equips the Christian as a witness to God and His Kingdom.

The work of scholars in many fields during the last hundred years, often misunderstood and even despised by those who enjoy the benefit of their discoveries, has resulted in a new apprehension of the original force of the Bible as the dynamic record of the creative and saving acts of God. This force comes through the words which express the faith of those who tell the story, enabling us with them to discern the working of God in historical events and in the lives of individuals. Thus light comes, not only upon the past, but also upon our path to-day. And with light comes power. Bible news is so good that it liberates mind and heart. This is true par excellence of the New Testament, whose words are the vehicle of that power of God which wrought in Christ and enters into our experience as the Holy Spirit.

To understand what we read, we must learn what we can of the mental world of the writers and their first readers. Here we depend upon scholars, and by the mercy of God we have to-day the help of many specialists, converging upon these words of life. Among books which make this help available, the latest and

v

best is the *Theologisches Wörterbuch zum Neuen Testament*, which began to appear in Germany in 1933 under the editorship of the late lamented Gerhard Kittel, and is now more than half completed. A very large body of writers is responsible for this immense work, and it is highly significant, in view of the fact that our Lord and His Apostles were Jews in a Greek-speaking world, that many of them are authorities on the Old Testament, the Septuagint, and first century Judaism. All of them are convinced that God is in Christ reconciling the world unto Himself, and this gives their work an inspiring quality not always found in writings of scientific integrity.

The present volume is the first of a series of manuals which it is hoped to publish, giving selected articles from the dictionary in English. Its subject is obviously central both for theology and for religion in a disordered world. In the preface to his translation of the first part of Anders Nygren's famous book, *Agape and Eros*, A. G. Hebert says, " There can be no right answer to the question, ' What is Christianity ? ' except by a clear view of the real meaning of the Agape of the New Testament, and its difference from pagan Eros." It is noteworthy that the two scholars, whose work on the Biblical doctrine of love is presented here, are both contributors to the article on God, and Gottfried Quell also writes the long and important section on " the LORD " in the Old Testament.

Dr. Gottfried Quell is Professor of Old Testament at Rostock. His best known books are—*Die Auffassung des Todes in Israel* (1925) and *Das kultische Problem der Psalmen* (1926).

Dr. Ethelbert Stauffer is New Testament Professor at Erlangen, author of *Grundbegriffe einer Morphologie des Neutestamentlichen Denkens* (1929), *Die Theologie des Neuen Testamentes* (1941), *Christus und die Caesaren* (1948).

The Hebrew approach is characteristic of the whole dictionary—as it is of Ethelbert Stauffer's recent book on N.T. theology—and reinforces what James Moffatt said in *Love in the New Testament*, pp. 6 f. : " What marks off Christianity is not the conviction that men have discovered a new depth in love divine, but that something has happened, something which has revealed that love in a new scope and reach. For the realization of this, let us confess at the outset, Christians were deeply indebted to the tradition of Hebrew religion. It was an inheritance which helped them in two special ways. The conception of the ' Covenant' as the bond between God and His people which involved His entrance into human life and history with a purpose of loving grace, made it possible to believe that the process of time could embrace a Divine Act of eternal significance. Human life was not a mere drift ; history was not an illusive series of happenings, too unsubstantial for a decisive Deed to be done among and for mankind. Furthermore, there were prophetic hopes and hints of a redemptive value attaching to the sufferings of the good, and even of atonement for sin being made through the loving obedience and spiritual agony of a Servant whose rôle was in a deep sense ethical. It was the grasp of such truths that enabled the primitive Church to understand the divine love as more than illustrated in the life of Jesus, and as something determinative of human destiny."

IN MEMORIAM GERHARD KITTEL

GERHARD KITTEL was born at Breslau on 23rd September, 1888, his father being the famous scholar Rudolf Kittel, editor of *Biblia Hebraica* and author of many important books on the Old Testament.

After studying theology and oriental languages at various universities, and writing a thesis on the Odes of Solomon, he became a lecturer at Kiel in 1913, and received his doctorate in 1917 at Leipzig, where he was appointed professor. In 1926 he was given a chair at Tübingen, where he died on 11th July, 1948.

His best known publications are *Jesus und die Rabbinen*, 1914 ; *Rabbinica*, 1920 ; *Die religiöse und kirchliche Lage in Deutschland*, 1921 ; *Der Midrasch Sifre zum Deuteronomium*, 1922 ; *Die Probleme des palästinensischen Spätjudemtums und des Urchristentums*, 1926 ; *Der " historische Jesus "*, 1930 ; *Das Urchristentum und die Religionsgeschichte*, 1932 ; *Die Judenfrage*, 1933 ; *Adolf Schlatter* (Rede), 1938 ; *Dichter, Bibel und Bibelrevision*, 1939 ; *Christus und Imperator*, 1939 ; and finally the *Theologisches Wörterbuch zum Neuen Testament*, from 1933 onwards.

When the first volume of the dictionary appeared, Kittel expressed his hope that the work might not only serve the scholar but also help the preacher, and in the preface to Vol. II he sees the labour which unites him and his colleagues as a contribution to the healing and true unity of the Church, " for both of these flow only from the message of the New Testament ". Before he died he had the satisfaction of knowing that all these aims were being realised. One of his fellow-workers has described him as " a genius of an editor, who knew how to bring together in the common task men of widely separated and often hostile groups ".

Like his father, Gerhard Kittel held views on the Jewish Question which were not shared by the majority of his fellow-Christians.* But, paradoxically, one of

* See J. R. Porter in *Theology*, Nov. 1947.

the outstanding merits of his dictionary is that it does full justice to the bearing of Hebrew and Rabbinical studies on the interpretation of the New Testament. So much so that these volumes are as indispensable to students of the Old Testament as they are to those of the New.

Gerhard Kittel will be remembered, not only as a great scholar, who illuminated the study of the New Testament by his work on Judaism in the Hellenistic period, but as a man of simple Christian faith, who could say of his imprisonment by the French after the war, in a letter to a German friend, that it was one of the most precious times of his life, for which he could only thank God. In 1938, when clouds were gathering, he wrote to me of the need to think much of one another, and of Him who has power even to break down the walls which separate nation from nation. We may well apply to him the word ἀκέραιος, whose meaning he himself gives as " one who maintains his integrity in the face of evil " (Inhaber der dem Bösen gegenüber bewahrten Integrität).

J. R. COATES.

CONTENTS

BIBLIOGRAPHY

J. Ziegler : Die Liebe Gottes bei den Propheten, 1930.

G. Winter : Zeitschr. A.T. Wiss. IX, 211 ff., 1889.

W. Lütgert : Die Liebe im N.T., 1905.

B. B. Warfield : Love in the N.T. (Princeton Th. Rev., XVI, 153 ff.), 1918.

P. Battifol : Etudes d'histoire et de theologie positive, I, 283 ff., 1926.

H. Preisker : Die urchristliche Botschaft der Liebe Gottes, 1930.

A. Nygren : Agape and Eros, 1932, 1938, 1939 (Swedish, 1930, 1936.)

E. Stauffer : Sittlichkeit des Urchristentums (R.G.G., V, 530 ff.).

H. Riesenfeld : Etude bibliographique sur la notion biblique d' ΑΓΑΠΗ (Conjectanea Neotestamentica, V).

H. Sahlin : I Esdras iv et I Cor. xiii (Conj. Neot. V).

H. Riesenfeld : Note sur I Cor. xiii (Conj. Neot. X).

Maximus Confessor (d. 662) : κεφάλαια περὶ ἀγάπης (Migne P.G. XC, 960 ff.).

S. Kierkegaard : Works of Love, 1946. (Danish 1847.)

M. Scheler : Wesen und Formen der Sympathie, 1926.

H. Scholz : Eros und Caritas, 1929.

L. Grünhut : Eros und Agape, 1931.

H. Reiner : Die Goldene Regel (Z. f. Philos. Forsch., III, 1).

[R. H. Charles : Rel. Dev. betw. the O. and N.T., 133-158, 1914.

J. R. Coates : The Christ of Revolution, 1920.

W. A. Curtis : Jesus Christ the Teacher, 179-190, 1943.

C. Gore : The Philosophy of the Good Life, chap. vii, 1930 (Murray) ; 1935 (Dent).

T. W. Manson : The Teaching of Jesus, 285-312, 1931.

J. Moffatt : Love in the N.T., 1929.

J. Oman : Grace and Personality, 93-138, 1925 (3rd. ed.).

F. C. Porter : The Mind of Christ in Paul, 1930.

O. S. Rankin : Israel's Wisdom Lit., 35-52, 1936.

C. E. Raven : Jesus and the Gospel of Love, 1931.

C. A. A. Scott : [N.T. Ethics, 1930].

Square brackets, here and elsewhere, indicate additions by the translator.

I

LOVE

BY

GOTTFRIED QUELL &
ETHELBERT STAUFFER

Translated from the German
first edition, Stuttgart, 1933
and with additional notes
by J. R. Coates

I. LOVE IN THE OLD TESTAMENT

1. LINGUISTIC MATERIAL

THE idea of love is most commonly expressed in the O.T. by the root *'ahebh*[1] and its derivatives *'ohebh*, *'ᵃhabhim*, *'ahᵃbhah*. As in our own language, the same word is used in relation to both persons and things or actions, and its employment for religious purposes is very enlightening. The LXX equivalent is generally *ἀγαπᾶν*,[2] occasionally in secular usage *φιλεῖν* (ten times ; *φιλία* five times for *'ahᵃbhah*), *ἐρᾶσθαι* and *φιλιάζειν* (once or twice).

Next we have the root *rḥm*, common to all Semitic languages, the verb appearing in the O.T., with one exception,[3] only in the Piel. This usually indicates sympathy with those who need help,[4] and is therefore often used to express the love of God. *Raḥum*

---

[1] The etymology is obscure ; for various theories see J. Zeigler, Die Liebe Gottes bei den Propheten (1930), 13 f.

[2] *Ἀγαπᾶν* occurs frequently in the LXX, generally as the translation of *'ahebh* and its derivatives, five times of *riḥam*, twice of *hapheç*, once of *raçah*, and occasionally of other roots, sometimes with a certain relevance (e.g. *ṣuth* Hiph., *pathah* Pi., *shaʿaʿ* Pilp.), but sometimes quite irrelevantly (e.g. *boʾ* Hiph. at II Sam. vii, 18 ; I Chron. xvii, 16 for theological reasons, *hataʾ* and *ʿasch*).

The noun *ἀγάπη* occurs about twenty times, and *ἀγάπησις* about ten, the MSS. often differing in their usage. Both represent *'ahᵃbhah* in all cases except Hab. iii, 4, where *ἀγάπησις* is a paraphrase for *ḥebhion*, either for theological reasons or by mistake. There is no Hebrew equivalent in Wis. iii, 6 ; vi, 18 ; Ecclus. xlviii, 11.

[3] Psalm xviii, 1 (2), Qal, of love to God.

[4] The relation of the verb to the noun *rehem* (womb) and to the abstract plural *raḥᵃmim* is obscure and disputed. (Cf. Ziegler, op. cit. 36 f.) No conclusions can be drawn from it as to the interpretation of particular passages.

(merciful) is applied almost exclusively to God.[1]
Ἀγαπᾶν appears in the LXX as a translation of *rhm*
only five times ; the ordinary equivalents are ἐλεεῖν
(twenty-six times) and οἰκτειρεῖν (ten times).

Other roots to be considered are *hapheç*[2] (LXX
mostly ἐθέλειν, sometimes βούλεσθαι, βουλεύεσθαι, εὐδοκεῖν
and ἀγαπᾶν) and *raçah*[3] (LXX εὐδοκεῖν, προσδέχεσθαι,
παραδέχεσθαι, εὐλογεῖν, ἀγαπᾶν), which are both followed
by the preposition *b*ᵉ to indicate the person or thing
in which pleasure is taken ; *hashaq*[4] means " to be
lovingly attached to " (LXX προαιρεῖσθαι, ἐνθυμεῖσθαι,
ἐλπίζειν) ; *habhabh*[5] is common in Aramaic, but only
occurs at Deut. xxxiii, 3 in the O.T. ; *'aghabh*, meaning
woman's bodily desire (except Jer. iv, 30), is confined
to secular usage,[6] like the nouns *dodhim* and *y*ᵉ*dhidhoth ;*
yadhidh (beloved) also occurs in the phrase *y*ᵉ*dhidh*
Yahwe (beloved of Yahwe).[7]

Love is thus shown in the O.T. to be fundamentally a spontaneous feeling [8] which impels to self-

[1] Ps. cxii, 4 is an exception. A favourite expression is *rahum*
*w*ᵉ*hannun.*

[2] With erotic meaning Gen. xxxiv, 19 ; Deut. xxi, 14 ; Esther
ii, 14 ; for friendship I Sam. xix, 1, etc. (For religious use see
note 2, p. 16.) In I Sam. xviii, 22 it is synonymous with *'ahebh.*

[3] *raçah* emphasises the idea of acceptance. *raçuy* means
" beloved " rather than " loved " (Deut. xxxiii, 24 ; Job xx, 10 ;
Esther x, 3) ; cf. I Sam. xxix, 4, Hithp., " makes himself acceptable ". This fits the word for use in worship. Cf. note 1, p. 16.

[4] With erotic meaning Gen. xxxiv, 8 ; Deut. xxi, 11. With
God as subject only Deut. vii, 7 ; x, 15, where it goes with *bahar,*
" choose ". In Psalm xci, 14 it indicates piety. Elsewhere the
meaning is weakened to " wishing " (I Kings ix, 1, 19 ; II Chron.
viii, 6). The Pi. and Pu. are used as technical building terms in
Exod. xxvii, 17 ; xxxviii, 17, 28.

[5] LXX ἐφείσατο.   [6] LXX ἐπέθετο, " attached herself ".

[7] See notes on page 15.

[8] Cf. e.g. Jer. xxxi, 20 : " my bowels are troubled ". Similarly
Exod. xxxiii, 19 can be understood untheologically : " I will
show mercy on whom I will show mercy ".

sacrifice[1] or, in the case of things, to grasping the object which awakens desire, or to performing the action which gives pleasure. Love is an inexplicable personal force : $m^{e'}odh$, " might " (Deut. vi, 5). To give this feeling its right, means to love with all the heart and soul and might (Deut. vi, 5 ; xiii. 4). Life swings on the poles of hate and love (Eccles. iii, 8 ; ix, 6). Rooted as it is in the sex life,[2] love finds its proper objects in persons. Where things or occupations are said to be loved, the language seems faded and metaphorical,[3] and it is reasonable to suppose that the ultimate ground and origin of the idea are only found in the love of person for person. This is always the case where the word is used in a religious sense. Everywhere in the O.T. God's love implies his personality ; just as loving him without an image means loving God himself and this is the root of love for his Word, Law, Temple, etc. Indeed love means such a strong expression of personal life that even when the word is used in connection with things there is a suggestion of passion except in the case of the most trivial objects.[4]

Both secular and religious love meet us in the O.T. The former includes sex, family, friendship and social relationships, and we shall study this first, as being

---

[1] Cf. Lev. xix, 18, 34 : " thou shalt love . . . as thyself ".

[2] This may be assumed for *'ahebh*, though etymological support is lacking, from its widespread use in an erotic sense.

[3] Examples are plentiful. See e.g. Gen. xxvii, 4 : Jacob loves savoury meat ; Is. lvi, 10 ; Prov. xx, 13 : men love sleep ; xxi, 17 : wine ; xviii, 21 : the tongue ; xv, 12 : reproof ; xxix, 3 : wisdom ; Ps. cix, 17 : cursing ; xi, 5 : violence ; Amos iv, 5 : hypocritical worship ; Hos. ix, 1 : the gains of harlotry. The " love of good or evil " also belongs here (Amos v, 15 ; Psalm lii, 4, etc.).

[4] This applies least to *hapheç* and *raçah*, though they show numerous examples.

simpler ; then we shall proceed to investigate the religious side of the subject in the light of what we have learnt from the secular.

2. SECULAR LOVE

(a) First come those cases in which love simply means the vital urge of the sexes towards each other, standing out as an independent force over against law. Sexuality is often strongly emphasised, especially by Ezekiel, who generally uses the Piel (intensive) of 'ahebh to indicate sexual desire.[1] Hosea and Jeremiah also often speak of love in this sense,[2] and the imperative of 'ahebh in Hosea iii, 1 is used euphemistically for sexual intercourse.[3]

All love between man and woman,[4] and especially that which binds husband and wife together,[5] is simply recognised as the gift of nature, with no suggestion of a lack of restraint, and the fact that it was a favourite subject with poets shows that it played an elevating part in the life of Israel.[6] It is in the Song of Songs (viii, 6) that passionate love receives its finest

[1] Qal only Ezek. xvi, 37 ; elsewhere always Pi. part. (xvi, 33, 36, 37 ; xxiii, 5, 9, 22). The use of 'aghabh is confined to Ezek. xxiii (Oholah and Oholibah), apart from Jer. iv, 30.

[2] Hosea ii, 7 ; iii, 1 ; iv, 18 ; ix, 10, etc. Jer. xxii, 20, 22 ; xxx, 14 ; ii, 25 (Qal). Cf. Jer. ii, 33 : " to seek love " means " to follow instinct ".

[3] Also the passive participle in the same verse.

[4] Cf. e.g. Gen. xxix, 18, 20, 30, 32 ; xxxiv, 3 ; Judges xvi, 4, etc. The record concerning Solomon (I Kings xi, 1-3)—unless intended as a gentle caricature—in giving the number of his wives, treats " love " in a very dry judicial manner as legalised sexual intercourse.

[5] E.g. I Sam. i, 5, 8.

[6] The famous eulogy of the virtuous woman in Prov. xxxi, 10 ff. has an undertone of quiet irony, since the opening question can only be answered honestly in the negative.

description, in words like those of a hymn : *'azzah khammaweth 'ah^abhah*, " love is strong as death ". In the sphere of sex it stands over against the negative, hate, as a positive primitive force of unknown origin. The brutal nature of both is unveiled in the story of Amnon and Tamar (II Sam. xiii, 1-22) ; the same ominous note sounds in the hysterical words of Delilah, " thou dost but hate me, and lovest me not." (Judges xiv, 16) ; and finally the Law finds it necessary to deal with the symptoms of sexual attraction and repulsion (Deut. xxi, 15 ff. ; xxii, 13 ff. ; xxiv, 1 ff.).

(*b*) It seems to be an entirely different matter when the same word *'ahebh*, or *raçah* or *hapheç* is used of personal relations which have no possible connection with sex. Love without *libido* operates in the spheres of family relationship, friendship and legal association. It is difficult to determine the psychological connection of this with sexual love. Perhaps the O.T., like our own language, uses these terms to connect things which naturally have nothing to do with each other, so that properly one should say they are employed as metaphors : personal attachments other than sexual are compared with what is erotic when they are described in the same terms. Yet this would appear to be going too far, in view of the fact that in Hebrew, so far as we know, it is quite impossible to express the difference between Eros and Agape, although the difference is recognised (II Sam. i, 26). The O.T. writers were so impressed by what is common to both that they felt no need to use different words. The exact nature of this quality may be expected to come to light in those cases where the spontaneous and irrational nature of love shows it to be a feeling that springs out of the depths of personality. Jonathan comes to love David *'ah^abhath naphsho*, i.e. with the love that is peculiar to his own soul and goes out from it

(I Sam. xx, 17).   Saul loves David *m^e'odh*, i.e. according to a force that works in him (I Sam. xvi, 21).   Or Jonathan loves David *k^enaphsho*, " as his own soul " (I Sam. xviii, 1, 3) ; i.e. his relation to David was not only very close, it was of the very stuff of his life, as vital to him as his own soul ; he and David were identical, as it were, like a man and his soul.   It might seem as if nothing could go further than this as an expression of personal fellowship, and this adds to the impressiveness of the poetical expression of the same thought in David's lament over his friend : " thy love to me was wonderful ".[1]   This brings out the irrational element to perfection, although it has not reached the stage of showing the connection with religion.[2]

(*c*) Linguistic usage does not always convey such a strong impression of intense feeling, even when, e.g., a friend [3] or a relation [4] is called *'ohebh*.[5]   But the dominant position given to the idea of love constitutes the great glory of O.T. ethics.   Love is regarded as inseparable from humanity, and therefore set forth as the norm of social relationship and included within the scope and shelter of the divine law.   It makes very

---

[1] II Sam. i, 26.

[2] The latter is hinted at by the author of Eccles. ix, 1, when he solemnly affirms that the most elementary human feelings of love and hate remain a mystery, immediately after pointing out that all the works of the righteous and the wise are in the hand of God.

[3] E.g. Prov. xiv, 20—where the " love " is insincere. But the high level of the Wisdom teaching on this subject is shown by such sayings as " Love covereth all transgressions " (Prov. x, 12) and " There is a lover that sticketh closer than a brother " (xviii, 24).

[4] Cf. combinations like " My lovers and my friends " (Ps. xxxviii, 12 ; lxxxviii, 19).

[5] The institution of comparisons particularly involves a considerable weakening of the idea, as in Gen. xxxvii, 4 and xxix, 30 (sexual).

little difference that such regulations only refer to the treatment of fellow-nationals and resident aliens. The limitation is necessary in order to make the law valid within that circle. This of course is bound to appear objectionable from the point of view of the paradox involved in the use of an entirely non-legal idea in a legal prescription, for love is fundamental to life itself.[1] Therefore, although Lev. xix, 18 (thou shalt love thy neighbour as thyself) is in the form of a law and contains the clearly defined legal term " neighbour ", it is not strictly a law, because love is a matter of feeling and cannot be legally commanded. If it were to be taken legally, the word " love " would have to be interpreted as meaning to behave as if one's actions were dictated by love. But this cannot be taken seriously, and the analogous prohibition of hatred, with its reference to the heart (Lev. xix, 17), shows that it is the inner life that is in view.[2] The idea of legality must therefore be abandoned, and the juridical form regarded simply as an oxymoron, intended to stab the reader broad awake to the ultimate object of the whole of the social legislation, viz. brotherhood : its protection, cultivation, and sometimes also its creation. Love is to be the foundation of legal relationships, and to obey this commandment can only mean not to repress the feeling of love, which arises instinctively apart from the will, but to bring it to bear upon the neighbour as if upon the self.[3] The lawgiver who is concerned with the

[1] The strengthening of the divine law with the words " I am the LORD " hardly makes any difference, for they belong to the style of the so-called " Holiness Code " and generally add nothing to the substance of the commandment.

[2] Cf. also Zech. viii, 17.

[3] Ecclus. xxxiv, 15 (xxxi, 15) introduces this motive into a simple matter of etiquette, prescribing good table manners : νόει τὰ τοῦ πλησίον ἐκ σεαυτοῦ.

regulation of social life along these lines knows that legal ordinances only take you half-way and that the desire for power is always tending to disrupt fellowship ; so, whether conscious or not that it is a legal monstrosity, he resorts to the paradox of commanding love.

There is obviously a danger of this breeding a very much diluted—and therefore legally more manageable—idea of love in the sense of patronage or the like.[1] But if anyone had been inclined towards such an interpretation, he would have found it hard to support it by any analogy drawn from the law. Lev. xix, 34— the same law of love applied to resident aliens—is attended by the same difficulties.[2] More in harmony with what has been said is the view of Jesus that this is one of the two commandments on which the whole law hangs (Matt. xxii, 40). He separates it from everything else in the law and strips it of all attempts at legal interpretation, since these can only do violence to it. The command to love, wearing the clothes of the law, reduces the law itself to absurdity, since it shows the boundary beyond which there can be no legislation, human or divine, and establishes the claim of a way of life that is above the law.

This amounts to a definite judgment upon the particularism, which would make the law more applicable to the home-born than to the resident alien. Although he is obviously concerned exclusively with quite concrete legal relations, nevertheless the lawgiver introduces a thought which extends far beyond the literal meaning of his words, by emphasising the recognition of those who have rights within the community, not on account of their legal status, but simply

---

[1] This misfortune has actually occurred in the case of the " popular maxim " (Strack Billerbeck) of Matt. v, 43 : " Thou shalt love thy neighbour and hate thine enemy ".

[2] Similarly Deut. x, 19. The imperative of 'ahebh only at Prov. iv, 6 ; [Hos. iii, 1 ; Am. v, 15 ; Zech. viii, 19 ; Ps. xxxi, 24.]

as human beings with a claim upon love. It was hardly a mistake on the part of the LXX translator when he virtually abandoned the legal force of re‘ᵃkha by using the phrase ὁ πλησίον σου. The reference is actually to any human being in the immediate neighbourhood.

From this we can go on without hesitation to say that the same " neighbour " or " alien " can even mean enemy and hater from the human point of view, and yet he must be treated according to the law of love. This certainly seems to be the true inference from a comparison of Deut. xxii, 1-4 with Exod. xxiii, 4 f., the former prescribing help to the brother, i.e. the fellow-Israelite, and the latter to the enemy. Whatever may be the literary relationship between these two passages—whether we have in Exodus an interpolation improving upon Deuteronomy or, vice versa, in the latter a weakened form of the Exodus passage—in any case the comparison justifies us in including the love of enemies in Lev. xix, 18. The neighbour may be friend or foe, and the right attitude to him should be one of love and not of legality. That means that a man must be regarded as a human being rather than as a person of legal standing. Thus Exod. xxiii, 4 f., and still more Prov. xxv, 21,[1] serve to inculcate the love of enemies, though ostensibly they are merely concerned with behaviour. In the story of Joseph also the hero illustrates the ideal of returning good for evil, and attention is drawn to his religious obedience (Gen. l, 19).

[1] The words which follow in ver. 22 characterise this ironically as a form of revenge : meat and drink are the coals of fire which the wise man, with perfect self-control, heaps upon the head of his enemy, to annihilate him. Prov. xxiv, 17 also belongs here : " Rejoice not when thine enemy falleth, and let not thine heart be glad when he is overthrown "—although this is rather a measure of prudence, as appears in ver. 18.

The O.T. affords plenty of examples of failure to love enemies.[1] The most impressive of these is Ps. cix, with its agonised complaining. The speaker recalls his love,[2] but that only serves to fan the flame of his hatred—a grim illustration of Ecclus. xxxvii, 2 : " 'Tis a grief unto death when a bosom friend becomes a foe ". The poor often had this experience, as noted in the cutting words of Prov. xiv, 20 ; [3] and the tribal organisation, with its ritual exclusiveness, made it almost impossible to have full personal relations with foreigners.[4] But occasional failures in practice cannot detract from the greatness of the ethical demand, especially when it is remembered that it has divine authority, and love plays a vital part in religion.

3. RELIGIOUS LOVE

(a) When love takes its place in the vocabulary of religion, it becomes highly important in theology, because of its close connection with life. That holds good in general for the O.T., although mutual love between God and man can easily be undervalued in the case of Israel because the expression of it is apt to be very restrained or narrowed by theological specu-

[1] Cf. Joab's blunt words to David, II Sam. xix, 6 (Heb. 7).

[2] In Ps. cix, 4 f., the second half of ver. 4 is corrupt. It seems to mean " while I pray (for them) " : but this does not make sense. The only possibility would be to take the words as referring to the past—" whereas I prayed ".

[3] " The poor is hated even of his own neighbour."

[4] Elisha's advice concerning the captured Syrians (II Kings vi, 22)—according to the Hebrew text—can be understood as a human protest against the ban (cf. I Kings xx, 42, etc.). The story of the Ethiopian, an alien without the full rights of citizenship, who was so moved by sympathy for Jeremiah that he saved his life when his fellow-countrymen tried to put him away, might serve as an illustration to the parable of the Good Samaritan.

lation. This restraint is due to the overwhelming weight of the Covenant idea, which controls the theological thinking of Biblical authors to such a degree that they are seldom free from its legal categories and hardly ever give a clear presentation of love as a pure expression of psychical reality apart from legality, abounding in religious truth and unique in its power. There can be no doubt that the Covenant is an expression in juridical language of the experience of God's love : the whole Covenant theory is based on the idea of love.[1] It is characteristic of the religion of Israel that so often this is only tacitly recognised, as if it were improper to ascribe to God an emotion so typical of the creature or to attempt the evaluation of what happens in communion with God. Not less notable are the attempts to assimilate love with various conceptions transplanted from law into theology, such as mercy, judgment, righteousness, truth. The result of this is a considerable levelling of religious ideas which hinders the fruitful theological development of the idea of love in the O.T., though it has not prevented its appearance in full glory in certain sayings.

These proclaim on the one hand that man loves God, and on the other that God loves man. A logical connection between the two is characteristically not worked out. Deuteronomy alone makes attempts of that sort, basing the appeal for love to Yahwe on Yahwe's love to the patriarchs (x, 14-16), and promising Yahwe's love as a reward for loyalty to the law. The two groups of sayings are here presented singly, without regard to any order of precedence, since it is inadvisable to begin their investigation with an estimate of their hortatory value.

[1] The same can be said of the closely related idea of Election, and of the religious use of the juridical term *hesedh*, which gives love its widest scope.

(b) The O.T. is familiar with love towards God as a fundamental element in piety, but does not enter into any learned definition of the content of this feeling. When it is brought into close connection with fear,[1] that is merely rhetorical, and is obviously a misuse of language; for love in the O.T. is the opposite of fear,[2] striving to overcome all separation[3] and playing its part as a fundamental motive in all communion with God.[4] To love God means to enjoy him and seek him instinctively.[5] Fundamentally, those who love God are the truly pious, whose life of faith bears the stamp of originality and genuineness : they seek God for his own sake. When Abraham is called a friend of God because of his familiar intercourse with him, that marks him out as a model of piety.[6] Because of the definite pattern of their inner life, the same title is applied to all members of the community of Yahwe-worshippers.[7] This designation denotes the active side of religion, apart from ritual and morality. Obviously it is not in any sense à piece of theology : its origin is to be found in simple experience. It is

[1] In Deut. x, 12 love is one of the elements of " fear ", along with obedience and service. These ideas are already well worn and closely intermingled. The struggle between fear and love finds classical expression in the words of David (II Sam. xxiv, 14).

[2] Cf. in the New Testament I John iv, 18 ; II Tim. i, 7.

[3] Cf. Deut. xi, 22, etc. : " to cleave unto him ".

[4] Typical examples are Ps. xviii, 1 ; cxvi, 1. In the latter the verb " I love " has no object in the Hebrew, and it is better to retain the absolute use, in spite of its difficulty, and not to substitute words of one's own, however poetical. (See Gunkel [and Kirkpatrick] ad loc.) [Cf. pp. 46, 50, 63.]

[5] Cf. Jer. ii, 2 : " the love of thine espousals " ; Ps. xci, 14 (ḥashaq).

[6] Isaiah xli, 8. LXX understands this as passive : " whom I loved ". Cf. II Chron. xx, 7 (LXX) : " thy beloved " ; James ii, 23 : " friend " ; Judith viii, 22 (Vulg.) : " friend ".

[7] 'ahebh also in heathen religion, Jer. viii, 2.

an attempt to describe an activity of the religious consciousness [1] which leads beyond creaturely passivity —or apart from it—to that pure joy in believing which is the goal of the devout and a motif in all his hymns. [2] Love sees salvation in the Godhead, and is the strongest basis of trust. [3] That this form of piety was highly valued and richly cultivated in the worship of Yahwe is shown in the rich variety of O.T. hymns ; though this point may easily be missed, because the use of the idea of love in exhortations or confessions, especially outside the books of the prophets, makes it appear much more a product of reason than it really is. Favourite combinations are, e.g. " who love Yahwe and keep his commandments " ; [4] " to love him and serve him " (Deut. x, 12 ; xi, 13 ; Is. lvi, 6) ; " to love him and walk in his ways " (Deut. x, 12; xi, 22 ; xix, 9 ; xxx, 16 ; Josh. xxii, 5 ; xxiii, 11). A rather forced coupling of love with acts of worship and moral conduct is apt to interfere with a deeper understanding. [5] On the other hand in Deut. xxx, 6,

[1] For the purposes of analysis the magnificent simile of Judges v, 31 (" let them that love him be as the sun when he goeth forth in his might ") is open to objection, since it is the antithesis to the perishing of Yahwe's enemies. But the figure of an irresistible natural process may have been suggested to the poet by the word " love ".

[2] We are dealing here with one of the forms of what is called " fascination " (cf. Otto, The Idea of the Holy, chap. vi).

[3] Ps. xl. 16 ; lxx, 4. When reference is made in Psalms of lamentation to God's wonderful works in the past (xl, 5) it is impossible to say whether this recollection gives rise to the Psalmist's confidence or whether it comes in to support a spontaneous feeling. Both are possible in the life of prayer and it is a question of mood.

[4] E.g. Exod. xx, 6 ; Deut. v, 10 ; vii, 9 ; xi, 1 ; I Kings iii, 3 ; Dan. ix, 4 ; Neh. i, 5.

[5] It is tempting to interpret the conjunction as explicative : " love him—that means, keep his commandments ". Is it possible that this was the original meaning ?

love to God is impressively shown to be something
which springs from the very depths of a man's being
and is ultimately the work of God himself : Yahwe
circumcises Israel's heart, so that she may love him
with all her heart and soul.　The prophetic metaphor
in Jer. iv, 4, originally directed against the seculari-
sation of the idea of the Covenant, serves with a
significant modification in the sense of Jer. xxxi, 33
(and Ezek. xi, 19) to indicate the irrational origin of the
most powerful vital forces of the community.

Often, however, as in the examples already given, the
language employed seems to indicate the very opposite
of this.　The O.T. obviously sets the deed, the
expression in conduct, above the feeling as such, and
the impression is conveyed that man has it in his own
power either to love or not to love.　This is specially
the case in what Jesus calls the greatest of the commandments, Deut. vi, 5 : Thou shalt love the Lord thy God
with all thy heart and with all thy soul and with all thy
might.　The paradox is the same as in Lev. xix, 18
and 34, and what has been said above about that applies
here also.　That which is prescribed as law [1] really
lies outside the province of legal regulation.　Of course
nobody can understand that, who lacks the quality
of which the law speaks.　This is presupposed, and
the demand is for complete devotion.　The emphasis
is on the word " all ", and the sentence might be
paraphrased : Thou shalt exert all thy powers, so
that love may produce a disposition which will
determine thy conduct ; the cultivation of thy relationship to Yahwe requires the devotion of thy
whole personality, heart (*lebhabh*) and soul (*nephesh*).
The personal nature of this relationship is of course

---

[1] This is strongly brought out in Deut. xxx, 16, where the
pronoun " I " is emphatic.　The idea is more natural in poetry,
e.g. Ps. xxxi, 23.

indicated by the expression " thy God ". It is the
business of the law-giver to make it clear that this
involves demand and duty. As teacher and leader
he knows that theory without practice is worthless, and
he therefore seeks by means of his paradoxical formula
to enlist the most positive force of religion in support
of loyalty to the Covenant. Yahwe himself will
be the judge of love's sincerity (Deut. xiii, 3). Ideas
like this differentiate Deuteronomy from Jeremiah,
who founds the New Covenant between God and His
People upon the law written in the heart, that is, a
law which has ceased to be a law (Jer. xxxi, 33).
He means simply the natural instinct of love to God.

(c) The message of God's love in the Old Testament
is addressed both to the people and to the individual.
The former comes first in point of time, but the latter
throws more light on the nature of love. It is remarkable how little the O.T. speaks of God's love for a
particular person. The expression " beloved of
Yahwe " (yᵉdhidh Yahwe) only occurs twice [1] (apart
from II Sam. xii, 25) ; in three cases God is said to
love ('ahebh) kings, viz. Solomon (II Sam. xii, 24 and
Neh. xiii, 26) and Cyrus (Is. xlviii, 14 ?), but here we
may have to do with the theory that kings are sons of
God, a theory undoubtedly derived from heathen
mythology [2] and spiritualised in Israel, and therefore
we cannot interpret these passages in terms of the
religion of Israel. Otherwise 'ahebh is never used in
individual utterances concerning the love of God.
The term employed is either raçah, an expression
connected with the offering of sacrifice which shows

---

[1] Ps. cxxvii, 2 of an ordinary individual ; Deut. xxxiii, 12 as an
attribute of the tribe of Benjamin.   (Plural at Ps. lx, 5.)

[2] Cf. II Sam. vii, 14, ; Ps. lxxxix, 27 f. ; ii, 7 (see Gunkel). Perhaps the name Jedidiah (beloved of Yahweh) given to Solomon is
intended to designate him for the throne (II Sam. xii, 25).

nothing like the immediacy of feeling,[1] or *ḥapheç*, which also includes the idea of approval.[2] It can indeed be said that Yahwe's love is not thought of fundamentally in relation to individuals. When men pray for personal blessings, they prefer the thought of Yahwe's majesty, might or graciousness to that of his love, or else address him as " my King ",[3] hiding in a pronoun their longing for the loving attention of their God.

This agrees with the fact that usually only collective objects of God's love are mentioned. On the border-line stand certain designations of individuals as types : the resident alien (" stranger "), the pure in heart, he who hungers after righteousness, etc. ;[4] these Yahwe loves or corrects like a father (Prov. iii, 12). It may be that genuine faith lies behind such didactic utterances—like the trust motif in the Psalms—but it is not possible to assess accurately their religious value, because their " love " looks so much like mere approval or, in the case of the resident alien, patronage.[5] The

---

[1] Cf. e.g. Lev. vii, 18 ; Amos v, 22 ; Jer. xiv, 12 ; Ezek. xliii, 27. " The LORD thy God accept thee " (II Sam. xxiv, 23) is a polite formula, wishing David a successful sacrifice. At Job xxxiii, 26 *raçah* means the hearing of prayer ; at Prov. xvi, 7 Yahwe's recognition of the merit of a life of piety.

[2] Ps. xviii, 19 (" he delighted in me ") is to be understood in the sense of xxxvii, 23 (" he delighteth in his way ")—as is shown by the claim to righteousness made in the following verse. Cf. the same association of ideas in Ps. xl, 11 and 12.

The Queen of Sheba's polite formula (I Kings x, 9 ; II Chron. ix, 8) is no doubt connected with the idea that the king is a son of God. (See p. 15 on II Sam. xii, 24 ; Neh. xiii, 26 ; Is. xlviii, 14 ; and cf. II Chron. ii, 11 (Huram of Tyre addressing Solomon).

[3] Ps. v, 2. Cf. also Hos. ii, 23.

[4] Deut. x, 18 ; Prov. xxii, 11 LXX ; xv, 9. Wis. vii, 28 clearly points towards the exclusiveness which characterises many sayings of this sort : " Nothing doth God love save him that dwelleth with wisdom ".

[5] Here belong Ps. lxviii, 5 ; ciii, 13.

father-son idea obviously became current coin among pedantic teachers,[1] and this also seems to rule out the deeper conception of love. The thought of God as Father never established itself in the personal religion of ancient Israel.[2]

(d) What the O.T. has to say about God's love is concerned mainly with the nation; that is its natural sphere. Hosea is the first, so far as we know, to have realised and set forth love as the fundamental motive in Yahwe's treatment of his people. It is true that Isaiah also makes use of the thought of God as Father (Is. i, 4 ; xxx, 1, 9), but for him the emphasis is rather on the idea of authority than on that of an inner feeling of affection, which is only faintly heard in Yahwe's severe words concerning the ingratitude of his sons.[3] On the other hand, Hosea clearly recognises the flowing forth of divine love at the heart of the election of Israel and the Covenant. When he represents Yahwe as a man wooing an unworthy woman in defiance of convention, law and reason, he makes it clear that he understands that no legal forms or guarantees can adequately set forth God's relationship to his people (Hos. iii, 1). He himself must love his adulterous wife as Yahwe loves the children of Israel. This means that the official religion had collapsed long ago, and that the national existence was

---

[1] Job v, 17—the same teaching in the mouth of Eliphaz.

[2] The occurrence of the word " father " in the caricature of Canaanite prayer in Jer. ii, 27 naturally suggests that under the influence of the prophets the idea of God's Fatherhood came to be purposely avoided in personal religion among the Jews, because it was impossible to dissociate it from beliefs connected with the fertility cults. Cf. J. Begriff in Zeitschrift für A. T. Wissenschaft, 1928, p. 256.

[3] Sayings like Exod. iv, 22 (" Israel is my first-born ") or Deut. xiv, 1 (" Ye are the children of Yahwe ") do not belong here ; they make no appeal to feeling, but simply illustrate Yahwe's claims from the law of the family.

only maintained by an unfathomable divine love which to normal understanding must appear grotesque. Even if objection be taken to this reading of the third chapter, a similar lesson is taught by the experience with Gomer. The prophet must marry the harlot, because only such a stupid and degrading union can give a true picture of Yahwe's relation to the land of Israel (Hos. i, ii). The ominous names of the children show that what had happened was far from being an accident, that on the contrary the adulterous mother was wantonly playing with fire, heedlessly (ii, 8) incurring the doom of a mother accused by her children (ii, 2). So she becomes an object of pity. He who presides over the whole pitiable situation understands her misery better than she does, and takes her under his legal protection (ii, 19 " betroth ") for ever " in mercies ". Then shall she know him to perfection (ii, 20). In this way Hosea seeks to expound Yahwe's rule. He pulls down the theory of the Covenant, in order to expose God's love as its foundation, and then builds it up again with righteousness, judgment, loving-kindness and faithfulness. But the foundation-stone is mercy.[1]

✳ With similar tenderness and depth Hosea works out other aspects of the love of God, which suggest the picture of a loving father, although he avoids the terms " father " and " son ", perhaps intentionally, and strictly speaking only describes a fatherly teacher who is disappointed in his pupil but for that reason loves him all the more passionately.[2] Israel was once

---

[1] It must remain an open question how far Hosea's own physical propensities may have predisposed him to employ Eros as a symbol for Agape. Cf. A. Allwohn, Die Ehe des Propheten Hosea in psychoanalytischer Beleuchtung, 1926, 54 ff. [See W. Robertson Smith, The Prophets of Israel, 159-178.]

[2] For determining the exact nature of the picture in Hos. xi, 1 ff., the important word is not " my son " (the reading is un-

young, and won the affection of Yahwe in her early days (xi, 1). It was Yahwe's hand that helped Ephraim to walk (xi, 3) ; he drew them with " cords of love ",[1] though they heeded neither call nor guidance. In the hour of their self-prepared doom, when it seemed to be Yahwe's duty to turn his just wrath into action, the love of God breaks through with loud complaint : " How shall I give thee up, Ephraim ? How shall I surrender thee, Israel ? Mine heart is turned within me, my compassions are kindled together. I will not execute the fierceness of mine anger, I will not again destroy Ephraim : for I am God and not man, the Holy One in the midst of thee " (xi, 7-9). That sentence, in which Yahwe explains his behaviour, states perfectly the final consummation of the O.T. conception of love. It establishes the superiority of divine to human love. This means that divine love is not swayed by passion or by the fear of consequences. It operates irresistibly as a moving principle in the character of God. /God is not less divine and holy when love directs his actions. Therefore he can be said to suffer because of his people's lovelessness, when he finds their loyalty to be as a morning cloud and as the dew that goeth early away (vi, 4). Face to face with sin he may even be said to experience something like a feeling of helplessness : " O Ephraim, what shall I do unto thee ? O Judah, what shall I do unto thee ? " (vi, 4).

This motif of the suffering love of God gives a special quality to all Hosea's pronouncements of doom. It shows the depth of his despair when he

certain) but " taught (a little child) to go " in verse 3—which does not go well with *na'ar* in ver. 1.

[1] The bad state of the text makes the nature of the illustration doubtful. Perhaps it is taken from the ox-team, in view of the word " yoke ". But this is not really satisfactory.

utters a threat like that in ix, 15 : " I will love them
no more ".[1] Words like these really announce God's
intention to be God no more, i.e. complete chaos.
Therefore when the last chapter of the book withdraws
all the threatenings by saying " I will love them freely "
(xiv, 4), it can hardly be questioned that this is in line
with the fundamental tendency of Hosea's message—
whatever view we take of that chapter.

Jeremiah also makes use of the motif of the suffering
love of God, but seems to me to alter it and weaken it
(Jer. xii, 7-9). Yahwe hates his heritage because it
growls at him like a lion. Yet he calls it " the dearly
beloved of my soul ", and the whole poem is a lamentation. Yahwe cannot explain why Ephraim is such
a dear son that his heart is moved whenever he thinks
of him, and he cannot help showing mercy to him.[2]
With everlasting love he loves Israel his wife, and this
love is the ground of his faithfulness. Jeremiah also
adopts other motifs from Hosea, whether consciously
or unconsciously. He too knows that Jerusalem-
Israel once was young, and celebrates her espousal to
Yahwe as a time of love, in this connection comparing
the Word of Yahwe to a fountain of living water (Jer.
ii, 2 ff., 13). He shows how Yahwe waited in vain to
hear from his beloved the tender words " my Father ",
and how he must feel that she only utters them hypo-
critically, and how in spite of all he never grows weary
of calling her to repentance (Jer. iii, 19 ; iii, 4 ; iv, 1).

Deutero-Isaiah also seizes upon the theme of the
young bride, taken back by Yahwe with everlasting
mercy (Is. liv, 5-8), but significantly avoids the adultery
motif. Here the wedded wife is " forsaken and grieved

---

[1] Cf. i, 6 : " unpitied " ; xiii, 14 ; " repentance shall be hid
from mine eyes ".

[2] Jer. xxxi, 20 ; cf. also xxxi, 9. [See Skinner, Prophecy and
Religion, 64-73, 198-230.]

in spirit " ; her husband has left her, not she him, and that it happened " in wrath " is only added as it were out of pity, without any indication of the reason for wrath. Perhaps the idea of Zion as the wife of Yahwe is also implied in the prophet's most moving reference to God's love when he says it is like that of a mother— nay, goes beyond it : " though mothers may forget their children ", Yahwe says to Zion, " yet will I not forget thee ".[1] Again, it sounds like a variation of the father-son motif when Yahwe uses the masculine pronoun in announcing Israel's redemption : " I give Egypt as thy ransom, Ethiopia and Seba for thee, since thou art so precious to me, so honourable, and I love thee " (xliii, 3 f.).

Whereas the prophets, with all their differences, present on the whole a simple type of piety, unencumbered by theory,[2] the case is different when we come to the sayings about the love of God in Deuteronomy. The great ideas are presented in the form of teaching, with a view to making them fruitful, and this makes a certain qualification inevitable, since the law cannot know the wealth of experience out of which the prophets speak. Experience is transformed into dogma. As already stated, the thought of love is mainly used in Deuteronomy to support that of election and the Covenant, and thus love's non-rational genius is rendered ceremonious and ineffective. We read that Yahwe chose Israel out of all the nations on earth to be his own peculiar people ; not, however, because

[1] Is. xlix, 15. The same motif also at lxvi, 13 : " As one whom his mother comforteth, so will I comfort you ". On the other hand Deut. xxxii, 18 (" the God that bare thee ") looks like something foreign. [See A. B. Davidson, The Theol. of the O.T. 170-174.]

[2] Zeph. iii, 17 has suffered damage, and is therefore not clear. Ezekiel likes to win the favour of Yahwe by means of the cult : xx, 40 f. ; xliii, 27. Cf. also Ps. cxlvii, 11 ; cxlix, 4.

Israel was more in number than any people—it is on the contrary the smallest of all—but because he loved Israel ; that explains his attachment (*hashaq*, Deut. vii, 7). But in the same breath the speech goes on to refer to the oath sworn to the patriarchs, and creates the impression, only too easily, that the really important point is the legal guarantee given with the oath, particularly when the exhortation follows immediately with the suggestion that all this shows that Yahwe, the true God, is also the faithful one who will abide by the Covenant with all who on their side love him and keep his commandments. Deut. vii, 13 actually puts the love of God beside his blessing ; he will give them both as the reward for loyalty to the Covenant. Without intending it, this introduces into the idea of love an incongruous flavour of bargaining, which it never has among the prophets. It thus becomes part of the orderly arrangement of the life of piety, and is thereby robbed of its best part, viz. its freedom. A more fortunate expression of the same idea is found in Deut. x, 14 ff., where there is no reference to an oath, and it is simply asserted that Yahwe had a delight in the Patriarchs to love them, and chose their seed after them.[1] The demand for circumcision of the foreskin of the heart is more harmonious with the message of God's love because it has nothing to do with the sphere of law. The figure which corresponds most closely to the didactic aim of Deuteronomy is unquestionably that of the Father. "Consider in thine heart", we read in Deut. viii, 5, " that as a man educates his son, so Yahwe will educate thee ". Obviously this form of the idea differs somewhat from that which is found in Hosea.[2]

[1] Similarly the statement in Deut. xxiii, 5.

[2] It is also found at Deut. xxxii, 6—though only with reference to Yahwe's creation of Israel. [See Driver, Deuteronomy pp. xix-xxxiv.]

The development of the idea of love into a dogma, noticeable in Deuteronomy, led to important consequences. Owing to its close association with the dogma of election, it was involved in the hardening to which that was subject. This is illustrated by its use in the book of Malachi, which begins with the direct and attractive words, " I love you, saith Yahwe ". But this is not understood in the deep sense, and with the full range of the word 'ahebh ; it is used to introduce a remarkable discussion of the question how this love works—or on what ground it rests [1]—in terms of legal significance and not of ultimate reality. The inquiry is concerning the consequences or the presuppositions of the fact indicated in the words " hast thou loved us ". Violence is thus done to the tenderness of the idea, and its power is broken. What follows in the text shows that the real value of the good news consists only in its legal consequences. This is to be found in the preference of Jacob to Esau. The misfortune of Esau (Edom) makes it clear that he is " hated " by Yahwe ; Jacob is to learn that his escape from a similar fate is proof of the " love " of Yahwe. Even if the antithesis owes something to the conventional use of the words " loved " and " hated " in marriage laws,[2] the fact remains that it is a distortion of the idea of love to argue that Yahwe loves because he hates. The idea of the father is also mutilated in this book, being expounded as involving a legal claim against the priests : " If I be a father ", Yahwe says to them, " where is mine honour ? " (Mal. i, 6). Or else it is practically identified with the authority of a man who employs his son to work for him (Mal. iii, 17).

---

[1] The first question in Mal. i, 2 can mean either " On what ground dost thou love us ? " or " How dost thou show thy love for us ? " What follows proves that the second is intended.

[2] Cf. Deut. xxi, 15 ff.

(e) The prophetic idea of God's love is, however, strong enough in itself to paralyse such excrescences. Finally, like the prophetic conception of God, it has within it the tendency towards universality. Actually the Old Testament nowhere speaks of the love of God reaching out beyond Israel. To say that it did, one would have to dig it out of a Messianic context which might be supposed to imply it.[1] But this is too violent a proceeding, for when Messianic teaching abandons particularism and moves towards the idea of humanity as a whole, it is still too thin and general to allow of its being credited with so vital a motif.

The short sentence, " He loveth the peoples " (Deut. xxxiii, 3), where the verb is *habhabh*, can be understood in a universal sense, according to the Hebrew text and the versions. But the context shows that this is not intended, and that there must be some error. In any case it is doubtful whether *'ammim* can mean peoples.

The international question in Mal. ii, 10 (" Have we not all one father ? ") does not refer to God's love but to his work as creator, as is shown by the second question : " Has not one God created us ? " The story of the Tower of Babel even opposes the idea of the unity of mankind (Gen. xi, 1-9).

[1] The passage which lends itself most plausibly to this interpretation is Is. xlii, 6. *Berith-'am* means " covenant of mankind " as is shown by the use of *'am* for " mankind " in v, 5. (*'abhi-'adh* in Is. ix, 5 is too problematic.)

II. THE WORDS FOR LOVE IN
PRE-BIBLICAL GREEK

THERE are really three important words for " to love "
in pre-Biblical Greek : ἐρᾶν, φιλεῖν, ἀγαπᾶν.

(1) ἐρᾶν means passionate yearning after another
person. The Greeks have always sung glowing
hymns to sensual demonic Eros, the uncontrollable
all-controlling god. He played a great part in the
cultus, became the last word in philosophy, after the
time of Plato, for the uplifting and fulfilment of life, and
was sublimated in the mysticism of Plotinus, becoming purely spiritual and meaning the overwhelming
desire for union with the One.

Ecstasy is what the Greek seeks in Eros ; this for him
is religion. Self-control is indeed the most lovely
of all heaven's gifts to the heart of man (Sophocles,
Antigone, 683 ff.)—the very perfecting of manhood.
But Eros is more glorious, for it puts an end to all self-
control, raises all the senses to a pitch of frenzy, bursts
all the bounds of manhood humanistically conceived,
and transports man above himself. The great tragedians praise it with pious awe as well as with ardour :
" Invincible Eros . . ., who drivest mortals and immor-
tals mad, thy violence ruins the true heart, making
it untrue " (ibid. 781 ff.). This is a god, and he rules
the gods : " Tyrant over gods and men " (Euripides,
Fr. 132, Nauck). All other powers in heaven and
earth are inferior to the one and only omnipotence,
Eros. Under the tyranny of this almighty power, a
man loses his ability to choose, his will, his freedom—
and finds his supreme blessedness in being thus
overpowered.

Where the demonic force of the sensual ecstasy is

celebrated with religious enthusiasm, religion conversely will seek its culminating point in sensual ecstasy. Eros occupies a central position in the fertility rites as generator, and sacred prostitution flourishes in the temples of the great goddesses, often under oriental influence. Sexual intercourse between gods and men not only figures in mythology, but is a concrete reality in the cultus. The " sacred marriage " in the Mysteries means that the worshipper is physically united with the world of the god.[1] Religion and ecstasy are the same thing when erotic experience is explained in terms of religion.

But the ecstasy sought by the Greeks in Eros is not necessarily sensual. Already in the Greek Mysteries erotic ideas—as so often in mysticism—are frequently dissolved into pictures and symbols for intercourse with the supernatural. Plato carried this further when he devoted a whole dialogue to Eros. He too thinks of Eros as ecstasy which lifts man above rationality, springing from an elementary necessity and finding relief in the generative act (Symposium 200, 206 ; Phaedrus 237 ff., 242 ff.). But physical beauty, which sets Eros on fire, only points the way to " the divine goodness itself ", which is the meaning and goal of all love, the eternal, the summum bonum (Symp. 210 f.). Plato definitely raised Eros above the sensual sphere ; Aristotle considered it as a cosmic function, apart altogether from human experience. For the latter it is the power of attraction by means of which the First Cause keeps all things in orderly motion : " He moves it as a thing beloved ". This sort of love which holds the world together, has nothing to do with ecstasy ; it is an exercise of will-power : the Prime

---

[1] O. Kern, Religion der Griechen I (1926) 53 ff ; Griech. Mysterien der klassichen Zeit (1927) 71 f. ; A. Dieterich, Mithrasliturgie [3] (1923) 121 ff., 244.

Mover is not to be thought of in terms of desire but of will, being at the same time the absolute goodness (Metaph. XII, vii, p. 1072a, 27 f.).

Later Platonism shows the same effort to cleanse Eros of its original demonic traits and subordinate it to the ideal of humanity. A typical example is found in the tractate, Socrates on Love, by Maximus of Tyre. He is more Platonic than Plato himself (Symp. 181 f., 208 f.) when he contrasts lust with the love of beauty : " The latter is Greek, the former barbarian ; one is the unwilling victim of a disease, the other a willing lover " (Max. Tyr. xix, 4, Hobein) ; and puts it perfectly in xx, 2 : " Eros is a matter of free choice". The mystical understanding of Eros again finds perfect expression in Plotinus Ennead III, v, Concerning Eros, (Volkmann) : " The urge of the soul away from the world of sense and reason towards the Above and Beyond (cf. V, v, 8), past all frontiers towards the point where love and the beloved come together and are one " (VI, viii, 15)—this upward flight is the true Eros, the meaning of all love. At a time when Eros was holding its popular orgies, looking for piquant stories among the myths of the gods, or seeking romantic adventures in the temples, Maximus was bringing it under the discipline of humanism and Plotinus sublimating it in mysticism. Yet it remains the same Eros, the natural impulse to overcome the limitations of the individual life. That is why erotic religion exalts frenzy in its lower form and ecstasy in its higher.

(2) φιλεῖν, φιλία on the other hand generally indicate liking or caring, as of gods for men, of friend for friend, the love that is given to all kinds of human beings, the love of Antigone when she says she was made for mutual affection.[1] This sort of love is a

[1] Sophocles, Ant. 523. Here it is φιλία that speaks, in 683 ff. it is ἔρως—both in the name of the truth, which is mightier than Necessity and Reason.

noble vocation, a task from which a man can excuse himself, not an irresistible urge or frenzy.

(3) ἀγαπᾶν carries with it for the Greek none of the magic power of Ἔρως and hardly any of the warmth of φιλία. Its etymological origin is unknown. Its meaning is colourless and indefinite. The verb often means no more than to be content with something,[1] or to welcome somebody with a courteous greeting, the reference being to outward behaviour. But it also has a deeper meaning when it indicates striving after something, or liking somebody or something,[2] and frequently it denotes sympathy, the mutual respect and friendship of equals.[3] Specially characteristic are the instances where it takes on the idea of preference, and means to put one value or aim above another, to esteem one person more highly than another. So it can be used of God's special love for an individual.[4] The " beloved of God " enjoys special privileges, and receives special gifts and blessings.[5]

This brings us to the distinguishing quality of Agape. Eros is promiscuous and finds its satisfaction here, there and everywhere ; but Agape is the love that makes distinctions, choosing its object and holding to it.

[1] Suidas s.v. ἀγαπᾶν : " to be satisfied with something, wanting nothing more ".

[2] Themistios Περὶ φιλανθρωπίας 9a Dindorf : " those who love the same things are friends of one another ".

[3] Hierocles, Carm. Aur. 56 (Mullach).

[4] Cf. also Dio Chrys. Or. xxxiii, 21 : " Zeus said he loved that best of all the cities under the sun ".

[5] Wilcken, Chrestom. I, cix, 12 (Ptolemaios IV) : " immortal, beloved by Isis ". Dittenberger, Or. Gr. Inscr. xc, 4 (Rosetta Stone, Ptol. V) : " beloved by Ptah " along with " immortal " (cf. xc, 8 f., 37, 49). Constant. Porphyrog., De ceremoniis I, 97, cd. Reiske 43 (greeting of the president of the Senate at the Byzantine court) : " Welcome, faithful servant and friend of the king . . . beloved of the king . . . beloved of Caesar ".

Eros is led by a more or less indefinite impulse towards
a definite object ; the exercise of Agape is a free act,
definitely chosen by the subject. Eros at its highest
means man's upward urge, his love towards the divine,[1]
Agape is specially seen in God's love, the love of one on
high, exalting them of low degree.[2] Eros seeks in
others the satisfaction of its hunger for life ; Agape
often means kindness, practical generosity, doing good
to others.

The same general scope and the same shades
of meaning are found in the case of the adjective
as in that of the verb just considered. The word
" beloved " (ἀγαπητός) can be applied to a thing of
which one approves or to a human being of whom
one is fond ; an only child is particularly apt to be so
described.

The use of ἀγαπᾶν along with ἐρᾶν and φιλεῖν,
however, shows how vague and variable its meaning is.
Quite frequently it is a mere synonym, being added to
the other verb for the sake of impressiveness, or substituted for it as a stylistic variant.[3] In the case of
Plotinus it does seem as if he intentionally used ἐρᾶν
for the love which strives upwards and ἀγαπᾶν for
that which comes down.[4] But while poets and
philosophers from Homer to Plotinus were for ever

---

[1] Dio Chrys. Or. xii, 60 : ἰσχυρὸς ἔρως . . . ἐγγύθεν τιμᾶν
τὸ θεῖον. Cf. xii, 61 : ἄνθρωποι ἀγαπῶντες δικαίως.

[2] Plotin. Enn. V, i, 6 : ποθεῖ δὲ πᾶν τὸ γεννῆσαν [τὸ γεγεν-
νημένον] καὶ τοῦτο ἀγαπᾷ, καὶ μάλιστα ὅταν ὦσιν μόνοι τὸ
γεννῆσαν καὶ τὸ γεγεννημένον.

[3] Xenoph. Mem. II, vii, 12 : ὡς κηδεμόνα ἐφίλουν, ὡς ὠφε-
λίμους ἠγάπα. Corp. Herm. I, 19 : ὁ ἀγαπήσας ἐκ πλάνης ἔρωτος
σῶμα. Dio Chrys. Or. xii, 32 : θαυμάζειν καὶ ἀγαπᾶν τὸ
δαιμόνιον.

[4] Cf. Plotin. Enn. VI, vii, 31 passim, but also VI, v, 10 : ὁ Ἔρως
ἀγαπῶν ἀεὶ οὕτως ὡς δύναται μετασχεῖν . . . τὸ γὰρ ὅλον ἦν τὸ
ἐρώμενον.

busy with Eros, hardly anyone treated Agape in a fundamental way. It is striking enough that there is hardly any occurrence of the noun ἀγάπη in pre-Biblical Greek.

The instances hitherto adduced for ἀγάπη are very small in number, often doubtful, often difficult to date. The older indices quoted Plutarch, Quaest. Conv. VII, vi, 2 (II, 709e), but this is now untenable since Wyttenbach has shown that ἀγαπήσων should be read instead of ἀγάπης ὧν. (Cf. Dubner's edition, p. 865.) The scholion to Thucydides II, li, 5 is late. Late also and uncertain is the occurrence of the word on a pagan inscription from Pisidia, where ἀγαθόν should perhaps be read instead of ἀγάπην (see Deissmann, Light from the Ancient East, pp. 18, 70).[1] Philodemus of Gadara, Concerning Courage, xiii, 3, is pre-Christian, but the reading is not quite certain.[2] The latest discovery is the most important,[3] viz. a papyrus from the beginning of the second century A.D., containing a large ancient Isis-liturgy. It enumerates the names under which Isis is worshipped in different places : in the Egyptian coastal town of Thonis she is called Agape (l. 28) ; what was at first thought to be a second instance must now be abandoned, reading ἀγαθήν ἄθολον (l. 109) and not ἀγάπην θεῶν ;[4] but it remains fairly certain that Agape [5] was one of the cult-names of Isis (cf.

---

[1] See Papers of the Amer. School ii, 57 ; W. H. Hatch in the Journal of Biblical Lit. 1908, pp. 134 ff.

[2] Philodemus, c. 60 B.C., from the charred papyri of Herculaneum, edited by Olivier (1914) 52.

[3] On ἀγάπη in pre-Biblical Greek see additional note on p. 31. See further for the Christian era Reitzenstein, Poimandres 297 ; Nachr. Ges. Göttingen (1919) 18, 138 f. ; P. M. Meyer, Jurist Pap. (1920) 30 (bottom) ; Preisigke, Wörterbuch s.v.

[4] G. de Manteuffel, in Revue de Philologie 54 (1928), 163 No. 10. [Cf. Pap. Oxy. XI (1915), 1380.]

[5] Reitzenstein, Nachr. Ges. Göttingen (1917) 130 f. compares

φιλίαν in l. 94). 'Αγαπησμός and ἀγάπησις are more frequent, apparently older, and in any case better attested than ἀγάπη : both mean love or the demonstration of love.[1]

with this Inscr. Gr. XII, v, 217 : " I (Isis) joined together wife and husband . . . I caused women to be loved by men ".

[1] Suidas s.v. ἀγαπησμός : ἀγαπησμὸν λέγουσιν καὶ ἀγάπησιν τὴν φιλοφροσύνην. See Passow-Crönert s.v.

Additional Note communicated by Dr. Stauffer, July 13th, 1949. (See p. 30, n. 3.)

Earlier evidence is found in Pap. Berlin 9869 (Berliner Klassikertexte 2 (1905) 55), a fragment, not completely understood, of a philosophical dialogue of the Ptolemaic period, probably second century B.C., which contains the words ΜΑΛΙΣΤΑ ΑΓΑΠΗΣ . . . . Cf. also Pap. Paris 49.

III. LOVE IN JUDAISM

(1) A totally different picture is presented when we look at the Old Testament (see pp. 1-24). The primary Hebrew word is *'ahebh*, which can mean the over-whelming passion that unites husband and wife (Song viii, 6 f.), the unselfish loyalty of friends (I Sam. xx), or resolute devotion to righteousness (Ps. xlv, 7). The Hebrew term thus comprises all the wealth of the three Greek ideas. The one feature that is missing is religious eroticism ; Old Testament religion thus differs not only from what is so typical of the Greeks but also from the fertility cults of its environment. God's love for Israel (Deut. vii, 13) is not instinct but will ; the love to God and man enjoined upon Israel (Deut. vi, 5 ; Lev. xix, 18) is not ecstasy but service.

The essential characteristic of love (*'ahªbhah*) in Israel is actually its tendency towards exclusiveness. The Greek Eros is fundamentally universal, undis-criminating, undisciplined, broadminded. The love which is commended in the Old Testament is the jealous love which chooses one object among thousands and holds it fast with all the strength of its passion and its will, brooking no relaxation of the bond of loyalty. It is just this jealousy which reveals the divine strength of such love. It is no accident by which in the Song of Songs (viii, 6) love strong as death is inseparably connected, in the poetic parallelism, with jealousy hard as Hell. Jacob has two wives, but his love is only given to one of them (Gen. xxix) ; he has twelve sons, but loves one of them more than all the others (Gen. xxxvii, 3). God has set many peoples in the world, but gives his love to the elect nation. With this he makes a covenant which he loyally keeps and

32

jealously guards—as if it were a bond of marriage
(Hos. i ff.). To break the law is a breach of faith,
to worship strange gods is adultery, calling forth the
passionate jealousy of Yahwe. For he is " a jealous
God ", punishing iniquity, but showing mercy (*ḥeṣedh*)
unto them that love him and keep his commandments
(Exod. xx).

The principle of loving one's neighbour is marked
by the same motif of exclusiveness. It is a love that
makes distinctions, choosing, preferring, rejecting—
not a cosmopolitan love, embracing millions. The
Israelite begins his social activity at home, loving
Israel first as God does, and bestowing his love upon
the stranger who is admitted to membership in his
house and nation (Exod. xx, 10 ; xxii, 20 etc.). I
must also go to the help of my enemy (*sone'*, hater)
if he meets with misfortune and appeals to me (cf.
Exod. xxiii, 4 f.). The scope of social responsibility
is thus always defined in terms of a particular organism
and a concrete situation. The cosmopolitan Greek
loves all the world ; the patriotic Israelite his neighbour ; the impulse working centrifugally in the one
and centripetally in the other.

The Septuagint almost always employs ἀγαπᾶν to
translate the Hebrew *'ahebh* (see p. 1).[1] The noun
ἀγάπη now becomes more frequent, as the translation
of *'ahᵃbhah*, while ἔρως and φιλία and their cognates
tend to disappear. The victory of the inoffensive
ἀγαπᾶν is no doubt due to its previous usage, which
made it a suitable vehicle for the ideas of choice,
special attention and willingness to help, which are
integral to the Old Testament understanding of love.
But the real victor in this competition is the old
Hebrew *'ahebh*, which enriched the vague Greek word
with the full strength of its meaning. It used to be

---

[1] Zech. xiii, 6 LXX, ἀγαπητός for *mᵉahebh*.

thought that ἀγάπη was a new word coined by the
Septuagint, but this view is no longer considered
probable. What is much more important is the fact
that the Greek translation of the O.T. has given new
values to the whole ἀγαπᾶν family of words.

(2) *Hellenistic Judaism.* (a) In the widespread Jewish
world Greek and oriental ways of thought and speech
are intermingled with the predominant influence of
the Old Testament.[1] God's love is a frequent theme.
He loves his creation more than any man ever can ;
but he loves Israel by name : " Thy love is upon the
seed of Abraham ".[2] His special good pleasure again
rests upon the pious (ἠγαπημένος in the Prayer of
Azariah, v. 12 — Dan. iii, 35, LXX). Josephus says
upon the " good " when he is writing his best Greek,[3]
but upon the " penitent " when he is thinking in
Biblical terms (Ant. II, 23 [3, 1]). The Wisdom
literature and related writings teach that the way to
earn God's love is to fulfil the commandments and
particularly to practise mercy. He who treats the
orphan like a father will be loved by God as a son
(Ecclus. iv, 10 f. ; cf. Test. Napht. viii, 4 and 10).
But in the highest sense ἀγάπη is a relation of mutual
loyalty between God and man. " The faithful shall
abide with him in love " (Wis. iii, 9). The martyr
who devotes himself to God without reserve, enduring
every torture for his sake, reaches a deeper level in the

[1] For what follows cf. Kauffman Kohler in Jew. Enc. VIII
(1904), 188 ff. ; [R. H. Charles, Rel. Dev. (1914), 133–158].

[2] Ps. Sol. xviii, 4 ; cf. Josephus, Ant. VIII, 173 [6, 5] : θεὸν
ἀγαπήσαντα . . . τὴν χώραν. Schlatter, Wie Sprach Josephus
von Gott (1910) 63 ff., compares the Rabbinic ḥibbebh with
Josephus' use of ἀγαπᾶν.

[3] Ant. VIII, 314 [12, 6] ; τὸ θεῖον . . . ἀγαπᾷ τοὺς ἀγαθούς,
μισεῖ δὲ τοὺς πονηρούς. How thoroughly Greek this is, appears
from a comparison with Julian Ep. lxxxix b, p. 129, 4 (Bidex-
Cumont).

experience of the divine faithfulness in the midst of his agony—and will receive eternal life in the world to come.[1] " The Lord is faithful to those who love him in truth, enduring . . . his discipline."[2] Love to God is bound up with God's love. But it is God who takes the initiative, according to the Letter of Aristeas (229) : " Piety's power is love, which is the gift of God ". Similarly one can speak of love towards wisdom and truth (Ecclus. iv, 12). Love of wisdom is the keeping of her laws (Wis. vi, 18). Love the truth, and it will preserve you (Test. Reub. iii, 9). Josephus is specially fond of circumlocutions which have a metaphysical sound, and speaks significantly of the mind that loves God.[3] That sounds like the religion of a cultured Greek. Philo speaks in the tone of a mystic about the love which seeks the absolute, by which man is lifted above all fear and attains to true life (Deus Immutabilis 69) ; " Ascend, O soul, to the vision of the Real, fearlessly . . . lovingly " (Migr. Abr. 169 ; cf. Cherub. 73).

(b) *Neighbourly Love* is a favourite theme of Hellenistic Judaism. Not only is it God's commandment ; it also, like love to God, is rooted in God himself. Hate is of the devil ; love is of God. He who loves his neighbour,

---

[1] Wis. iii, 9 ; Dan. LXX, ix, 4 ; Bel xxxvii (xxxviii) ; IV Macc. xvi, 19 ff. ; xv, 2 : τὴν εὐσέβειαν μᾶλλον ἠγάπησε (more than life itself).

[2] Ps. Sol. xiv, 1, as a formula ; cf. iv, 29 ; vi, 9. Love to God also Tob. xiv, 7.

[3] Ant. VII, 269 [11, 3] ; Ap. ii, 296 [41] : " to love truth ". Otherwise in Ant. XVI, 158 [5, 4] : " accustomed to love righteousness instead of glory " (cf. μᾶλλον ἠγ. in n. 1 above). Typically Greek in Bell. Jud. V, 438 [10, 3] ἀγαπητόν, " something with which one must be content ". Sometimes Josephus, like the profane Greek writers, uses ἀγαπᾶν promiscuously with ἐρᾶν, φιλεῖν or their cognates ; cf. e.g. Bell. Jud. IV, 319 [5, 2] : Ἄνανος . . . ἠγαπηκὼς τὸ ἰσότιμον καὶ πρὸς τοὺς ταπεινοτάτους φιλελεύθερός τε καὶ δημοκρατίας ἐραστής.

and only he, is secure against the assaults of Beliar
(Test. Gad v, 2 ; Benj. iii, 4 ; cf. viii, 2). Hatred leads
to death ; love through long suffering to salvation
(Test. Gad iv, 7). The reference is often to relatives,[1]
but more frequently to neighbours in general—particularly in the case of the Golden Rule in " Menan-
der ".[2] Love of enemies is also expressly enjoined
(Ep. Aristeas 227). The fact remains, however, that
the Jews of the Dispersion found difficulty enough in
reconciling their inherited idea of love with the Hellenistic ideal of humanity. Philo devotes a long chapter
to this problem in De Virtut. 51 ff. under the significant
title, " Of Philanthropy " ; and comparison with
Josephus, Apion II, 209 [28 ff.], etc. makes it probable
that this is a classical passage in Jewish apologetic.
Everything that can be extracted by a tendentious
exegesis from the Old Testament in support of philan-
thropic motives is here assessed by Philo and presented
in the form of a unified system. The Jew must first
show love to his fellow Israelite : he stands at the centre ;
round him are proselytes [3] and resident aliens ; then
follow enemies (109 ff.), slaves, beasts and plants in
ever-widening circles until at last we arrive at the
love of all creation. That must have impressed the
Greeks. And yet, consciously or unconsciously, this
very arrangement displays the peculiar quality of the
Jewish love of neighbours—its fundamentally centripetal character. Hellenistic Judaism is ready to
adapt itself in external details, but remains rooted in

[1] Test. Sim. iv, 7. Cf. also " beloved and only son ", Philo,
Som. i, 194 ; Abr. 168 ; Vit. Mos. i, 3.

[2] Men. 40 in a negative form. Similarly Tob. iv, 15 and Philo
in Euseb. Praep. Ev. VIII, vii, 6. For an approach towards the
positive form, see Ep. Arist. 207 ; cf. Kittel, Probleme 109 f.

[3] 103 : κελεύει δὴ τοῖς ἀπὸ τοῦ ἔθνους ἀγαπᾶν τοὺς ἐπηλύτας
μὴ μόνον ὡς φίλους καὶ συγγεγεῖς ἀλλὰ ὡς ἑαυτούς.

the ancient Jewish understanding of love. Thus the frontier is held firmly against the Eros of the " corrupt Greeks " (Sib. iii, 171).[1] Eros is no god : he is a destroyer (Phocylides 194). The strongest enemy of all forms of eroticism is to be found in the purity of Agape (Test. Benj. viii, 2).

The noun ἀγάπη occurs more frequently in the Testaments of the XII Patriarchs (Gad iv; 7 ; v, 2 ; Benj. viii, 2 ; Reub. vi, 8 f.), but is only found once in the Psalms of Solomon (xviii, 4), once in the Epistle of Aristeas (229) ; and once in Philo (Deus Immut. 69). Josephus uses neither ἀγάπη nor ἀγάπησις.[2] Cf. further Wis. iii, 9 ; vi, 18 f. ; Sib. ii, 65 .

(3) *Rabbinical Judaism.* (a) So far as Hebrew is concerned, 'ahebh remains the fundamental word for loving, but in Rabbinic writings the Aramaic word hibbebh has become naturalised.[3] Both words carry on the idea of an exercise of will and the old religious quality ; indeed these are often deepened by the endurance of persecution and by a century of discipline in willing and doing.

Love marks the relation between God and man, but specially between God and his people. " Beloved (habhibh) is man, for he is made in the image of God . . . Beloved is Israel, for they are called children of God— yea, specially beloved because they are told that they are God's children." So said Akiba (Aboth iii, 18 ; cf. Bab. Yoma 52a). Other illustrations show even more clearly the warmth and constancy of this love. God's everlasting mercy towards Israel is like the love

---

[1] Josephus loves piquant stories, but tells them in a tone of moral indignation, e.g. Ant. XVIII, 72 ff. [3, 4].

[2] Cf. Thackeray, Lex. Jos.

[3] Cf. the Blessing of Moses (Deut. xxxiii, 3) : 'aph hobhebh 'ammim. Besides 'ahebh and habhabh also raham, hesedh, etc. Cf. Levy, Neuhebr. & chald. Wörterbuch üb. d. Talm. u. Midr.

of a king who after a short interval graciously seeks again the favourite wife who had been divorced (Midrash 51 to Exod. xxxviii, 21). God is the beloved of the Song of Songs, always near, always ready to forgive (Bab. Shab. 88*b*). Therefore Israel must love its God with all its heart and soul and might (Deut. vi, 5). The Shema' plays as important a part in later Jewish piety as in Rabbinical exegesis and theology.[1]

The Law is itself an outstanding proof of God's love for his people. " Beloved are Israel, for unto them was given the desirable instrument; but it was by a special love that it was made known to them that that desirable instrument was theirs, through which the world was created ; as it is said, ' For I give you good doctrine ; forsake ye not my law ' (Aqiba in Aboth iii, 18)." The Law is Israel's patent of nobility—like all God's gracious gifts, a privilege involving responsibility. Love of the Law brings God and his people together (*ḥabhibh* in Bab. Men. 99*b*) and classical examples [2] like Moses and Jethro provide a powerful inspiration for wholehearted and unconditional devotion (Bab. Shab. 130*a*, etc.).

Suffering, however—and particularly martyrdom—is the point at which love between God and his people has its decisive revelation. " How precious are chastisements." [3] For sufferings are for the correction of those whom the Lord loves, and must be understood as the chastisements of love (Mek. Exod. xx, 23 ; Bab. Ber. 5*b*). Not only so ; sufferings are the means of earning God's good pleasure, they atone for sin and

---

[1] Cf. Targ. Onq. Deut. vi, 5 (*tirḥam*) ; Sifre Deut. 32 on vi, 5 (Kittel, 54 ff.) ; Strack-Billerbeck IV, 189 ff.

[2] Bab. Sota, 13a, etc.

[3] Sifre Deut. vi, 5. *ḥabhibh* in formula in Exod. Rabba 27 on xviii, 1 ; Deut. Rabba 5 (end) ; Bab. Yoma 52a, etc.

guarantee a portion in the world to come.[1] But above
all they are the decisive testing by fire of our love for
God's law and for God himself. " When the Scripture
says that those who love him are like the sun rising
in splendour, it refers to those who, when humiliated,
refrain from humiliating others, who suffer abuse
without retaliating, who fulfil the commandments out
of love and rejoice in chastisement."[2] It is obvious
that such loyalty must affect the future lot of the
martyr. But the outstanding point is that God is
loved for his own sake. It is related that all through
his life Aqiba was dominated by the thought that only
martyrdom could finally and perfectly express the love
" with all thy soul " demanded by the Shema'. He
taught the Law without a care for his own safety . . .
When the hour came for repeating the Shema', he was
dragged to the place of execution—and died under the
iron combs with the word *'eḥadh* (One) upon his lips,
almost finishing the first sentence of the Shema' (Bab.
Ber. 61*b*). This fine story gives us an incomparable
picture of suffering Israel's pure, strong-minded,
absolute love for its God.

But the thought of the Rabbis always turns back
to God's love. It may be hidden in this time of stress—
all the more glorious will be its revelation when its
own time comes. Love is strong as death. Only the
triumphant words of the Song of Songs come anywhere

[1] Lev. Rabba 32 on xxiv, 10 : " It is for these strokes I am loved
(*'ahebh*) by my Father in heaven ". So in Mek. Exod. xx, 6
(Wünsche 213). Further Mek. Exod. xx, 23 : " Sufferings are
precious, because they obtain the law, the land and the world to
come ". Similarly Sifre Deut. vi, 5 (Kittel 54 ff.) and Bab.
Sanh. 101a-b. Very significant is the answer to the question, " Do
you like being chastised ? "—" Neither chastisement nor com-
pensation ! " (Bab. Ber. 5b, *ḥabhibh*). Cf. O. Wichmann, Die
Leidenstheologie (1930).

[2] Bab. Shab. 88b ; cf. also Mek. Exod. xx, 23 (Wünsche 227 f.).

near giving a true idea of the elemental strength of this
love. A magnificent exposition of the Song puts into
words all the bitter facts of experience which God's
persecuted people have in mind when they speak of
his love as being strong as death to the generation
of the persecuted. Hard as Hell is God's jealousy
when idolatry flourishes. Many waters cannot quench
love ; and the peoples of the world cannot tear
Israel away from the love of its God. If a man would
give all the substance of his house for love, he would
utterly be contemned ; and the love with which Aqiba
and his companions sacrificed themselves is more
precious than all the treasures of the world.[1] Romantic
religion has always looked for mystical thrills in the
Song ; Judaism has made of it a hymn to the brave and
faithful love which unites God and his tortured people.

(b) Jewish expressions for love strike another note
when they deal with man's relations to man.[2] Love
to God is perfected in suffering, whereas love to one's
fellow man is perfected in the giving of practical help.
" To practise love means to perform acts of kindness."[3]

Who is the neighbour who has a claim upon the help
of an Israelite ? Primarily he is the fellow-Israelite
or the proselyte—just as he is in the ancient Hebrew
centripetal conception of the matter.[4] Again as in the
Old Testament, readiness to help an enemy is demanded
if the latter is a fellow-Israelite, and even, in certain
circumstances, if he is a foreigner (Mek. Exod. xxiii, 4)[5].

[1] Song Rabba viii, 6 f. (Wünsche 183 f.) ; cf. also Peṣiqta 28
(Wünsche 262).

[2] Sexual love e.g. Bab. Ket. 56a (ḥibbah).

[3] Bab. Sukk. 49b. ; cf. g^emiluth ḥaṣadhim in Bab. Ber. 5b, etc.

[4] Many examples in Strack-Billerbeck I, 353 ff. ; cf. also IV,
536 ff., 559 ff.

[5] This and other important passages in Kittel, Probleme 110 ff.
For historical parallels, etc. see Haas, Feindesliebe in der ausser-
christlichen Welt (1927).

This last interpretation, however, did not remain unquestioned. The love of neighbours of which Judaism speaks generally halts at the frontier. Hillel is therefore perfectly consistent when he adds to his attractive words about loving God's creatures a saying about making the Law widely known and increasing the number of God's people : " Loving ('*ahebh*) peace. Striving after peace. Loving thy fellow-creatures and drawing them near to the Law " (Aboth i, 12). The centripetal motif is still dominant.

Jewish love of neighbour is originally the duty which Israelites owe to one another. But as such it reaches its highest significance. " Upon three things the world is based ; upon the Law, upon divine service, and upon the practice of charity " (Simon the Just in Aboth i, 2). Aqiba taught that love of neighbour is the great all-comprehensive rule (Sifra Leviticus xix, 18).[1] Hillel does the same when he gathers all the commandments together in the Golden Rule : " Do not unto thy neighbour what is hateful unto thee ; that is the whole Law. All the rest is commentary." [2]

The Rabbis are not content with commending the love of neighbours and drawing up formal rules for it ; they speak also about its motives and grounds. " Practise love to others, so that they may practise love to you."[3] A deeper level is reached when it is suggested that love, and not clever calculation, should be the mainspring of our behaviour. It is love that gives meaning and value to works of charity. " Do all

[1] But cf. also the equalisation of all commandments in IV Macc. v, 20.

[2] Bab. Shab. 31a ; Targ. Pseudojon. Lev. xix, 18. Positive formulation in Ab. R. Nathan xv, 1 f. ; xvi, 2 (Kittel, Probleme 110).

[3] Cf. G. Klein, Der älteste christl. Katechismus (1909) 86, A.1 ; for the idea of a reward see Strack-Billerbeck IV, 562 ff.

that you do for the sake of love." [1]   It is widely
recognised that love cannot be commanded. It
cannot properly fall under rule and compulsion, but
must be more deeply grounded. The Rabbis have
shown its foundations, and thereby brought Jewish
understanding of love to its culminating point.

(c) The love of which the Rabbis speak is neither
love between God and man alone, nor love between
man and man alone, nor both side by side, but both
inseparably together. It is the fundamental principle
of the threefold relationship : God, man and man.[2]
" As the Holy One, blessed be He, clothes the naked,
visits the sick, comforts the mourners, buries the dead—
so do thou clothe the naked, visit the sick, comfort the
mourners, bury the dead " (Bab. Sota. 14a). And
again," He who has mercy on his fellow-man, himself
receives the mercy of Heaven". [3]   Man's mercy is
nothing else but emulation of the mercy of God,
imitation of divine behaviour.[4]   God treats men on the
principle on which they treat their fellow-men. Love
is the principle divinely ordained for the relation
between God, I, and Thou ; unless it is in constant
control the relation is ruined. First and last it is God
who maintains this principle. Yet there are times
when it is man's business to maintain the standard of
divine kindness before God. This is indeed one of

---

[1] Sifre Deut. 41 on xi, 3 (Str.-Bill. III, 306).

[2] [Cf. C. H. Dodd, The Johannine Epistles, p. 117 : " The
energy of love discharges itself along the lines which form a triangle
whose points are God, self and neighbour " ; Kierkegaard 87 ff.].

[3] Bab. Shab. 151b. ; cf. Bab. Ber. 5b : Deeds of love count for
the blotting out of sins . . . like the sufferings of the martyrs !

[4] Cf. also A. Marmorstein, Die Nachahmung Gottes, in Jüd.
Stud. für J. Wohlegemuth (1928) 25 ff. ; G. F. Moore, Judaism
II, 109 ff. ; [I. Abrahams, Studies in Pharisaism ii, 138 f. ;
Schechter, Some Aspects of Rabbinic Theology 199-202.]

Judaism's most daring ideas—or perhaps we should call it a desperate appeal.

Esdras reaches the climax of the powerful third dialogue with the angel when he says, " I know that the Lord is called . . . the merciful, in that he hath mercy upon them which are not yet come into the world. . . . If he did not forgive of his goodness, that they which have committed iniquities might be eased of them, the ten thousandth part of men would not remain living " (II Esdr. vii, 132, 138). The angel's retort makes no difference : " Thou comest far too short of being able to love the creation more than I " (vii, 47). The fact remains : it is Esdras who must appeal to the mercy of God, declaring that the whole human world would fall to pieces if God were to measure by righteousness and not by love.[1] Rabbinic Judaism also gives us the same insight, the same attitude. The good man, loving righteousness and hating wickedness, intercedes for God's creatures in the confidence that God's mercy is greater than Israel's sin, assured that without love God cannot uphold his world.[2]

This assurance could not be given its full range and scope without shattering the basis of the Jewish view of God, world and life. But these it was never given. The great words about love remain isolated. In spite of all, righteousness continues to provide the foundation for Jewish theology and ethics.[3] It was

[1] Cf. Apoc. Sedrach 8 (end) in Texts and Studies (1893) II, 2, 3, p. 133 ; Apoc. Elias 17 in Texte u. Untersuchungen (1899) XVII, 3a, p. 63 ; obviously echoes and expansions.

[2] Peṣiqta 16 f. (Wünsche 171 f., 178). The thought of intercession for the wicked is expressed otherwise in Bab. Sanh. 37a.

[3] It is significant that the same thing is true of Zoroastrianism. " The best possession known is that of Zarathushtra Spitama, which is that Mazda Ahura will give him through the Right the glories of blessed life unto all time, and likewise to them that

Jesus who first broke down the old foundation walls
and undertook the daring task of a complete rebuilding.

practise and learn the words and actions of his Good Religion."
" Whoso therefore in the future lightly esteemeth the Daevas and
those mortals who lightly esteem him—even all others save that
one who highly esteemeth him—unto him shall the holy Self of the
future deliverer, as Lord of the house, be friend, brother, or father,
O Mazda Ahura." (Yasna liii, 1 ; xlv, 11 ; trans, J. H. Moulton,
Early Zoroastrianism (1913).) Cf. Sacred Books of the East
XXIV, 73 ff. ; 113.

IV. JESUS

(1) *The New Demand.* (*a*) Jesus summarised the meaning of the old and new righteousness in two sentences : " Thou shalt love God ; thou shalt love thy neighbour " (Mark xii, 28 ff. ; Matt. xxii, 40). Both are well-known Old Testament sayings, and both are often expressly emphasised by the Rabbis. And the new formula for neighbourly love which Jesus set up (Matt. vii, 12) only differs from Hillel's famous rule by being couched in positive terms.[1] Jesus stands clearly and consciously in the line of his nation's ethical tradition. But he demands love with such exclusiveness that all other commandments are included in it ; love is the final criterion of righteousness. For him also love is an affair of willing and doing. But he requires wholehearted decision for God so uncompromisingly as to discourage his hearers.

The question of love to God presents two radical alternatives : " No man can serve two lords :[2] for either he will hate the one and love the other, or else he will hold to one and despise the other " (Matt. vi, 24). According to this, loving God means attending to him like a slave (Luke xvii, 7 ff.), faithfully obeying his orders, submitting to his lordship and seeking the extension of that lordship before every other aim in life (cf. Matt. vi, 33). But it also means regarding God as the ground of one's whole existence, depending upon him without reserve, leaving all care and final responsibility to him,[3] living out of his hand. In any

[1] See n. 2, p. 41.

[2] Notice Matt. xxii, 37 : " Thou shalt love the Lord ".

[3] On the problem of the relation between love and anxiety, see W. Koepp's discussion with Heidegger in Seeberg-Festschrift (1929), 99 ff.

case it means hating and scorning everything which neither serves God nor comes from him, breaking with all merely prudential considerations, cutting off everything that hinders (cf. Matt. v, 29 f.), breaking every tie except that with God.

Jesus mentions two enemies against which war must be declared by the men who mean to love God : Mammon and pride. The man who seeks to pile up riches is a man of little faith, a heathen, hopeless for the Kingdom of God (Matt. vi, 24b, 30 ff.). And Jesus pronounces a Woe over the Pharisees " because ye love the first seat in the synagogues and greetings in the market-place ".[1] The desire for prestige is not consistent with love to God. But there is yet a third danger which threatens love to God, and that is the distress of a time of persecution. Like the great Jewish martyr-theologians, and above all Aqiba, Jesus knows that the opposition and hostility, slander and suffering, which await his disciples, will constitute the crucial test of their loyalty to God (cf. Matt. x, 17 ff. ; v, 10 ff.). When the great, final tribulation comes upon the world, " Then shall many stumble [2] . . . and the love of the many shall wax cold : but he that endureth to the end shall be saved " (Matt. xxiv, 10, 12 f.).[3] These words make absolutely clear what it means to love God. It means glowing with a passion for God, the passionate eagerness to suffer that characterises a little flock which holds on, faithful and undismayed, in spite of all its problems and the menace of powerful authorities—until HE comes, whom they love.

---

[1] Luke xi, 43. Matt. xxiii, 6 has φιλεῖν. The basic word is of course 'ahebh ; cf. 'ehabh in Aboth i, 10 : " Love working, hate lording it ".

[2] Cf. Matt. v, 29 f.

[3] [See p. 12, note 4.] For the absolute use of ἀγάπη cf. also Ep. Aristeas 229 (see above p. 35). [Cf. I John iv, 19 R.V.]

(b) Love to God is the great, fundamental demand of Jesus. " And a second is like unto it : thou shalt love thy neighbour as thyself " (Matt. xxii, 39). Like a good Jew, he takes the sober view of the matter, and simply tells us to love our neighbours as ourselves— avoiding the fanaticism both of a vague universalism and of the impracticable idealism which says, " Thou shalt love thy neighbour more than thine own soul " (Barnabas xix, 5). But he sets love free for ever from its limitation to fellow-nationals, and brings it to bear again upon the case that lies at our feet. He takes the question out of the sphere of legal controversy and puts it to the heart with an impressiveness that admits of no evasion.

The Golden Rule (Matt. vii, 12 ; Luke vi, 31), taken by itself, might be wrongly understood as mere philanthropy, as it is in humanistic ethics from Aristotle to Kant. But the story of the Good Samaritan makes this impossible (Luke x, 29 ff.). The lawyer asks, " Who is my neighbour ? " Jesus does not reply with a systematic grading of mankind in groups ranging from fellow countrymen close at hand to foreigners far away, after the manner of Philo (see above p. 36). Neither does he proceed to extol the love of those afar, which regards all men equally as brethren. His answer is to turn the lawyer's question round : " Who is neighbour to the man in need of help ? " Jesus destroyed the old centripetal grading system, in which the centre was " I ", but retained the idea of the neighbour as organising principle and founded a new system, in which the centre was " Thou ". But his grading is not a scheme that can be applied mechanically to all men and all occasions ; it is concerned only with the concrete, and functions from case to case, whenever a man is in need. Whoever " by chance " (Luke x, 31) is nearest to the sufferer, it is his duty to act as neighbour. Of the three who found themselves close to the wounded man in the story, which did his duty as neighbour ? The Samaritan—an alien. Why so ? Because " when he saw him he was moved with compassion ". The final decision lay with the heart. It was the one whose heart felt pity for the stranger, who did his duty as a neighbour. What is here demanded is an absolutely unsentimental readiness to help. Without any excitement the Samaritan does what the moment requires, and provides for the immediate future—neither more nor less. He is one who " shows mercy ", neither refusing to act nor wasting words on the duty or guilt of others. Here is one who does what has to be done and what he can do. That is precisely what gives the story its inescapable impressiveness : " Go and do thou likewise ".

(c) When Jesus demands *love of enemies*, he sets himself consciously in opposition to Jewish tradition. Though so brief, the record in Matt. v, 43 f. and Luke vi, 32 f. makes three points quite clear. First, the new demand belongs to a new time : " It was said . . . but I say ". Secondly, it involves χάρις (Matt. v, 46 f. : " reward ", " more "). Thirdly, it is addressed to a group of " hearers " (cf. Luke vi, 27) who are sharply separated from " sinners " (publicans, Gentiles, Matt. v, 46 f.). The love of enemies, demanded by Jesus, characterises the attitude of the sons of the new people of God, to whom the future belongs, towards the children of this world. They must practise love without expecting any return, lend where there is no hope of repayment, give away with boundless generosity. They must willingly accept the world's hostility in a sacrificial spirit of non-resistance (Luke vi, 28), even doing good to those who hate them, countering curses with blessings and praying for their persecutors (Luke vi, 27 ff. ; Matt. v, 44). It is possible to find isolated parallels to some of these rules in the Rabbinic world. They mean nothing over against the closely-knit programme of Jesus. This unparalleled will to martyrdom goes far beyond the martyr-spirit of God's ancient people, the Jews. A new task of intercession is here laid upon the martyr : he is to pray for the hostile world, which hates God and kills the faithful.[1]

There have always been utopians. But here speaks one who gave concrete reality to the love of neighbours, without illusion or sentimentality. He speaks of these impossible claims in a tone of consistent earnestness and realism, as meaning what everybody can and should do. There have always been visionaries, dreaming of universal love and a better world. Jesus knows the world as it is, and yet calls on men to live the life of perfect love in this world. He does it in sober, objective seriousness. That is what is so mysterious in his demand for love—this new way of treating the matter as self-evident. The secret must lie here.

(2) *The New Situation.* (a) If the matter is self-evident, that implies that Jesus has more to proclaim than a new demand. He proclaims, he creates a new world-situation. Jesus proclaims the divine mercy, not as the temper in which God always acts—pardonner, c'est son métier—but as an unparalleled event, the possibility of which is grounded in God alone, placing man here and now in a perfectly new situation. Jesus brings the forgiveness of sins, and when a man experiences that, a completely new power of overflowing love is released within him. It is in this sense that Jesus says of the woman that was a sinner, " Her sins, which are many, are forgiven ; for she loved

[1] [See F. Jackson and K. Lake, The Beginnings of Christianity I, 77 ff., 288 ff.]

much " : the latter is evidence, showing that the former has taken place.[1]

It is striking that in this instance ἀγαπᾶν is twice used without a direct object, specially as the absolute use of the verb is not found elsewhere except in the first Epistle of John.   This only makes it all the clearer what Luke vii, 47 is about.   The point is that the new life is here awakened in a human being, who now has love, is full of it, under its guidance in everything. The question as to who is the recipient of this love is secondary.   In this case love is directed by a spontaneous impulse towards him who is the author of it (cf. the absolute use of ἀγάπη in the Epistle of Aristeas 229, and in Matt. xxiv, 12, where similarly God is its primary object).   But that is not the important thing in our story, and certainly it is not the motive of the divine act of forgiveness.

God has, by his act of forgiveness, introduced a new order into the world, which entirely surpasses the old, doing away with its scale of values, and creating new tasks and possibilities.   The new relation of God to man lays the foundation for a new relation of man to man : " Be ye merciful, as your Father is merciful " (Luke vi, 36).   The peacemakers shall be called sons of God.[2] If a man sits in judgment over his fellow, he rules himself out of the new order and falls under God's unmerciful judgment.   " For with what measure ye mete it shall be measured to you again."[3]   The prayer for forgiveness, which we ever need to pray afresh, demands the daily renewal of readiness to forgive " everyone that is indebted to us ".[4]

---

[1] Luke vii, 47.   The love is evidence of forgiveness.   See E. Klostermann's commentary (2nd ed.) ad loc.

[2] Matt. v, 9.   Cf. υἱοί at Matt. v, 45.

[3] Luke vi, 38 ; cf. Matt. v, 22 ff.

[4] Luke xi, 4 ; cf. also Matt. v, 7 ; xviii, 21 ff.

According to the Synoptic Gospels, Jesus hardly ever[1] uses the noun ἀγάπη for God's love, and never the verb ἀγαπᾶν (nor indeed φιλία or φιλεῖν). He proclaims and brings forgiveness (ἄφεσις), and speaks of God showing pity and being merciful (ἐλεεῖν, οἰκτίρμων εἶναι). Consistently with this, whenever the imitation of God is involved—the threefold relation of God, man and man—the exhortation to be merciful and conciliatory stands in the foreground.

(b) God's love, which breaks into the world at this great moment of history, is pardoning love. But Jesus knows a divine love of another kind, viz. the preferential love, which includes a setting apart and a peculiar calling. This is God's love for Jesus himself, bestowed on him alone. Jesus refers to this in the parable of the Wicked Husbandmen, when he speaks of a " beloved son " (υἱὸς ἀγαπητός, Mark xii, 5, cf. Matt. xii, 18). But the calling of the " only son " is to tread to the end the pathway of the prophets, on which they met their death. The beloved son is the unique martyr,[2] standing at the turning-point of time, whose death brings judgment upon the world and lays the foundation for the new ordering of all things (Mark xii, 8 ff.). Thus Jesus himself becomes the founder of the new people of God : ·it is the attitude towards him which decides whether or not a man will belong to the world to come. Love that is ready to help the humblest is equivalent to readiness to help the Son of Man, whereas lovelessness is nothing else than despising the Son of Man. He will pass judgment on both when his Day arrives (Matt. x, 40 ff. ; xxv, 31 ff.).

---

[1] Luke xi, 42 should perhaps be compared with Ps. Sol. xviii, 3. Yet see Matt. xxiii, 23.

[2] Here, surely, we have an echo of ancient ideas concerning the final martyr. See Zeitschr. f. syst. Theol. VIII (1930, 1931), 212 A.4.

So Jesus can pronounce beatitudes upon the disciples
who must suffer persecution for his sake (Luke vi,
22 f.), and calls for unconditional devotion to himself, the following of him even unto death, with the
same radicalism with which he summons men to be
ready for God : " He that loveth father or mother
more than me is not worthy of me . . . and he that
doth not take up his cross and follow after me is not
worthy of me " (Matt. x, 37 ff., cf. Luke xiv, 26 f.).
The point which we have been considering makes all
that Jesus said about love perfectly clear, and gives it
unity.   God sends the " beloved son " into the world
" to proclaim the acceptable year of the Lord ".
The son brings the forgiveness of sins, to which man
responds with grateful love, and is bound to respond
with unconditional readiness to help and forgive his
fellow-man.   Jesus calls for unreserved decision for
God and gathers round him a " storm troop " (Matt.
xi, 12) that clings to him, forsaking all and loving God
with a burning passion.   He creates a new people of
God, which abjures all hatred and violence, and must
tread the sacrificial way through all opposition with
an invincible will to love.   And he himself dies,
according to an ancient tradition, with a prayer for the
hostile world upon his lips (Luke xxiii, 34).

The Synoptic Gospels employ the word ἀγαπητός
exactly as Jesus does, when they report the utterance
of the expression " beloved son " at the beginning of
the public ministry and again at the beginning of the
period of the Passion (Mark i, 11 ; ix, 7).   And
Mark puts the connection between love, calling and
stern demand in a nutshell : " looking upon him
loved him and said " (x, 21).   Jesus loves the rich
young ruler with the love of God, which calls man to
his noblest task.   But the demand is too alarming
and he cannot face it !   The only other instance of the

use of the verb ἀγαπᾶν by the Synoptists, apart from
the words of Jesus, is Luke vii, 4 f. ; [1] they never use
the noun ἀγάπη. In the Book of Acts the only form
found is ἀγαπητός (xv, 25),[2] and it uses φίλος with
kindred meaning (xxvii, 3) and above all ἀδελφός
(i, 16). 'Αγάπη and ἀγαπᾶν do not occur at all, but
we find ἀφίημι, etc. (viii, 22 ff.), and the same idea of
forgiveness put in a negative form in the intercession of
the first Christian martyr for his enemies : " Lord, lay
not this sin to their charge " (vii, 60).

[1] But cf. Matt. x, 37.
[2] The " golden rule " is given later in the same section (xv, 29).

V. THE APOSTOLIC AGE

1. *Paul.* (*a*) Paul is perfectly clear in his understanding and description of the new situation created by God's act of love. The mighty argument of the Epistle to the Romans setting forth the theme of the new age now inaugurated, fitly culminates in a hymn which starts with the love of the elect towards God, proceeds to the love of Christ, and comes to rest in perfect assurance of " the love of God that is in Christ Jesus our Lord " (Rom. viii, 28, 31 ff.). This assurance rests upon three facts. (i) God has sent his own son,[1] and this act of love was perfected on the Cross in the self-offering of the son " who loved us ". (ii) God has called the apostle and goes on calling those whom he has fore-ordained ; his loving will is set upon them ; they are ἠγαπημένοι, ἀγαπητοί. (iii) God's love is shed abroad in our hearts and is henceforth the decisive reality of our existence.

As Jesus did not distinguish between his own activity and that of God, but rather did what God alone could do, in the forgiveness of sins, so for Paul the love of God is fundamentally one with the love of his Christ (Rom. viii, 37 ; II Thess. ii, 16). God's loving work is revealed and realised in the loving work of Christ : " God commendeth his own love toward us in that . . . Christ died for us " (Rom. v. 8). The eternal love of God becomes, in the love of Christ, a world-changing event, of which Paul is fond of speaking—using the verb, always in the Aorist tense.[2]

---

[1] Ἴδιος υἱός, Rom. viii, 32 ; υἱὸς τῆς ἀγάπης, Col. i, 13 ; cf. Eph. i, 6 : ὁ ἠγαπημένος. Paul never calls Christ ἀγαπητός.

[2] Ἀγαπήσαντος, Rom. viii, 37 ; II Thess. ii, 16 ; also Gal. ii, 20. The influence of this is seen in Eph. v, 2, etc. With Eph.

54

God's love involves predestination. Paul quotes the Old Testament passages concerning God's unconditioned sovereignty in loving and hating, choosing and rejecting (Rom. ix, 13, 25), and himself uses ἀγαπητοί and κλητοί, or ἐκλεκτοὶ καὶ ἠγαπημένοι in formal parallelism (Rom. i, 7 ; Col. iii, 12). It is relevant also to observe that the idea of the love which elects gives force and value both to the divine decision made long ago [1] and to the actual calling which now takes place through the agency of the fact of Christ : " . . . brethren beloved of the Lord, for that God chose you from the beginning unto salvation in sanctification of the Spirit . . . whereunto he called you through our Gospel to the obtaining . . ." (II Thess. ii, 13 ; cf. Eph. i, 4 f.).

The community of the elect, whom God in his " goodness and severity " (Rom. xi, 22) has separated out of the general mass of " sinners ", stands in unbreakable fellowship with the God of love and peace. He is livingly at work in their midst (Rom. viii, 35 ; II Cor. xiii, 11 ff.). The love of Christ constraineth us (II Cor. v, 14) ; but more than that : " the love of God hath been shed abroad in our hearts through the Holy Spirit which was given unto us " (Rom. v, 5). It is impossible to give more weighty expression to the reality of this new life-force than Paul has done in these words.

What Paul means by the love of God is clear. It is the directing of God's sovereign will towards this world and its salvation. Love in action is the goal towards which God has been striving from the very beginning. Ever since Abraham's days God has envisaged a people

---

ii, 4 (ἀγάπη ἦν. ἠγάπησεν) cf. Tosefta Ber. iii, 7: 'ahᵃbhathᵉkha she'ahabhta.

[1] Cf. ἐκλογή at I Thess. i, 4 (ἠγαπημένοι) ; Rom. xi, 28 (ἀγαπητοί) ; Rom. ix, 11 ff.

free from the domination of the law. He has created this people through the sending of the Son and finally of the Spirit. So runs the story according to the Epistle to the Galatians. And in the magnificent conclusion of the epistle the Spirit is seen to be the spirit of love (Gal. v, 2–vi, 10).

(b) The aim of God's loving action is the new man. But this is not achieved without loving action on the part of man himself. For every act of God, creation as well as redemption, assumes both the possibility and the necessity of human activity. God's will does not exclude the exercise of man's will ; on the contrary, it includes it, and is carried out most successfully when the latter is in a state of extreme tension. God's sovereign call is a call to freedom. God's new man is a free man. What the apostle says about the relation between divine and human love can only be understood in the light of this fundamental principle, seen in its purity in the fact of Jesus, and said by Paul to govern the relations between divine and human activity (cf. Phil. ii, 12 f.).

God has the first word. It is he who founds the relationship. That is established once for all in Romans viii. His design, his choice, his calling—these are decisive. All that Agape can mean proceeds from him. When men love God, that is the immediate reflection of the love which streams down from heaven upon the elect. Or rather, it is an act of choice like the original act of love itself. In it the covenant is concluded between God and his elect—the bond which defies all powers between heaven and earth : " to them that love God all things work together for good even to them that are called according to his purpose " (Rom. viii, 28 ; cf. 37).

It is the same fundamental relationship which leads Paul to coin the pregnant formula : " If any man

loveth God, the same is known of him " (I Cor. viii, 3).
We can only take the active step of turning to God in
so far as we are passive before him. The same
correlation of the passive with the active serves the
development of the same theme in Gal. iv, 9 ; I Cor.
xiii, 12 ; Phil. iii, 12.

God produces in us that kind of life which makes us for
the first time really alive as responsible human beings.
God awakens in man the faith with which he is entirely dependent upon God. But faith first comes into
operation, and finds its realisation " through love "
(Gal. v, 6). God introduces the Spirit into his elect
(Rom. v, 5 ; II Thess. ii, 13). Again passivity
characterises the human being. But the Spirit sets
him free for the highest form of activity—in love.
Freedom binds and perfects itself in love.

The idea that love is the work of the Spirit, which
sets it free, finds classical expression in Gal. v, 22 :
" The fruit of the Spirit is love " ; and also in phrases
like " the love of the Spirit " (Rom. xv, 30) and " love
in the Spirit " (Col. i, 8) ; it is hinted at more deli-
cately in I Cor. iv, 21. On the relation between the
Spirit and freedom, see Rom. viii, 2, and on love as the
criterion and goal of freedom, Gal. v, 13. There can
be no question that in this liberation to love, the law is
fulfilled, surpassed and left behind, and a new order
of life created, which brooks no lapse or violation.

The purpose of divine love, however, is not that we
should return love to God,[1] nor that we should attain
freedom for our own sakes ; it is that he who is called

[1] Paul very rarely speaks of love to God. In addition to Rom.
viii, 28 and I Cor. viii, 3 cf. II Thess. iii, 5. " Love of the Truth "
(II Thess. ii, 10) occurs in a passage strongly influenced by
tradition (see p. 35). Philem. 5 is to be read as an example of
the figure of speech known as chiasmus, and " Love " connected
with " the saints ". Finally cf. Eph. vi, 24 (iv, 15).

should put himself in love and freedom at the service of his neighbour : " Through love be servants one to another ; for the whole law is fulfilled in one word— thou shalt love thy neighbour as thyself" (Gal. v, 13 f.).[1] Paul takes up Jesus' demand for the love of neighbours, and establishes it in the same sense as the Lord. But his main interest is in brotherly love : " Let us work that which is good toward all men, and especially toward them that are of the household of the faith " (Gal. vi, 10). The organic principle, laid down once for all in the law of neighbourly love, is here completing its organising task : once the readiness of an Israelite to help those who share with him the life of the Covenant nation, it now means serving fellow-members of the new people of God—making the salvation of the brotherhood the supreme object in life.[2] " Beloved " and " Brother " become interchangeable terms (I Thess. ii, 8 ; Philem. 16).

The decisive importance of brotherly love is seen in relation to the unique moment in cosmic history (καιρός, Gal. vi, 10 ; Rom. xiii, 11) which makes it imperative. During the whole of this age of decision between the Cross and the " End ", brotherly love is the only relevant behaviour—the only principle that is sure of the future. Its sign is the sign of the Cross. It is willingness to serve and sacrifice, to forgive and make allowances, to share and sympathise, to lift up the fallen and restore the erring [3] in a community which owes its whole existence to the mercy of God and the

[1] For the love of neighbour see further Rom. xiii, 8 ff. and cf. I Thess. iii, 12.

[2] For the love of the brethren see I Thess. iv, 9 ; Col. i, 4 ; Philem. 5 ; cf. Eph. iv, 2 ; vi, 23. ἀγαπᾶν for married love in the Social Code, Col. iii, 19 (Eph. v, 25). Cf. Delatte Anecdota I (1927), 423 : ἀγάπην ἀνδρὸς πρὸς φιλίαν τῶν γυναικῶν. [Cf. I Pet. ed. E. G. Selwyn (1947) 105, 432.]

[3] Gal. v, 25 ff. ; Rom. xii, 9 f. ; I Cor. xiii, 4 ff.

sacrificial death of his Christ.[1] The apostle's own
highest ambition is to help forward the salvation of the
Church by the imitation of Christ. He is willing to
fill up that which is lacking of the afflictions of Christ
(Col. i, 24).[2] At the same time the humblest act of
human love finds its place in the service of the great
loving activity of God—in harmony with Paul's
fundamental idea of the relation between divine and
human operations. It is in love that the working
of God and man achieves unity. Love builds up
(I Cor. viii, 1)—it builds the work of the future.
Love's sign is the sign of the end. That is the great
truth of I Cor. xiii. Therefore love is the greatest of the
gifts of the Spirit, " the more excellent way " ; it not
only stands at the centre of the triad, faith, love, hope,
but is more than faith, more than hope. Faith and
hope are under the sign of this passing age ; " Love
never faileth ".[3] Love is the power of the coming age
already breaking into this world. For Paul, as for
Jesus, love is the only life-force that has a future in this
age of death.

The triad—faith, love, hope—seems to be a formula
in I Thess. i, 3 ; v, 8 ; Col. i, 4 f.[4] In all these cases
love comes in the middle. Wherever the relations of
these three are defined in detail, love is shown to play
the principal part. Thus on the one hand in Gal. v, 6
we have " faith working through love ", and on the

---

[1] Phil. ii, 1 ff. ; I Cor. viii, 11 ; Col. iii, 14 f. (Eph. v, 2 ; also
married love in the same connection, v, 25).

[2] Cf. II Cor. i, 3 ff. (viii, 7 f.).

[3] Cf. (only as a form of expression) Aboth v, 19 : love that is not
dependent upon a material cause will never pass away.

[4] See Harnack, Preus. Jahrb. 164 (1916) 1 ff. ; Reitzenstein,
Nachr. Ges. Göttingen, 1917, 130 ff. ; P. Corssen in Sokrates vii,
(1919), 18 ff. ; Lietzmann, Kor. ad loc. ; A. Brieger, Die urchristl.
Trias Glaube, Liebe, Hoffnung, theol. dissertation Heidelberg
(1925). [Further references in Nygren, Agape, etc. I., 100.]

other hand in Rom. v, 5 " hope putteth not to shame
because the love of God hath been shed abroad . . ."
Paul assigns faith and hope unequivocally and obviously
to this age : " We walk by faith and not by sight "
(II Cor. v, 7) and "we hope for that which we see not"
(Rom. viii, 25). In Rom. viii, 28, 35 ff., on the contrary, God's victorious love saves us through all
distresses and our love to him defeats every assault.
In I Cor. xiii it is brotherly love, without which all
good deeds and all spiritual gifts lack value and content,
that never fails. At verse 8 the argument moves on to
the consideration of the end, when all other gifts will
become meaningless. The provisional nature of knowledge and its ultimate decay are similarly displayed,
as sharing the interim character of faith and hope.
The conclusion is introduced by the typically eschatological idea of " abiding ", which means " enduring "
(e.g. I Cor. iii, 14). " Now abideth "—from what has
gone before, and from all that Paul says elsewhere, we
expect the next word to be " love ", the subject of the
chapter, to which the whole hymn of praise is devoted.
Instead of this we find the favourite triad, stylistically
very impressive, but neither strictly relevant nor
suitable from the point of view of syntax—the verb
being in the singular. Paul seems to have sacrificed
precision for the sake of effect. The result is that he
has to rescue his main idea by adding a sentence, which
certainly makes a brilliant ending, but lacks the cosmic-
historical note of that opening word : " The greatest
of these is love ". The original purpose, lost sight of
for a moment through the introduction of the triad, is
thus fully recovered : love is no longer of this world ; it
reaches out beyond into the coming age—love alone.[1]

[1] On I Cor. xiii see I Clem. 49 f. ; Apoc. Sedrach 1 ; Augustine,
Sermon 350 De Caritate (Migne, Patr. Lat. xxxix, 1533) ;
Melancthon's Commentary (C. Ref. XV. 1134 ff.) ; Calvin's

(2) *James*. Faith grows strong in proportion to
its practical activity in love. Paul sees that to be
absolutely essential (Gal. v, 6). James has translated
the truth into practical propositions, whose sober
clarity rules out all pious and comfortable evasions.
The very first meaning of love is to do your plain duty
to your neighbour and to give the labourer his rights
(James v, 1 ff.). It means to take seriously the fundamental proposition : He who loves God is my brother,
the equal of all, even though he wears vile clothing
(ii, 1-4). God has thought him good enough to
call into his kingdom (ii, 5). Love is indeed the law of
the new realm—" the royal law " (ii, 8). This love
is an act of faith, demanded by faith, made possible
through faith, counted for righteousness because of
faith (ii, 14 ff.). The love towards God that lies behind
all brotherly love is also an act of faith. It holds fast
to God and his commandments in the fight against
worldly passions, and trusts in his promises through
the long days of anxiety and opposition. It is strong in
patience (i, 2 ff.).

(3) *John*. Paul regards love as the principle of the
future ; for John it is the principle of the Christ-
world which is being built up in the midst of the contemporary cosmic crisis. " God so loved the world
that he gave his only-begotten son that . . . " (John iii,
16 ; I John iv, 9 f.). John and Paul (Rom. viii, 32) are
at one in this fundamental idea. But John differs
from Paul in ever new representations of the love of the
Father to the Son.[1] All love finds its true centre in
him ; his sole function is to mediate God's love. John

Commentary (ed. Tholuck V, 1834) ; Harnack, Sitz. Preuss.
Akad. Berl. 1911, 132 ff. ; E. Lehmann-A. Fridrichsen, Theol.
Stud. u. Krit. 94 (1922) 55 ff.

[1] John iii, 35 ; x, 17 (ἀγαπᾶν). Ἀγαπητός never in this
connection.

therefore hardly ever speaks of the love of the Son to
the Father (John xiv, 31).   What he stresses is the love
of the Son to those whom the Father has given him—
his " friends ".   God's love reaches the human world
through the Son.[1] But this love is at the same time
glorified and set free through his death.   Through the
death of the Son, God fulfils his purpose of salvation
for the world.[2]

The Johannine Agape is explicitly the love which
comes down (see p. 29).   More than that, it is a
heavenly reality which comes down into this world
as it were from stage to stage.   But this cosmic reality
effects its revelation and achieves its victory in moral
action.   John takes the same view of the matter as
Paul does when he is considering the problem of the
relation between God's work and man's.   The world
of light and life breaks through into this world in
the form of love.   John, therefore, not merely finds it
possible to emphasise the ethical character of Agape in
the life of Christ and of Christians—he is bound to do so.

Consequently in John, love to God or Christ [3] takes
second place after love to the brethren, which springs
from God and has its prototype in Christ.[4]   In brotherly
love the circle which consists of the Father and the Son
and those who belong to him becomes a fellowship
which is not of this world.   God's love is life's ultimate reality for this fellowship, and to abide in his love
is the law of its life.[5]   " He who loveth not abideth in

---

[1] John xvii, 23 ff. ; xiv, 21 ff. ; I John iv, 19.   Personal affection in John xi, 5 ; xiii, 23.

[2] On John xiii, 1 see A. Debrunner in Gnomon 4 (1928), 444.
On John xv, 13 see Dibelius in Festschrift f. Deissmann (1927)
168 ff.   Further cf. I John iv, 9 f. ; iii, 16,

[3] John v, 42 ; viii, 42 ; xiv, 28.

[4] John xiii, 34 f. ; xiv, 15 ff. ; xxi, 15 ff. ; I John iv, 20.

[5] John xv, 9 f. ; I John ii, 10 ; iii, 10 ; iv, 11 ff.   On the last see
R. Schütz, Die Vorgeschichte d. Joh. Formel, $\theta\epsilon\grave{o}s$ $\mathring{a}\gamma\acute{a}\pi\eta$ $\mathring{\epsilon}\sigma\tau\acute{\iota}\nu$

death." [1] The verb is used without a direct object—
and not only in this verse (I John iii, 14). This
absolute use, which in Luke vii, 47 is exceptional, is
quite regular in I John (iii, 18 ; iv, 7 f. ; iv, 19).
This love is a movement of life, a form of existence,
a realisation of God in this world.

Thus love is the one commandment which includes
all others, being repeated and set before the reader
with magnificent monotony. It is seldom defined
more closely in terms such as those used in I John iii,
18 ; " love . . . in deed and truth ".[2] Frequently,
however, in the Johannine Epistles the exhortations are
interrupted and made more emphatic by the affecting
term of address, " beloved ", which here has nothing
to do with the doctrine of election but simply indicates
the relation of brother to brother (III John, 5 ; I John
iv, 7).

In the Apocalypse the demand for brotherly love falls
far behind the passionate summons to hold fast to God
in this hour of crisis and suffering—and in death itself.
Love here means just what it did in the old martyr-
theology, which the contemporary distress has brought
to life again. The book begins with a hymn concerning
the faithful witness " that loveth us " (i, 5) ; then
follow visions of " the beloved city " (iii, 9 ; xx, 9), and
of the glory of those who have kept faith and love,
" and they love not their life even unto death "
(xii, 11), alternating with threats against God's
enemies and the accusation, " thou hast lost thy first
love " (ii, 4). The day has arrived when the love
of the many waxes cold (Matt. xxiv, 12).

in Diss. Kiel (1917). [See C. H. Dodd, The Joh. Epistles, 106-113.]
    [1] I John iii, 14 (B, Sin., A).   Cf. also ii, 15 ff. ; iii, 17 ; John
iii, 19. [See p. 12, n. 4.]
    [2] I John iii, 18, cf. II John i ; Test. Gad. vi, 1.   See additional
note on page 67.

VI. THE SUB-APOSTOLIC AGE

In the sub-apostolic age the formulae of the early Church are sometimes retained as authoritative, sometimes superseded as the result of eager speculation. The old word, Agape, sometimes receives a narrower interpretation, sometimes a broader. John's combination of theological breadth with moral severity has broken down. All the same, the growing Church retains its reverence for " the greatness and wonder of love ", and knows perfectly well the practical meaning of Agape for Church and world. The finest evidence for this is the hymn in the first Epistle of Clement (49 f.).

Ἀγάπη and ἀγαπᾶν are now fundamental for the understanding of God's treatment of man and of the work of Christ.[1] Ἡγαπημένος and especially ἀγαπητός are favourite expressions for Jesus, sometimes combined with υἱός or παῖς, sometimes as an independent title, " the only-beloved ".[2] The Church and Christians are loved by God, chosen by him, his good pleasure resting upon them.[3]

This age also uses " Agape " to denote Christian piety as a whole.[4] That is the response to the love with which God first loved us, and the imitation of his love of men ; " we love what he loved, abstaining . . . "[5]

[1] Ignatius, Rom. vii, 3 ; Trall. viii, 1 ; Act. Thom. 132, p. 239, 26.
[2] II Pet. i, 17 ; Herm. S. 5, ii, 6 ; 9, xii, 5 ; I Clem. 59, 2 f. ; Mart. Pol. 14, 1 ; Diog. 8, 11 ; Barn. 3, 6 ; 4, 3 ; Asc. Is. 1, 4 ; Act. Phil. 4, p. 3, 19.
[3] Jude 1 ; I. Clem. 8, 5, etc.
[4] Ign. Magn. i, 1 ; I Pet. i, 8 ; C. Schmidt, Gespr. Jesu in Texte u. Unters. 43 (1919), 121, 4. Ἀγαπᾶν used absolutely in the agraphon (?) in Didymus de Trin. I, 16, Migne Patr. Gr. xxxix, 333b, and in Ps. Clem. Hom. 3, p. 38, 6.
[5] Pol. ii, 2 ; Herm. M. 5. ii, 8 ; Diog. 8, 7 ; 9, 2 ; 10, 2 ff.

Love to God requires the despising and hating of the world. This tension may be relieved in martyrdom—here, as in Judaism, the ultimate proof of piety and devotion to God.[1] Ignatius, in his passionate epistle, seizes upon the Greek idea of Eros, to drag it forcibly, by a sharp antithesis, into the service of the idea of martyrdom : " I write to you in the midst of life, yet lusting after death. My lust hath been crucified " (ὁ ἐμὸς ἔρως ἐσταύρωται).[2] In another form the tension between God and the " fashion of this world ", between heavenly and earthly love, solves its problem by resorting to asceticism. Agape comes to mean purity or continence or even ascetic practices. Chaste Agape is mightier than Eros.[3]

The principal use of the word " Agape ", and its derivatives, however, is to denote the love of brethren.[4] The old sayings about faith, love and hope, about the meaning and fulfilment of the law, and about the love of enemies, are highly esteemed and reproduced in other forms.[5] " Thou shalt hate no man, but some

[1] II Tim. iv, 8 ff. ; Heb. i, 9 ; I Pet. iii, 10 ; II Pet. ii, 15 ; John iii, 16 (I John iv, 9 f.).

[2] Ign. Rom. 7, 2 (cf. 2, 1 ; ad Pol. 4, 3). See Origen, Comm. on Song. Sol. Prol. (Baehrens, p. 71, 25). On the relation of φιλία, ἀγάπη, ἔρως see Justin Dial. 8,1 ; Clem. Al. Strom. VI, 9, 73, 3 ; Origen, Comm. on Lam. i, 2 Fragm. XI (Klostermann). Cf. Harnack in Sitz. Akad. Berl. (1918) 81 ff.

[3] I Clem. 21, 8 ; Pol. 4, 2 ; Herm. S. 9, 11, 3 (on this see Jerome, Ep. 22, 14, p. 161, 17 Hilberg : agapetarum pistis) ; Act. Joh. 29 ; 63 ff. ; 68 ; 109 ; 114 ; Act. Paul, 6 ; 9 ff. But asceticism without Agape is useless : Act. Gr. S. Melaniae Jun. in Anal. Boll. 1903, p. 30 f., par. 43.

[4] Cf. I Pet. i, 22 ; II Pet. i, 7 ; I Clem. 47, 5 ; 48, 1 (φιλα-δελφία) ; I Pet. ii, 17 (ἀδελφότης) ; Test. XL. Mart. 2, 4.

[5] Didache i, 2 f. (negative form of Golden Rule) ; Pol. 3, 2 f. (triad) ; Diog. 5, 11 ; 6, 6 ; II Clem. 13, 4 (love of enemies, cf. Clem. Al. Strom. IV, 13, 93, 3) ; II Clem. 16, 4 (alms, cf. J. Nicole, Papyrus de Genève I (1896), 14, 7) ; II Clem. 4, 3 (ἀγ. ἑαυτούς, cf.

thou shalt reprove, to some thou shalt show mercy, and for some thou shalt pray, and some thou shalt love more than thyself" (Didache ii, 7). Brotherly love means finally " desiring not only your own salvation, but also that of all the brethren " (Martyrd. Polycarp. i, 2). The leaders of the community strive at all times to strengthen the will to fellowship among the brethren— in service, reconciliation, the overcoming of evil with good.[1] Ἀγαπητός is a common form of address.[2] Agape becomes a technical term for the fraternal " love-feast " which is developed out of the primitive common meal and leads to important social consequences.[3]

Agape among the Greeks meant the mutual respect and sympathy of equals. Christian Agape is charged with a twofold consciousness, viz. a sense of unworthiness before God and a realisation of his mercy. This spirit of charity sets the tone of the brotherhood in all its ways. So in the midst of a world everywhere doomed by Eros, striving in vain for a way of escape by sublimation, these young brotherhoods spring up, a

Test. XI. Mart. 1, 6) ; Dion. Chrys. Or. 74, 5, II, p. 194, 8 ; 47, 20, II, p. 86, 12 f. ; Barn. 1, 4 ; 19, 5 (ὑπὲρ τὴν ψυχήν) ; Herm. Vis. 3. 8, 5. 7 ; S. 9, 15, 2 (Ἀγάπη) ; Didache xvi, 3 (ἀγάπη στραφήσεται).

[1] I Pet. iv, 7 ff. ; I Clem. 49 ff. ; Barn. 1, 6.

[2] Ἀγαπητοί specially in I Clem. Ἀξιαγάπητος (not vocative) in I Clem. 1 ; 21, 7. Προφήτας ἀγαπῶμεν Ign. Phil. 5, 2. Cf. specially Mart. Pol. 17, 2 f. (against suspicion of martyr-worship) : " It is Christ whom we worship ; the martyrs we love as disciples and imitators of the Lord ".

[3] Cf. the much discussed passages, Jude 12 ; II Pet. ii, 13 ; Ign. Sm. 8, 2 ; 7, 1 (see Leclerq in Dict. d'archéol. Chrét. I (1907) 775 ff.) ; R. L. Cole, Love Feasts, History of the Christian ἀγάπη (1916) ; R. Schütz, Z.N.W. 18 (1918) 224 ; Lietzmann on I Cor. xi, 23 ; K. Völker, Mysterium und Agape (1927). [See A. J. Maclean in E.R.E., I, 166-175.]

Church springs up, knowing the love whose way is not to covet but to give. The twilight of the Mystery cults gives place to " the mysteries of Agape ".[1]

[1] Clement of Alexandria speaks of " the mysteries of love " in Quis Dives salvetur 37, 1. The Stromata is specially rich in discussions about the love that flows out freely towards Reality, which finds its perfection in the true gnostic. Numerous motifs are evident here, which are met with in Philo and Plotinus, and also in the Hermetic writings, the Odes of Solomon and the Mandaean liturgies. Clement gives us a typical synthesis of mystical Agape with spiritual Eros—the synthesis which is familiar in all romantic religion. [See Nygren, Agape and Eros II, 137-152.]

Additional note communicated by Dr. Stauffer. See p. 63, n. 2 :

The stereotyped phrases in which the Johannine writings speak of ἀγάπη and ἀγαπᾶν betray their author's debt to the pre-Christian priestly tradition, above all to the world of the Testaments of the XII Patriarchs (Stauffer, Theologie des N.T., 5th ed., 1948, pp. 26, 318 ff. ; cf. J. Behm, Th.L.Z., 1948, pp. 1 ff.). E.g. Dan. i, 5 ; Jos. i, 4 ; Sim. ii, 6 : ἠγάπη αὐτὸν ὁ πατήρ (John xvii, 23, 26) ; Benj. iii, 1 ; Gad, v, 2 : ἀγάπη τοῦ θεοῦ (John v, 42 ; I John iv, 20) ; Iss. v, 2 ; Dan. v, 3 : ἀγαπήσατε τὸν κύριον καὶ ἀλλήλους (I John iv, 21) ; Dan. v, 3 ; Gad, vi, 3 ; vii, 7 ; Jos. xvii, 2 ; Zeb. viii, 5 : ἀγαπᾶτε ἀλλήλους (II John 5) ; Zeb. iv, 7 : ἀγαπήσατε τὸν ἀδελφόν (I John ii, 10) ; Gad, iv, 2 : ἐντολὴ περὶ ἀγάπης (John xiii, 34 ; xv, 12) ; Gad, vi, 1 : ἀγαπήσατε ἐν ἔργῳ (I John iii, 18) ; Ash. ii, 4 : ἐν ἀγάπῃ εἰσίν (I John iv, 16) ; Jud. xxi, 1 : ἀγαπᾶτε ἵνα διαμείνητε (John xv, 9 ; I John iii, 14 ff. ; iv, 16) ; Gad, iv, 6 f. : ἀγάπη καὶ τοὺς νεκρούς θέλει ζωοποιῆσαι . . . τὸ πνεῦμα τῆς ἀγάπης συνεργεῖ τῷ νόμῳ εἰς σωτηρίαν τῶν ἀνθρώπων (John iii, 16 ; I John iii, 15 f. ; iv, 9 f.). Thus R. Bultmann's anachronistic " parallels " from later Gnosis (Johannes, 1941, pp. 120, 404, 416) are seen to be irrelevant and unnecessary.

INDEX OF WORDS AND REFERENCES

II

THE CHURCH

BY

KARL LUDWIG SCHMIDT

Translated from the first
edition, Stuttgart, 1938,
and with additional notes
by J. R. Coates

PREFACE

AMONG the key words of the Bible, ἐκκλησία holds a place of special importance, indicating as it does the concrete phenomenon in which are seen those acts of the Creator which give meaning to history, the immediate objective for which Christ gave his life, and the organ of the Holy Spirit for the furthering of the Kingdom of God on earth.

" If the revelation of God in Christ is of supreme moment for mankind, the Christian community is also supremely significant. For the revelation occurred only within the life of that community. God did not manifest himself in Jesus alone, but in the life of the group which was formed about him and in whose creation he was himself the decisive factor. It was in Jesus *as known in the Church* that the fresh activity of God among men, which we call the revelation in Christ, occurred. And that revelation is not merely remembered in the Church ; it is constantly present wherever there is genuine Christian fellowship." (Prof. John Knox, Union Theol. Seminary, N.Y. : *The Christian Answer*, 1946, p. 242.)

The Church is the clue to the Bible as history, and it is also the culmination of the Bible as theology. Biblical theology is not one of a number of possible interpretations of the universe, provoking thought ; it is good news, a message and a call, an offer and an invitation, demanding action. The challenge of the Bible is not, " Do you agree ? " but " Do you believe ? " and " Will you join up ? " God is in Christ reconciling the world to himself, even through the Church, which is his body.

It might be said that the Church is both the theme of the Bible and its writer. Bible and Church explain each other, judge each other, need each other. Both are organs of the living God, and neither can function properly without the other. If the Church fails, it is because it is not Biblical enough, and if Bible study becomes pedantic and arid, it is because it is divorced from worship and service in the living fellowship of the Church.

In what sense did Christ found the Church? When did it actually come into existence? How are we to understand the Matthaean account of the incident at Caesarea Philippi? What was St. Paul's attitude towards the Church in Jerusalem? What is the relation between the Church and the Churches? What is implied in the expression, "the body of Christ"? What does the Old Testament contribute to the Christian doctrine of the Church? Is the New Testament idea of the Church eschatological?

Prof. K. L. Schmidt has already done, and is still doing, much to help us to answer these and other questions concerning the Church. The present volume is a translation, slightly abridged, of his article on ἐκκλησία in the *Theological Dictionary of the New Testament*, begun by Gerhard Kittel, who died in 1948, and now under the editorship of Gerhard Friedrich. It first appeared in 1936, and its value is recognised by George Johnston, in his important book, *The Church in the New Testament* (1943), and by other British and American scholars, who have expressed their desire for an English version of it. My warmest thanks are due to the author for his friendly assistance. He assures me that he still maintains the theses here set forth and says there is a good account of recent discussion in a revised and enlarged translation of *Aspects Nouveau du Probleme de l'Eglise*, by F. M. Braun, O.P., under the title, *Neues Licht auf die Kirche, die protestantische Kirchendogmatik in ihrer neuesten Entfaltung* (Benziger, Einsiedeln/Köln, 1946).

At a time when the Church is widely and deeply concerned about its true nature and proper function, it will be well if Dr. K. L. Schmidt's arguments—with their practical implications—receive the most earnest consideration. They cannot fail to help theology to be Biblical, and may help the Church to be Christian.

BIOGRAPHICAL NOTE

Karl Ludwig Schmidt was born at Frankfurt a.M., 5th February, 1891 ; studied at Marburg and Berlin ; served in the 1914-1918 war ; became Privatdozent at Berlin, 1918, and Professor at Giessen 1921, Jena 1925, Bonn 1929. As a member of the Social Democratic Party, he was dismissed from his post in 1933, and became a Pastor in Switzerland. Since 1935 he has been Professor of New Testament Theology at Basle.

Dr. Schmidt wrote articles for *Die Religion in Geschichte und Gegenwart* and *Theologisches Wörterbuch zum Neuen Testament* ; founded and edited *Theologische Blätter*, 1922-1937 ; and has been editor of *Theologische Zeitung* since 1945. His other principal writings are as follows—

Der Rahmen der Geschichte Jesu, 1919.

Die Pfingsterzählung und das Pfingstereignis, 1919.

Die Stellung der Evangelien in der allgemeinen Literaturgeschichte, 1923.

Die Stellung des Apostels Paulus im Urchristentum, 1924.

Die Kirche des Urchristentums, 1927 ; 2nd ed., 1932.

Das Gegenüber von Kirche und Staat in der Gemeinde des Neuen Testaments, in *Theol. Blätt.*, 1937, Sp. 1-16.

Le problème du Christianisme primitif, 1938.

Die Polis in Kirche und Welt, 1940.

Ein Gang durch den Galaterbrief, 1942 ; 2nd ed., 1947.

Die Judenfrage in Lichte der Kap. 9-11 des Römer-briefes, 1943 ; 2nd ed., 1947.

Aus der Johannes-Apokalypse, 1944.

Kanonische und apokryphe Evangelien und Apostelgeschichten, 1944.

Die Verkündigung der Kirche an die Gemeinde, 1944.

Das Pneuma Hagion als Person und als Charisma, 1946.

Israels Stellung zu den Fremdlingen und Beisassen und Israels Wissen um seine Fremdling- und Beisassenschaft, in *Judaica*, 1946, pp. 269-296.

Die Natur- und Geisteskräfte im paulinischen Erkennen und Glauben, 1947.

Wesen und Aufgabe der Kirche in der Welt, 1947.

Homo imago Dei in Alten und Neuen Testament, 1948.

The proclamation of the Church to the Congregation, in *Scottish Journal of Theology*, September 1948.

J. R. Coates.

CONTENTS

BIBLIOGRAPHY

H. W. Beyer : " Die Kirche des Evangeliums und die loslösung des Katholizismus von ihr " in Der römische Katholizismus und das Evangelium, 1931.

C. G. Brandis : 'Εκκλησία in Pauly-Wissowa, V, 1905.

G. Gloege : Reich Gottes und Kirche im N.T., 1929.

K. Holl : Ges. Aufsätze zur Kirchengeschichte II, 44 ff., 1928.

G. Holstein : Die Grundlagen des evangelischen Kirchenrechts, 1928.

F. J. A. Hort : The Christian Ecclesia, 1897.

A. Juncker : Neue Kirchliche Zeitung, 126 ff., 180 ff., 1929.

F. Kattenbusch : " Der Quellort der Kirchenidee " in Festgabe für Harnack, 1921 ; " Die Vorzugsstellung des Petrus und der Charakter der Urgemeinde zu Jerusalem " in Festgabe für K. Müller, 1922.

W. Koester : Die Idee der Kirche beim Apostel Paulus, 1928.

L. Kösters (Catholic) : Die Kirche unseres Glaubens, 1935.

O. Linton (Swedish) : Das Problem der Urkirche in der neueren Forschung, 1932. Review by F. Kattenbusch in Theol. Stud. Krit., 97 ff., 1938.

E. Lohmeyer : Vom Begriff der religiösen Gemeinschaft, 1925.

W. Macholz : " Um die Kirche " in Theol. Blätt., 323 ff., 1928.

A. Médebielle : in Dictionnaire de la Bible, Suppl. II, 487 ff., 1934.

W. Michaelis : Täufer, Jesus, Urgemeinde, 1928.

E. Peterson : Die Kirche, 1929.

H. Schlier : " Zum Begriff der Kirche im Eph.", in Theol. Blätt., 12 ff., 1927.

K. L. Schmidt : Die Kirche des Urchristentums, 1932 ; " Das Kirchenproblem im Urchristentum " in Theol. Blätt., 293-302, 1927 ; art. in Forschungen und Fortschritte, 277 f., 1927.

F. Siegmund-Schultze (ed.) : Die Kirche im N.T. in ihrer Bedeutung für die Gegenwart, 1930.

H. E. WEBER : " Die Kirche im Lichte der Eschatologie " in
    Neue Kirchliche Zeitung, 299 ff., 1926.

H. D. WENDLAND : " Der christliche Begriff der Gemeinschaft "
    in Theol. Blätt., 129 ff., 1930 ; Die Eschatologie des Reiches
    Gottes bei Jesus, 1931.

[J. R. COATES : The Coming of the Church, 1929.

R. NEWTON FLEW : Jesus and His Church, 1938.

G. JOHNSTON : The Church in the New Testament, 1943.

T. M. LINDSAY : The Church and the Ministry in the Early
    Centuries, 1902.

A. LOISY : The Gospel and the Church, 1903.

T. W. MANSON : The Church's Ministry, 1948.

J. OMAN : The Church and the Divine Order, 1911.

C. A. A. SCOTT : The Fellowship of the Spirit, 1921.

B. H. STREETER : The Primitive Church, 1929.

A. M. RAMSEY : The Gospel and the Catholic Church, 1936.

C. E. RAVEN : The Gospel and the Church, 1939.]

DISCUSSIONS OF MATTHEW XVI, 17-19

R. BULTMANN : Z.N.W., 165 ff., 1919-1920.

A. DELL : Z.N.W., 1 ff., 1914.

H. DIECKMANN : Biblica, 189 ff., 1923.

S. EURINGER : A. Ehrhard Festgabe 141 ff., 1922.

K. G. GOETZ : Unters. z. N.T. XIII, 1927.

K. GUGGISBERG : Z. f. Kircheng., 276 ff., 1935.

TH. HERMANN : Th. Bl., 203 ff., 1926.

F. KATTENBUSCH : Th. St. Kr., 96-131, 1922.

G. KRÜGER : Th. Bl., 302 ff., 1927.

J. SICKENBERGER : Theol. Revue, 1 ff., 1920.

D. VÖLTER : Nieuw Theol. Tijdschr., 174 ff., 1921.

[F. H. CHASE : Hastings D. B. III, 758-760, 795 f.

S. SCHECHTER : J.Q.R., 428 f., 1900.]

Square brackets here, and elsewhere indicate additions by the
translator.

I. PRELIMINARY

THE Greek dictionary gives two meanings to ἐκκλησία:
(1) " gathering of the people ", (2) " church " ;
and calls the former secular, the latter Biblical or
ecclesiastical. The last edition of " Liddell and
Scott " retains this division, but sub-divides the second
part, bringing in the Septuagint : (1) " ' assembly
duly summoned ', less general than σύλλογος ",
(2a) " in LXX ' the Jewish congregation ' ", (2b)
" in N.T. ' the Church as a body of Christians ' ".

N.T. lexicons follow suit, but make a further distinction : (a) the whole body of believers, (b) the
individual congregation, e.g. one meeting in a house.
The question arises as to which of these came first,
and different answers are given. Grimm-Thayer
puts the local Church first : " those who anywhere, in
city or village, constitute such a company and are
united into one body " ; and gives the second place to
" the whole body of Christians scattered throughout
the earth ". Preuschen-Bauer does the same, but the
Catholic Zorell reverses the order : first " the whole
body of those who belong to the religious society
founded by Christ ", and second, " any particular
Church, i.e. believers in Christ in any region or city,
under their own bishop ; almost identical with
diocese ". It is sometimes hard to decide which of
these meanings to give to ἐκκλησία, and the dictionaries
do not always agree.

The question is generally decided on denominational
rather than scientific grounds. Anglicans like to
speak of the ἐκκλησία as the one Church, " the body
of Christians ". Roman Catholics start from the
universal Church, and immediately quote Matt. xvi,

18,[1] going on to emphasise the authority of the bishop over the individual congregation. The orthodox Protestant puts the universal first, the liberal the local, a certain confusion being due perhaps to reaction against the hierarchy. The same thing is found in translations and commentaries. A notable exception is Cremer's Biblico-theological Dictionary of N.T. Greek, revised by Kögel (1923), which digs deeper, here as elsewhere, and thus reaches a better lexical conclusion. Here ἐκκλησία in the N.T. is the " redeemed community " (*Heilsgemeinde*), this view being based on the use of the word in the O.T. for the whole community of the people of Israel (*Gesamtheit der israelitischen Volksgemeinde*). Sometimes it means the whole Christian body, and sometimes the same N.T. redeemed community localised (*in lokaler Begrenzung*—a careful and well-chosen phrase). This dictionary further points out that it is not always possible to differentiate clearly between the two meanings. Reference may be made here to Zorell's remark that Acts ii, 47 ; v, 11 and other passages may be understood in either sense, in view of the fact that at the beginning the universal Church and the particular Church were one and the same.

The piling up of a great variety of equivalents for ἐκκλησία is shown to be undesirable primarily by the simple but determinative fact that the N.T. always uses the same word, while we commonly say " Church " in some places and " Congregation " in others. Another fundamental argument in favour of confining ourselves to one single rendering is the

---

[1] An exception is found in L. Kösters' article on " Church " in the second edition of Lexicon f. Theol. u. Kirche V, 968 ff. : " no doubt used at an early date by the Hellenists in Jerusalem for the gathering of the local Christian congregation, and then for the whole Christian community ".

fact that secular Greek writers use the same word as
the Biblical writers, both O.T. and N.T. We must
examine the question whether we could not, or should
not, use either "Church" or "Congregation"
uniformly in the N.T. Such an investigation will
bring us face to face with the decisive questions concerning the Church in the N.T., viz., What is the
relation between the so-called Church and the so-
called Congregation? Which of the two is intended
at Matt. xvi, 18? Is the original company of Christians at Jerusalem Church or Congregation? What
is the connection between that original body and the
other companies of Christians throughout the Roman
Empire? What exactly does ἐκκλησία mean to
Peter's Jewish Christians, what to Paul's heathen
converts, what to the Catholics of the ancient Church?
We ought indeed to go further, and inquire whether
either "Church" or "Congregation" should not be
adopted as the one and only rendering of ἐκκλησία
throughout the whole Bible. This raises the whole
question of the relation of the N.T. to the O.T.
Just as a Hebrew expression lies behind the LXX
ἐκκλησία,[1] so there is Aramaic, the language of
Jesus and of the early Church in Jerusalem, behind

[1] E. Peterson, Die Kirche (1929), 19 : " It is not enough to
derive the technical meaning of ἐκκλησία from the LXX ; it
must rather be interpreted in the light of the new situation in
which the apostles found themselves ". Certainly the LXX alone
is not enough ; we must rather go back to the Hebrew text.
Peterson considerably weakens his case by not troubling about
either the Greek or the Hebrew O.T. His thesis, equating
Church with Church of the Gentiles, comes to grief on the very
fact that the same expression occurs in the LXX, and among
Jewish and Gentile Christians. He does not feel the need to show
how the same expression can mean different things.
  [On LXX usage see further pp. 51 ff, and cf. J. Y. Campbell
in Journal of Theol. Studies (1948), pp. 130-142, where he favours
the translation, " meeting ".]

ἐκκλησία in the Gospel, and this has to be discovered.
The search for it will be concerned with matters of fact.

Finally we ought to thrash out the question whether
there is not one single rendering to be found, which
could be used throughout the whole of Greek literature
both sacred and profane. Could it be " assembly "
or " gathering " ? This leads to the further question
why the Christians of the N.T. avoided a term expressly connected with religion, and chose a thoroughly
secular word.

The dictionaries show that in both religious and
secular Greek ἐκκλησία covers the two ideas of coming
together and being together, and this seems to point
to some such rendering as " gathering ", which has the
advantage of being available for the abstract as well
as the concrete.

II. NEW TESTAMENT

THE word ἐκκλησία is not found in the following
Books : Mark, Luke, John, II Tim., Titus, I Peter,
II Peter, I John, II John, Jude.[1] Its absence from
II Tim., Titus, I and II John is not surprising, since
I Tim. and III John have it—and Jude is too short to be
of statistical value. What is more remarkable is its
non-appearance in the Petrine Epistles. But it may
well be asked whether the thing itself is not there,
although the word is missing, since in I Pet. special
emphasis is laid upon the O.T. community and its
meaning, with the use of O.T. expressions ;[2] and the
same question forces itself upon our attention in the
case of the three Gospels, Mark, Luke and John.

1. ACTS OF THE APOSTLES

Since the Matthaean ἐκκλησία passages are disputed
and of doubtful interpretation, it seems better to start
from the frequent and varied use of the word in Acts.
The early examples are of the highest importance,
viz., ii, 47 ;[3] v, 11 ; vii, 38 ; viii, 1 ; viii, 3 ; ix, 31.
Here we read of " the ἐκκλησία which was in Jerusalem " (viii, 1) ; of Israel as " the ἐκκλησία in the
wilderness " (vii, 38), echoing Deut. ix, 10, where
LXX ἐκκλησία = Heb. qahal ; and of the ἐκκλησία
" throughout all Judaea and Galilee and Samaria "
(ix, 31).[4] While the individual congregation is

---

[1] I Pet. and II Pet. are overlooked in all editions of Cremer's
N.T. Wörterbuch.
[2] [See E. G. Selwyn, I Peter, pp. 81-90.]
[3] [R.V. omits ἐκκλησία here, with many MSS.]
[4] " Throughout . . . Samaria " is probably to be taken

5

generally indicated, in one example the reference is
to a group of congregations, and therefore " Church "
is a better rendering than " Congregation ". It
should be added that there is some good textual
evidence for reading the Plural at ix, 31, instead of the
Singular,[1]—ἐκκλησία and ἐκκλησίαι both mean the
same thing. The Plural is better attested at xv, 41,
where only B D pc have the Singular, and is undisputed at xvi, 5. Elsewhere the Singular predominates
and indicates, either explicitly or by implication, the
congregation at Jerusalem (xi, 22 ; xii, 1—D pc " in
Judaea " ; xii, 5 ; xv, 4, 22) ; or at Syrian Antioch
(xi, 26 ; xiii, 1 ; xiv, 27 ; xv, 3) ; or at Caesarea
(xviii, 22) ; or at Ephesus (xx, 17, 28). The phrase
κατ᾽ ἐκκλησίαν (xiv, 23) means " Church-wise "
(gemeinde-weise) and may presuppose the Plural use
of the word ; Luther translates " in den Gemeinden " ;
A.V. and R.V. " in every Church ". A specially
pregnant saying is Acts xx, 28 ; Nestle compares this
with Ps. lxxiii, 2 (Heb. lxxiv, 2) where, however, the
word is συναγωγή (Heb. ʿedhah).

The special peculiarity of the N.T. idea of the Church
comes out clearly in the passages just reviewed. It
must be emphasised that, without regard to any
question of precedence, the congregation at different
places is simply called ἐκκλησία. Mere localisation
is not the main point in these cases—as is shown by the
mention of an ἐκκλησία " throughout all Judaea
and Galilee and Samaria " (Acts ix, 31). It must

attributively with R.V., and not predicatively with A.V., the
omission of the second article being permissible in Hellenistic
Greek, though it is found at I Cor. i, 2 and II Cor. i, 1—and
is regarded as " better " Greek !

[1] Nestle unfortunately prints the Singular, without noting
the important Plural reading, while Bruder prints the Plural and
gives the Singular [as the reading of A B C etc.].

further be emphasised that Singular and Plural are used promiscuously. This does not mean that the ἐκκλησία is divided into ἐκκλησίαι, or that, *vice versa*, it is formed by the coming together of the latter. It means that *the* ἐκκλησία is present in a certain place, and this is not affected by the mention of ἐκκλησίαι elsewhere. When we translate, we must either say " Congregation " and " Congregations ", or " Church " and " Churches " ; and the former is to be preferred. The reason why we cannot entirely dispense with the word " Church " is that " Congregation " has come to be used to differentiate the smaller local group from the whole body of Christian people. It is significant that the same term is applied to the Jewish Christian Congregation, say, in Jerusalem, and to a Gentile Christian one, e.g. in Antioch. Ornamental epithets are never employed ; the only attribute, so to speak, is the Genitive, " of God ", which comes from the O.T. It is generally omitted, but always to be understood, in order to give ἐκκλησία its full weight. The ἐκκλησία of God is always regarded as being distinguished from, or opposed to, other forms of society—as is made clear at Acts ii, 47, where the Christians are distinguished from " all the people " (λαόν) or " all the world " (D reads κόσμον).

Three times in one chapter (xix, 32, 39, 40) ἐκκλησία means an assembly or gathering of the heathen, and is a purely secular expression. If we act on the fundamentally necessary and reasonable principle of consistency in translating passages from the same author, we shall have to reject the word " Church ". The word " Congregation " would be better, if we could use it, like the German " *Gemeinde* ", perhaps with a suitable adjective, to denote a political meeting. The simplest rendering is here the most satisfactory, viz., " gathering ".[1] [If we were all Quakers, we should have no hesitation in recommending " meeting " as the English for ἐκκλησία in every context. Cf. n. 1, p. 3.] This would give us the right starting-point for differentiating between Church gatherings and those of a worldly character. It would then be easy to see the obvious point implied by the use of both Singular and Plural : if you speak of gatherings, you must be thinking of people gathering themselves together. The mere gathering tells us nothing ; everything depends on the character of those who are gathered. The addition of the words, " of God " or " of the Lord ", points to him who gathers men, or allows them to gather themselves ; and when this is followed by the phrase, " which he purchased " (Acts xx, 28), it is clear that God gathers his own. The ἐκκλησία is composed of *all* who belong to him. The use of the adjective " whole " at Acts v, 11 and xv, 22 bears out this idea of corporate unity ; it adds nothing new, but serves to stress an idea already involved in the expression, " Church of God ". The contrast with other (worldly) ἐκκλησίαι is not a matter of quantity but of quality. Size is an object in the case of a national gathering, but not for the gathering of the people of God. The essential is that God gathers his own. Numbers depend upon him who calls, and only secondarily upon those who respond to the call.   " Where two or three are gathered together in my name there am I in the midst of them." (Matt. xviii, 20.)

[1] Nevertheless it cannot be suggested that we should abandon the use of the word " Church " or the word " Congregation ". Apart from the impossibility of such an undertaking, it is obviously sensible to preserve the rich associations of such expressions. But it is desirable to establish the precise meaning of ἐκκλησία, because this is a point at which linguistic accuracy makes a real contribution to Biblical theology.

2. PAULINE EPISTLES I

Paul's usage is practically the same as that of Acts. There is no divergence between Jewish and Gentile Christians in their way of looking at this subject. The use of the Plural might be taken as showing that congregations stand side by side on an equal footing ; good examples of this are " other Churches " (II Cor. xi, 8) and " the rest of the Churches " (II Cor. xii, 13) ; cf. " no Church " (Phil. iv, 15). But that is not the decisive point ; it is not simply juxtaposition, but incorporation, with which we are concerned. The idea of corporate unity, mentioned above, finds expression in a number of ways : " the whole Church " (Rom. xvi, 23 ; I Cor. xiv, 23) ; " all the Churches " (Rom. xvi, 4, 16 ; I Cor. vii, 17 ; xiv, 33 ; II Cor. viii, 18 ; xi, 28) ; " everywhere in every Church " (I Cor. iv, 17).[1] Other references show that it is easy to pass from Singular to Plural, and *vice versa*. The alternative readings at I Cor. xiv, 35 show that. In any case the Plural is found in the two verses immediately preceding. Paul tells how he has persecuted the " Church " in Gal. i, 13 (cf. I Cor. xv, 9 ; Phil. iii, 6) and goes on in Gal. i, 22 to speak of the " Churches " of Judaea. Singular and Plural appear to be interchangeable in I Cor. x, 32 and xi, 16.

The ἐκκλησία is often definitely localised : Cenchreae (Rom. xvi, 1) ; Corinth (I Cor. i, 2 ; II Cor. i, 1) ; Laodicea (Col. iv, 16) ; Thessalonica (I Thess. i, 1 ; II Thess. i, 1) ; Asia (I Cor. xvi, 19) ; Galatia (I Cor. xvi, 1 ; Gal. i, 2); Macedonia (II Cor. viii, 1) ; Judaea (Gal. i, 22 ; I Thess. ii, 14).

The omission of the definite article is frequent, but makes no difference : I Cor. xiv, 4 (followed

---

[1] Paul loves such hyperbole, but has good ground for it.

immediately, in vv. 5, 12, by ἐκκλησία with the
Art.) ; xiv, 19, 28, 35 ; I Tim. iii, 5, 15. Obviously
Ἐκκλησία has almost become a proper name. The
Article can also be omitted with the Plural, e.g.
II Cor. viii, 23, though it appears in vv. 19 and 24.[1]

A fellowship small enough to meet in a house can be
called ἐκκλησία, e.g., Rom. xvi, 5 ; Philem. 2. One such
finds a place beside the other larger Churches (I Cor.
xvi, 19), and it is important to notice that another is
included among the recipients of a profound discussion
of the true nature of the Church (Col. iv, 15).

Strong support is found in I Cor. i, 2 and II Cor. i, 1
for the contention that the Church is not a great community made up of an accumulation of small communities, but is truly present in its wholeness in every
company of believers, however small. The proper
translation in those verses is not " the Corinthian
Congregation "—taking its place beside the Roman,
etc.—but " the Congregation, Church, Gathering,
as it is in Corinth ". When it is said that in such a
gathering anyone is despised (I Cor. vi, 4), that
people come together (I Cor. xi, 18 ; cf. xiv, 23 and
Acts xiv, 27), that women must keep silence (I Cor.
xiv, 34), or that it must not be burdened (I Tim. v, 16),
it is not the local congregation, but the Church as a
whole, that is in view.

Practically the only attribute which Paul applies to
the ἐκκλησία by way of definition is the Genitive, " of
God ". He adds this both to the Singular (I Cor. i,
2 ; x, 32 ; xi, 22 ; xv, 9 ; Gal. i, 13 ; I Tim. iii, 5, 15)
and to the Plural (I Cor. xi, 16 ; I Thess. ii, 14 ; II
Thess. i, 4) ; that it is used with both is more important

---

[1] In the 6th ed. of Blass's N.T. Grammar, § 254, A. Debrunner
draws attention to the omission of the article with personal
designations like " God ", " Lord ", " dead ", " nations ".
It may be the same with ἐκκλησία.

than might appear at first sight. Distinguishing as we do between the Church as a whole and the individual congregation, we are accustomed to speak of " the Church of God ", but not of " the congregations of God ". The fact that Paul does so speak is another indication that he does not differentiate, as was done later, between " Church " and " congregation ". Again, if the words, " of God ", are omitted, as they often are, they are always to be understood, just as " Kingdom " in the N.T. always means the Kingdom of God, unless it is explicitly described as an earthly realm. It should be noted that in some MSS. they have suitably been added, e.g. at I Cor. xiv, 4 ; Phil. iii, 6. It is always God who works in and through the ἐκκλησία ; cf. I Cor. xii, 28.

God works " in Christ ", and so here and there the two names are both mentioned, the most perfect example being I Thess. ii, 14 : " the Churches of God which are in Judaea in Christ Jesus ". Gal. i, 22 has only " in Christ ", omitting " of God " ; Rom. xvi, 16 has only " of (the) Christ ", the Genitive having the same meaning as the formula " in Christ ".[1] In any case the Genitive τοῦ Χριστοῦ, should not be translated into the mere adjective, " Christian ". Paul is not speaking of a Christian Church or con- gregation, besides which there may be another Church or congregation, but of God's gathering in Christ. There is only one example of the addition of the words, " of the saints ", viz., I Cor. xiv, 33 (qualifying, as it happens, " all the Churches ") but this need cause no surprise, since at I Cor. i, 2

[1] Deissmann in his Paulus (1925), pp. 126 f. [pp. 93 f. in 1st ed.], rightly points to this interchange between the " in "-formula and the Genitive in many other passages, and suggests the phrase, Genetivus communionis or mysticus—which is open to criticism and at least superfluous.

the ἐκκλησία is identified with " them that are sanctified in Christ Jesus ".[1]

Before entering upon a discussion of the passages in Colossians and Ephesians, whose very richness and fulness have led some to deny their Pauline authorship, let us review those which have already been adduced, and compare them with the evidence of Acts. A thorough examination of the passages in which the word ἐκκλησία occurs in connection with the conflict between Paul and Jerusalem reveals a striking amount of agreement, from the statistical and lexicographical point of view. The relative frequency with which Paul adds the words, " of God ", brings him very close to the only instance in Acts, viz., xx, 28, where the quotation of Ps. lxxiv, 2 stresses a favourite idea of Paul's. So far as the actual words are concerned, Acts never connects the words, " Jesus Christ ", with ἐκκλησία, as Paul does.[2] But there is no real difference here ; it is merely a matter of expression. Paul elaborates that which he holds in common with the original disciples concerning the Church in the light of his practical experience. What distinguishes the " ἐκκλησία of God in Christ Jesus " is the fulfilment of O.T. prophecy in the New Covenant in the experience of a definite number of the disciples of Jesus, who have received special powers as witnesses of his resurrection. God's community of the New Covenant, first really in existence when Jesus Christ is risen from the dead, does not derive

[1] Cf. R. Asting, " Die Heiligkeit im Urchristentum " (Forschungen z. Rel. & Lit. d. A.T. & N.T., 1930) 134, 147, 204, 269.

[2] It may be remarked in passing that the bare simplicity of the ἐκκλησία sayings in Acts speaks for the high antiquity of the book. The obvious possibility that a later writer is reproducing very old sources without alteration does not apply in this case, for such a writer would be bound to introduce the richer language of his own age about the Church.

commission and claim from the enthusiasm of men of
spiritual gifts, but only from a definite number of perfectly definite appearances of the risen Lord.[1] This
is established, not only by Acts, which is open to
question on many points, but above all by Paul's own
statement in I Cor. xv, 3 ff., where the Apostle to the
Gentiles attaches supreme importance to the align-
ment of his own experience on the Damascus road
with the resurrection appearances to the original
disciples. Paul himself was endowed with spiritual
gifts, and knew what it was to have visions and
auditions, trance and ecstasy (cf. II Cor. xii). But
the source of his apostolate as service of God's ἐκκλησία
did not lie in that quarter ; it was to be found simply
and solely in the Damascus vision, the event which
set him among the original witnesses of the resurrection.

From this point of view Paul is seen to have had
the same view of the Church as the first Christians in
Jerusalem.[2] Consistently with this, he recognised that
the Jerusalem community and its leaders had special
powers and privileges. It is impossible to exaggerate
the importance of the collection which he made for the
poor in Jerusalem—which was not so much for " the
poor in Jerusalem " as for " the poor in *Jerusalem* ".
Paul here recognised an obligation. It was not just a
case of charity, though that came into it. Still less
can it be called a piece of diplomacy on Paul's part.
No : it shows a sense of duty on Paul's part, and of his
respect for the men who first constituted God's ἐκκλησία
in Christ. This respect was not based on personal
grounds, as is shown by the fact that this same Paul

[1] K. Holl, following A. Schlatter, is specially emphatic on this
point in his uncommonly helpful treatment of Paul's idea of the
Church. See his Ges. Aufsätze z. Kirchengeschichte II (1928)
44 ff.

[2] Holl's conclusions are vitiated, in my judgment, by his failure
to recognise this fact.

does not hesitate to speak ironically of " those who were reputed to be pillars ", and ultimately to accuse Peter of hypocrisy, when he stumbles in the matter of associating with Gentiles (Gal. ii). Yet Peter, entangled in sin as he is, remains for Paul the outstanding figure in the company of the faithful. It is not the individual so much as the community that is at stake—God's gathering in Christ. This " gathering " is not something to be dealt with by man's free will, or treated as an object of human speculation ; it is something ordained by God, utterly beyond our disposal. Psychologising value-judgments are of no avail in the case of a man far more highly endowed with the gifts of the Spirit than those who give him the appropriate label and then blame him for not breaking away from the primitive idea of the Church.[1]

Paul had recourse to a pattern whenever he spoke of the Church ; or rather, a pattern was given to him which he could neither disregard nor destroy. It was the Christians of Jerusalem who were in danger of destroying it, with their exaggerated idea of the importance of the original disciples as persons of authority and of Jerusalem as their holy place—their tendency, in a word, towards the rank theocracy against which all the prophets, from the great writing prophets to John the Baptist, and Jesus himself, had uttered warnings, never weary of drawing attention to the call of God to his people. Paul was in line with these, speaking more clearly than the original disciples of the ἐκκλησία in promise and fulfilment, and never dreaming of setting forth a new doctrine of the Church, opposed to that of Jerusalem. It was not he who was the innovator. The original disciples, who, of course, cannot be regarded as innovators, yet allowed innova-

---

[1] As H. Weinel does in the 1st ed. of Die Rel. in Gesch. u. Geg. III, 1130.

tions to become predominant. Paul agreed with those
among them who were true and had to be specially
on their guard at this point, that it is of the very essence
of the ἐκκλησία of God that its foundation and con-
tinuance are in its Messiah Jesus alone, and that its
Lord is Christ alone—not men in theocratic arrogance,
even though they have the gift of revelation to an
exceptional degree. It is possible that Paul had such
men in view when he added the words " in Christ
Jesus " or " of Christ ", to ἐκκλησία, and when he
said "the rock (πέτρα) was Christ" (I. Cor. x, 4).[1]

Paul, however, like Acts, gives no formal teaching
about the ἐκκλησία in these Epistles. What he talks
about is just the gathering of men as God's gathering in
Christ. The nature and significance of this are clear to
those who accept the fact of God's dealing with men,
and know how he does it in Christ, without the explicit
addition of attributes and predicates. An apparent exception to this is found in one passage only, viz., I Tim.
iii, 15, where the ἐκκλησία is characterised as " the
house of God ", with reference to " edification " (cf.
I Cor. xiv, 4 f., 12). But " house " is a colourless word,
when compared with ἐκκλησία ; and again everything
depends on what is conveyed by the words, " of God ".

3. PAULINE EPISTLES II : COLOSSIANS AND EPHESIANS [2]

The doctrine of the ἐκκλησία receives its first explicit treatment in Colossians and Ephesians. The

[1] Cf. Lietzmann's footnote in Holl's Ges. Aufsätze II, 63 :
" May there not be a special point in saying that the rock was
Christ ? In any case for (Paul) himself obviously Christ is *the*
rock." Cf. also I Cor. iii, 11. We shall return to both these
passages when we deal with Matt. xvi, 18.

[2] Cf. N. Glubokowsky, W. F. Howard, K. L. Schmidt, " Christus
und die Kirche (Eph. v, 25-32) " in Theol. Blätt. (1930) 327 ff.

ἐκκλησία is the body of Christ (Col. i, 24), and Christ is the head of this body (i, 18). It is the same in Ephesians i, 22 and v, 23. The characteristic juxta-position of Christ and the ἐκκλησία at Eph. iii, 21 and v, 32 involves the ideas of co-ordination and sub-ordination as expressed in Eph. v, 24, 25, 29 ; that explains the absence of " and " in many MSS. of iii, 21. The holiness of the Church is only mentioned by Paul at Eph. v, 27, though it is a commonplace among suc-ceeding writers of the early period. Language of this sort is excessive. Another example of it is found at Eph. iii, 10, where we read of the manifold wisdom of God being made known through the Church. It is hard to be sure of the precise meaning of such state-ments in Ephesians ; the figurative language seems to be employed without any logic. Christ is the ἐκκλησία itself, since the latter is " the body of Christ ". But then again he is also above the Church, being its head. Such statements are closely inter-related. Christology and ecclesiology are obviously on the same footing. There is no obscurity for us here, so long as we read simple words in a superficial way. But what the apostle has in mind is a mystery, wrapped in obscurity, around which the words of men revolve (Eph. iii, 4 f.). This is no flight into the numinous. This is God's revelation of the secret forever hidden from human eyes. What goes on in the communion of Christ and the ἐκκλησία is something conceived by God, created by God, maintained by God. All culminates in the final hymn (Eph. v, 25-32) : the familiar social code simply means that the relation between man and wife should be based on that between Christ and the ἐκκλησία which in turn it illuminates.

The figures to which reference has just been made have their origin in the language of con-temporary mythology. It has been established by

H. Schlier [1] " that a consistent world of ideas finds expression in Ephesians, the author of which speaks the language of a particular Gnostic circle. The redeemer, who ascends to heaven, overcomes the heavenly powers (Eph. iv, 8 ff.) on his way, and breaks through the wall which divides the world from the divine kingdom (ii, 14 ff.). He thus returns to himself, as to the higher man (iv, 13 ff.), who lives his independent life in the heavenly kingdom. He is, however, the head of the body. In this he raises his members ($\mu\acute{\epsilon}\lambda\eta$), creates the ' new man ' (ii, 15), and builds his body up into the heavenly building of his $\acute{\epsilon}\kappa\kappa\lambda\eta\sigma\acute{\iota}\alpha$ (ii, 19 ff. ; iv, 12 ff., 16), in which God's work is made manifest (iii, 10 f.). The saviour loves and cares for his Church, cleansing and saving it. She is his wife and he her husband ; they are bound to each other in obedience and love (v. 22-32)."

There are six separate points here, each obviously corresponding in only a limited way to the generally accepted Christian affirmations, viz. (1) the redeemer's ascension ; (2) the heavenly wall ; (3) the heavenly man ; (4) the Church as Christ's body ; (5) Christ's body as a heavenly building ; (6) the heavenly marriage. The view repeatedly emphasised, that the Church is the body of Christ, can scarcely be held to involve the transfer of the relationship in anything like a physical sense. The body of which Ephesians speaks is, strictly, only a torso. But it grows up in all things into the head, from which, on the other hand, all growth proceeds. On the one hand Christ is the

----

[1] " Zum Begriff der Kirche im Eph." in Theol. Blätt. (1927) 12 ff. ; " Christus und die Kirche im Eph " (1930). The Mandaean Liturgies speak of a heavenly building, which is the great place of light and also the $\check{\alpha}\nu\theta\rho\omega\pi\sigma\varsigma$, the $\dot{\alpha}\nu\grave{\eta}\rho$ $\tau\acute{\epsilon}\lambda\epsilon\iota\sigma\varsigma$, the $\check{\alpha}\nu\theta\rho\omega\pi\sigma\varsigma$ alternating with his $\sigma\hat{\omega}\mu\alpha$. See Lidzbarski, Mandaean Liturgies (1920).

head, and on the other he is the whole body—including the head. This complicated theory can hardly be regarded as a development of the Pauline teaching in Rom. xii, 4 ff. and I Cor. xii, 12 ff. Above all, the equating of body, flesh, wife, church, cannot be derived from Paul's way of putting things in his other writings. I Cor. xii is concerned with the relation of Christians to one another, whereas in Ephesians they are the body of Christ. This world of ideas is more or less clearly presented in the Valentinian Gnosis, the Odes of Solomon, etc. :[1] the redeemer brings the redeemed on high as his body ; Christ is the man whose body the faithful are, and he himself is the head ; the ἐκκλησία as the body of the man first comes into existence through him and in him ; the Church is on the one hand identical with the body of the man, or with the man himself, but on the other hand his feminine

[1] E.g. Theodotus, the Valentinian Gnostic, says, ὁ μέγας ἀγωνιστὴς Ἰησοῦς ἐν ἑαυτῷ δυνάμει τὴν ἐκκλησίαν ἀναλαβών τὸ ἐκλεκτὸν καὶ τὸ κλητόν . . . ἀνέσωσεν καὶ ἀνήνεγκεν ἅπερ ἀνέλαβεν (Clem. Al., Exc. Theod. lviii, 1). The idea that the faithful form the body of the heavenly man may be illustrated from the Odes of Solomon xviii, 14 ff. : " They received my blessing and lived ; and they were gathered to me and were saved ; because they were to me as my own members and I was their head. Glory to thee our head, the Lord Messiah." [Translated by Rendel Harris.] Schlier gives many other examples from Christian apocryphal, Gnostic and Mandaean writings. It is impossible to deny the connection of all this with our subject, even though details remain debatable. It would be a mistake to regard this way of looking at the matter as tantamount to handing Paul over to the Gnostics. Perhaps Schlier should have it made clearer that in Ephesians, as elsewhere in the N.T., the Christological language is polemical, being the first effective means of establishing the unique worth of Jesus Christ, who remains the subject, whatever new predicates are introduced. The same applies to the predicates " Lord " and " Saviour " and, above all, " Word ". The point is not that Christ is the *Word*, but that *Christ* is the Word. See the next two notes.

counterpart, generally called wisdom, sometimes takes his place. It is from this figure of marriage that we are to understand the remarkable words of Eph. v, 25-32, culminating in the affirmation that Christ nourishes and cherishes the Church.

A statement so elaborate and sublime conveys the impression that it must be the outcome of speculations in which the acknowledgment of God and his ἐκκλησία in Christ is largely determined by the pattern upon which it is superimposed. But such an impression must be firmly resisted. The treatment of wisdom has nothing to do with abstract speculation or esoteric knowledge. Similarly in Ephesians wisdom and the knowledge of God are not theoretical but practical, meaning the knowledge of the heart (i, 18), which is attained through obedience towards God—in a word, through faith.[1]

The discovery of the source from which Ephesians draws its ideology does not bring us to the end of our investigation ; we have still to ask why it was employed and to what end it was directed. Two closely related reasons may be suggested. (a) Gnostic ideology and vocabulary, as used in Ephesians, are well adapted to the purpose of setting forth the intimate relationship of Christ and Church, and are therefore brought into the service of a Christological ecclesiology. (b) Gnosticism provides a suitable background for the establishment of the high Christology which was necessary for dealing with the assault of false teaching and

[1] This may serve to correct Schlier's impression that in Die Kirche des Urchristentums, pp. 313, 315, I have failed to recognise " that the mythology of Ephesians is not used in the conventional way, viz., in the service of speculation ". In any case I entirely agree with him when he says that the mythology of Ephesians is the one medium through which the author and his hearers are able to understand one another. On p. 315 of my book I was only speaking of the limits of speculation concerning the Church.

the conflict between Jewish and Gentile Christians. All the same, Ephesians is in fact thoroughly Pauline— whether it was written by the apostle or by one of his disciples. All kinds of difficulty beset an apostle in those days, when he tried to explain the ἐκκλησία of God in Christ, and when these are understood, it is impossible to share the widespread critical certainty that Paul could not have been the author of (Colossians and) Ephesians. Paul had to fight against Jewish Christians or Jews at one extreme, and Gentile Christians or Gnostics at the other, the former not going far enough and the latter going too far. His language had to be strong and elevated, as it is in Ephesians. This was a struggle within the Christian community, which was always in danger of destroying the ideal of the ἐκκλησία. The Church that is from above must be set over against the Jewish claim for a privileged position, the movement towards giving central authority to certain men and one place, which was threatening to lead the original disciples astray. Bizarre Gnostic speculation about the marriage of Christ, as the male principle, with wisdom as the female, must be countered with the doctrine of the ἐκκλησία, which alone takes the place of the " female ". The Paul whom we know in the undisputed Epistles is quite at home in this kind of disputing. That last point, about the " female ", reminds us of II Cor. xi, 2, where Paul refers to his effort to espouse the Corinthian Church to one husband, to present it as a pure virgin to Christ. It has already been pointed out that Rom. xii, 4 ff. and I Cor. xii, 12 ff. show Christians in relation to one another as members of one body, and not in relation to Christ ; but this is only a formal contrast, like that between love to God and love to neighbour. The difficulty of attributing to Paul what is said about the Church in Colossians and Ephesians is not in the matter but in the form ; it is easy to understand the substance of it coming from him, to meet a controversial situation of a special character, but it is far from easy to accept the assumption that he could ever have made such free use of the vocabulary of this Gnostic mythology.[1]

At any rate the point is pretty clearly made that the ἐκκλησία as the body of Christ is not a mere fellowship of men. The true meaning of the gathering of God in Christ can never be understood from the standpoint of social science. The one essential is communion with Christ. To put the matter in a nutshell—a single individual could be—would have to be—the ἐκκλησία if he has communion with Christ. This is the basis of true human brotherhood.[2] Over against all sociological attempts to comprehend the Church, it must be noted that for Paul, for those who followed him, and for the Fourth Evangelist, ecclesiology and Christology are identical. Paul says very emphatically that among Christians—in the ἐκκλησία as the body of Christ—all human divisions disappear (Col. iii, 11 ; Gal. iii, 28). The next verse in Galatians says, " and if ye

---

[1] The much discussed question of authenticity finds its crux here, regard being had also to the peculiar relationship between Colossians and Ephesians. There are traditionalist theologians who hold Ephesians to be genuinely Pauline, crediting the apostle with development, perhaps even to the length of Gnostic ways of thinking. In this connection T. Schmidt, in his Der Leib Christi Σῶμα Χριστοῦ (1919) goes so far as to assert that " in fact, nowhere else does Paul rise to the height of such a comprehensive view of the world and of history, embracing heaven and earth, past, present, and future ". On the other hand there are critical theologians who are led, by the fact that Gnostic language is used without the adoption of Gnostic ways of thought, to deny the Pauline authorship of Ephesians, while holding fast to its Pauline character.

[2] This is well shown in a lecture by the old-Catholic theologian, E. Gaugler, " Die Kirche, ihr Wesen und ihre Bestimmung " (Internat. Kirchl. Zeitschr. (1927), pp. 136 ff., esp. 146).

are Christ's, then are ye Abraham's seed, heirs according to promise ". If we understand Paul aright, we
must speak of the body of Christ with reserve. From
Paul's time onwards one dared not speak too loud, or
too much, of the organism which the body of Christ
had to represent. It was necessary to refrain from
an excessive use of figurative language, in order to
avoid the possibility of giving a wrong impression by
suggesting that the higher growth under discussion
was a natural growth. To be God's organ [discharging
a function of the divine life], means to give heed to
God's call. There can be no such thing as an unrelated
Christology or ecclesiology, in the sense of a Christ- or
Church-mysticism, since the God who speaks in Christ
is the God of the old covenant, who then institutes
the new covenant, and the gathering of God in Christ is
none other than the fulfilment of the O.T. gathering
of God. The same God has spoken and is speaking to
Israel with the word of promise, and to Christians with
the word of the fulfilment of this promise. Along with
the so-called Christ-mysticism and Christ-cult there
remain the God of the O.T. and his worshipping
community. When holiness is ascribed to the ἐκκλησία
that does not mean that she possesses it as a quality.
In other words, the true conception of church, congregation, God's gathering in Christ, is bound up with
a true conception of justification. That is what Paul
is always fighting for, whether against Jews or Gnostics.

4. The few instances of ἐκκλησία in the rest of the
N.T. add nothing new to what has been said above.
It only occurs in the framework of the Apocalypse :
thirteen times in the Plural and seven times in the
Singular, referring to the Churches at Ephesus,
Smyrna, Pergamum, Thyatira, Sardis, Philadelphia and
Laodicea. III John has the word three times, twice

with the Article and once without, though this makes no difference. James v, 14, speaking of elders of the ἐκκλησία, does not refer to a particular congregation, but to the Christian community as a whole, to which the Epistle is addressed. Heb. ii, 12 is a quotation of Ps. xxii, 22, ἐκκλησία representing the Hebrew *qahal*. Heb. xii, 23 is the only passage in which ἐκκλησία denotes the heavenly Jerusalem, and it may be questioned whether it is used here in its technical N.T. sense, especially as it is coupled with πανήγυρις [which Moffatt rightly translates " festal gathering ".][1]

[1] H. Windisch in his commentary rightly avoids " Gemeinde " and translates " Festschar und Versammlung ".

III. GREEK USAGE

THE N.T. itself shows that ἐκκλησία is used in secular Greek for a gathering of the people (Acts xix, 32, 39 f.). The Biblical connotation is indicated by the addition of the words " of God ", with the further addition of " in Christ Jesus " in the N.T., whether expressed or understood. What is the significance of the fact that Greek-speaking Jews and early Christians chose this particular expression ? Could it already have been employed among the Greeks in a religious connection ?

From the time of Thucydides, Plato and Xenophon onwards, and then specially in inscriptions, ἐκκλησία is the gathering of the δῆμος in Athens and most Greek cities. The derivation is simple and significant : the assembled citizens are the ἔκκλητοι (called out), i.e. those who have been summoned by the herald.[1] This naturally suggests that in the Bible the reference is to God in Christ calling men out of the world.[2]

It is questionable whether ἐκκλησία ever meant a religious society in ordinary Greek.[3] If it did, we could well understand its appropriation by a Christian congregation. This would apply specially to Corinth, as pictured by Paul in I Cor. But, apart from the fact

[1] W. Koester, in " Die Idee der Kirche beim Apostel Paulus " (N.T. Abhandlungen xiv, 1—1928) follows others in referring to the form ἐκλησία which is not included even in the latest dictionaries. It would imply derivation from ἐκ-λαός, but it is so rare that no conclusions can be based on it.

[2] Cf. Deissmann, Light from the Ancient East, 112-114.

[3] Johannes Weiss believes it did (I Cor. p. xvii), relying on W. Liebenam, Zur Geschichte und Organisation des Römischen Vereinslebens (1890) ; E. Ziebarth, Das griechische Verein-swesen (1896)—though he gives no evidence for the word ἐκκλησία ;

that the evidence is too slight, Paul would never have used a word with such associations, feeling as he did that everything depended on God's gathering in Christ. Some Gentile Christian circles, unfamiliar with the LXX, may have thought of their fellowship in terms of the derivation of ἐκκλησία, or as a kind of club. It is altogether possible, indeed quite obvious, that Christian congregations would copy contemporary clubs in many matters of organisation.[1]

It was the Septuagint which really gave the word ἐκκλησία to the N.T., after it had acquired its specific value. As soon as converted Jews saw the connection between the O.T. ἐκκλησία and that of the N.T., it became regulative. The political assembly of the ancient Greeks corresponds to this in a formal way, but really only provides an analogy, neither more nor less [2]; just as the application, for polemical purposes, of the title " Lord ", to Caesar is to be seen

and F. Poland, Geschichte des griechischen Vereinswesens (1909). This evidence is not given in modern dictionaries like Preuschen-Bauer and Moulton & Milligan. Lietzmann says expressly (Cor., p. 4) that the word ἐκκλησία " does not appear as the designation of a religious brotherhood ; the three apparent exceptions prove this (Poland 332), since they use ἐκκλησία to denote, not the brotherhood, but its gathering for business".

[1] Cf. G. Heinrici, " Zum genossenschaftlichen Charakter der paulinischen Christengemeinden " in Theol. Stud. Krit. (1881) 505 ff. Against this it is justly urged that the matters involved are common to the formation of all fellowships, and are not peculiar to that age. For further detail see Johannes Weiss, I Cor., pp. xx ff.

[2] E. Peterson goes further than this in Die Kirche, p. 19, n. 19 : " It can be shown in a number of ways that the λαός of the Christian ἐκκλησία is a copy of the ancient δῆμος. I am not only thinking of the forms of acclamation which passed over from the δῆμος to the λαός, but would draw attention to J. Partsch's discovery that the form in which the liberation of slaves was proclaimed in the Christian ἐκκλησία goes back to a custom of the secular ἐκκλησία (Sitzungsber. Heidelb. Akad. (1916) 44 f.)." The connection may be rightly recognised in a single instance of this

as corresponding to the application of the same title to Christ, but not as its prototype. This view is not affected by the fact that the political assembly—at least in classical times—was not without a religious undertone, being regarded as one of the most important duties required by the gods when they founded the city. That this was so may be seen from the prayers which were customarily offered by the herald before the ἐκκλησία and then by each speaker before he made his speech.[1] The later adoption of secular practices by the ancient Church is an entirely different thing, and belongs to the history of the Church in Rome and Byzantium.

That the Greek expression ἐκκλησία, in the sense indicated, did become regulative, follows from the fact that it held the field as the only technical term for the Christian community. It was hardly necessary, even if it had been possible, to translate ἐκκλησία into Latin. Tertullian, who played so important a part in the formation of ecclesiastical Latin, says *curia* in his

sort, but that does not prove the truth of Peterson's thesis that the Christian ἐκκλησία was derived from that of the heathen. He writes rather more cautiously on pp. 14 f., in words that should be taken as a note with the passage already quoted : " The secular ἐκκλησία of antiquity is a recognised institution of the πόλις. It is the assembly of those who have full citizenship, met together for the performance of legal acts. Analogously the Christian ἐκκλησία might be described as the assembly of those who have full citizenship in the heavenly city, met together for the performance of prescribed acts of worship. . . . The public and legal character of Divine Service in the Christian Church shows that the Church owes much more to political models, like the kingdom and the city, than to voluntary fellowships and societies."

[1] Cf. G. Busolt-H. Swoboda, Griechische Staatskunde I (1920), 518 f. ; II (1926), 996. Evidence for prayer in the Athenian ἐκκλησία is found in Aristophanes, Equites, 763 ff. ; Demosthenes, Or. xviii, 1 ; Plutarch, Pericles 8 (I, 156) ; Praecepta Ger. Reipub. 8 (II, 803 f.) (Kleinknecht).

Apologeticum (39 end), and this is a perfectly sound
translation of the Greek word ; but it did not become
a technical term.[1] The same is true of Augustine's
civitas Dei.[2] Among other renderings found here and
there are *contio* and *comitia*.[3] *Convocatio* might have
been adopted as a literal translation. But not one of
these established itself as connoting the Church. The
Romance-speaking peoples have followed the example
of Rome, and modern Greeks have naturally kept the
old term. The word " Church " almost certainly
comes from the adjective κυριακός (of the Lord), but
a kind of popular etymology connects it with ἐκκλησία.
Why is that? Why did the Greek word persist?
Perhaps it was felt in non-Christian circles that there
was no Latin word exactly corresponding.[4] The
matter was not decided by interesting and attractive
analogies, but by the geneological descent of ἐκκλησία
from the Greek Bible. The same term was retained,
as κύριος was for " Lord ". The considerations here
submitted do not constitute a mathematical demonstration that the LXX is entirely responsible ; but probably
it was felt that what was required was more than just
the word used by Greek-speaking Christians ; it must
be a word hallowed by use in the holy Book.

[1] Cf. Harnack, Mission u. Ausbreitung.I (1924), 420, n. 1. [See
p. 30, n. 2. Ref. to Tertullian not in English trans., Mission and
Expansion (1908) I, 407, n. 3.]

[2] F. Kattenbusch, in Der Quellort der Kirchenidee (Harnack-
Festgabe (1921), pp. 142-172) says this is the first attempt to give
a translation denoting the actual meaning of the word. On the
other hand Kleinknecht says that " Civitas dei in Augustine gives
the political idea of πολιτεία, under Platonic influence, in all
its ancient many-sidedness, but certainly not that of ἐκκλησία ".

[3] Cf. Deissmann, Light from the Ancient East, 112-114.

[4] Deissmann recalls Pliny's letter to Trajan X, 110 (111),
where the Latinised *ecclesia* occurs ; and a bilingual inscription
at Ephesus, of A.D. 103-4, in which the Greek word ἐκκλησία is
simply transcribed.

At the same time, this very word ἐκκλησία, with its natural worldly associations, voices the greatest claim of the Christian community over against the world. Many Gentile Christians, like those who to-day write the history of religion, thought of themselves as an association for the worship of Christ, and might have given themselves some kind of cultic title. There were plenty to choose from, among contemporary religious clubs and societies.

Heathen writers did actually apply such labels to the Christian community. Lucian evidently regards it as a θίασος [a religious guild or brotherhood like that of the worshippers of Bacchus], when he calls the leader θιασάρχης.[1] Celsus calls Christ's disciples θιασῶται.[2] What is more striking is that Eusebius also twice calls Christians θιασῶται, and once even applies the term θίασος to the Church.[3] This is all the material of this sort that is known, and the greatest care must be taken to avoid the exaggeration of assuming that Christianity was just one among other religious brotherhoods.[4] In order rightly to assess the juxtaposition

[1] Lucian, De Per. Morte, 11 : τὴν θαυμαστὴν σοφίαν τῶν Χριστιανῶν ἐξέμαθε . . . προφήτης καὶ θιασάρχης καὶ συναγωγεύς.

[2] Origen, Celsus iii, 23 : ὁ δὲ ἡμέτερος Ἰησοῦς ὀφθεὶς τοῖς ἰδίοις θιασώταις—χρήσομαι γὰρ τῷ παρὰ Κέλσῳ ὀνόματι—ὤφθη μέν κατ' ἀλήθειαν.

Origen is evidently astonished that Celsus should have employed this expression. Similarly, in the Latin Church, in Minucius Felix, Octavius, 8 f. (Migne P.L. III), a heathen speaks of the Christian community as a *factio, coitio, consensio*—somewhat derogatory words. See p. 30, n. 2.

[3] Eusebius, Hist. Eccl. I, iii, 12 : (Χριστὸς) αὐτὰς γυμνὰς ἀρετὰς καὶ βίον οὐράνιον αὐτοῖς ἀληθείας δόγμασιν τοῖς θιασώταις παραδούς. Cf. I, iii, 19. The word θίασος stands for Church at X, i, 8.

[4] A striking example of such exaggeration and mistake occurs in Der römische Staat und die allgemeine Kirche bis auf Diocletian (1890), pp. 46 f. where the author, K. J. Neumann, asserts

of θίασος and ἐκκλησία, it must be remembered that
words denoting the various brotherhoods of the ancient
world were used with remarkable frequency, viz.,
θίασος, ἔρανος, κοινόν, σύνοδος, σύλλογος and many
others. None of these were appropriated by the
Christians. Further, although the names of individuals
were often derived from those of gods or other persons,
no such thing ever happened in the case of the name of
Jesus.¹ The name " Christians " is rarely found in the
N.T. (only Acts xi, 26 ; xxvi, 28 ; I Pet. iv, 16) ;
it became popular gradually at first, and in the form
" Chrestians " was connected with the proper name
" Chrestos ". Christians are partisans of Christ,
as Herodians, for example, are partisans of Herod
(Mark iii, 6 ; xii, 13 ; Matt. xxii, 16), supporters of one
particular movement among many.

The uniqueness of Christianity is much better
brought out by emphasising the ἐκκλησία (of God)
than by the choice of some cultic word, perhaps distinguished by the addition of a personal name. The
so-called Christ-cult was not, and did not wish to be,
one cult among others, but took its stand against all
cults, in the sense that it stood over against the whole
world, including the whole of the so-called religious
world. All that is guaranteed by the choice of the
designation ἐκκλησία, with which the words " of God "
are always to be understood.

The question may be asked, and has been asked,
who was the first within the Christian movement to
say ἐκκλησία ? Could it have been Paul who set the
fashion among Greek-speaking Christians ?² But it

that " it would actually have needed explaining, if Greek
Christians had not seen their new associations as religious brother-
hoods and *thiasoi* ". The presumable *abusus* on the part of certain
Gentile Christians, is, however, no *usus legitimus*.

¹ See the careful investigations of F. Poland (op. cit.).

² Kattenbusch (op. cit., p. 144, n. 1) is inclined towards this

seems difficult in this case to make any particular
individual responsible. It is more likely that the
expression arose among Greek-speaking Jewish Christians and their Gentile adherents, who formed congregations resembling the Hellenistic synagogues before
Paul's time.[1] As Jews, these Hellenistic Christians
were brought up on the LXX. They no longer
called themselves συναγωγή (about which more will
be said later) but ἐκκλησία. As Christians, they
seized upon the expression which was falling into
disuse among the Jews, who were tending more and
more to depart from LXX usage and confine συναγωγή
to its local meaning. That in itself made ἐκκλησία
preferable. The latter was also a more impressive
Greek word.[2] It should also be noticed that in the
LXX ἐκκλησία is made to stand out by the use of
laudatory epithets.[3]

view. Cf. F. Torm, Hermeneutik des N.T. (1930), p. 80. H.
Dieckmann's thesis, in De Ecclesia I (1925), p. 280 : " Nomen
Ecclesiae ad ipsum Christum ut auctorem reducitur " is also
rejected by Catholic scholars, on the ground that Jesus would
hardly have used Greek ; cf. K. Pieper, Jesus und die Kirche
(1932), p. 11.

[1] Cf. K. L. Schmidt, Die Stellung des Apostels Paulus im
Urchristentum (1924), p. 16.

[2] Wellhausen, on Matt. xvi, 18, expresses the opinion that " in
Greek ἐκκλησία is the more honourable word ". The passage
from Tertullian, Apologeticum 39, mentioned above, should be
understood as an emphatic paraphrase of the emphatic word
ἐκκλησία : " Hoc sumus congregati quod et dispersi, hoc
universi quod et singuli . . . cum probi, cum boni coëunt, cum
pii, cum casti congregrantur, non est factio dicenda, sed curia ".
Augustine's exposition of Ps. lxxxii, 1 is relevant here : he
says that convocatio (ἐκκλησία) is the word for the Christian
congregation and congregatio (συναγωγή) for the Jewish, because
the former is a nobler expression, meaning the calling together
of men, whereas the latter indicates the driving together of cattle.
See also Trench sub. voc. [and Schürer, G. J. V. 4th ed., II,
504 f.].

[3] Pointed out by Lietzmann on I Cor, i, 1 ; also by K. Pieper,

Why did the LXX translators almost always choose ἐκκλησία to represent the Hebrew *qahal* ? Quite apart from the fact that the verbal root in both cases has the same meaning, there is much to be said for the conjecture that the choice was influenced by the similarity of sound between the two words.[1] This is supported by the fact that Greek- and Latin-speaking Jews were fond of adding Greek and Latin names similar in sound to their Hebrew or Aramaic ones.[2]

op. cit., 20, and Harnack, Mission and Expansion, etc., I, 407, where, however, the suggestion that the choice of the word ἐκκλησία was a master-stroke is questionable, if not actually misleading.

[1] As with ἀκροβυστία [and perhaps ἀγάπη and ὅσιοι, the latter suggested by L. W. Grensted (see C. H. Dodd, The Bible and the Greeks, p. 64, n. 1)]. Cf. Cremer-Kögel s.v. p. 566 and G. Stählin, Skandalon, p. 44.

[2] The best-known example is Saul-Paul ; cf. Jesus-Jason, Silas-Silvanus (Aram. *Sheʻila'*, Heb. *Sha'ul*). Modern examples are Luser-Ludwig (Heb. *'El'azar*), Moses-Moritz, Isaak-Isidor (or Ignaz).

IV. PARALLEL EXPRESSIONS

'Εκκλησία being a Greek word for a Biblical matter, it is not surprising that the latter does not stand or fall with the former. Thus it often happens in the N.T. that the word itself is missing where the matter itself is under discussion. Most important in this connection is I Peter, which, though Pauline in its general attitude, nevertheless differs from Paul in not using the word ἐκκλησία [1]; for this Epistle contains a specially rich analysis of the nature of the ἐκκλησία of God : " An elect race, a royal priesthood, a holy nation, a people for God's own possession " (ii, 9—all from the O.T.) ; " A spiritual house " (ii, 5) ; " The people of God" (ii, 10). Cf. Paul's strong emphasis in Phil. iii, 3 : " We are the circumcision ". It is the same in other passages : " Israel " (Rom. ix, 6) ; " the Israel of God " (Gal. vi, 16) ; " Israel after the spirit " (implied at I Cor. x, 18) ; " Abraham's seed, heirs according to the promise " (Gal. iii, 29 ; cf. Heb. ii, 16); " Twelve Tribes " (James i, 1). The fact of the Dispersion brings a new aspect of the matter into view, showing that Christians, just because they are the ἐκκλησία, are " sojourners of the Dispersion " (I Pet. i, 1) and " the Twelve tribes that are in the Dispersion " (James i, 1).

Other designations, only loosely connected with the O.T., or entirely apart from it, do not conflict with the proper title of ἐκκλησία. Some of them describe the faith and ideals of Christians, e.g. " the saints "

[1] Cf. Th. Spörri, Der Gemeindegedanke im ersten Petrusbrief (1925), esp. pp. 271 ff. ; [E. G. Selwyn, I Peter, pp. 81-90, 153-168.]

(generally with a reference to the O.T.) ; " the faithful " ; " the brethren " ; " the brotherhood ". Others are related to special circumstances and disappear later, e.g., " the disciples " (μαθηταί) ; " the poor ". The designation of Christians as " disciples " is applied to the first followers of Jesus, then widened, then narrowed and finally relegated to the background, simply because of the special relationship between the first followers and their master. There is no ground for speaking of a development from one designation to another, culminating in ἐκκλησία.[1]

The expression συναγωγή stands in a class by itself ; it will be treated here only in its relation to ἐκκλησία. The superficial view commonly held is that the latter means the Christian Church and the former the Jewish Synagogue. But this neat distinction first came into vogue in later centuries, and continues into our time. It looks as though the Christian congregation could call itself συναγωγή (James ii, 2, and v, 14).[2] Less questionable than this is the fact that the Jewish Christians in Trans-Jordan used the word both for their Church fellowship and for their Church building.[3] Apart from this more or less isolated instance, Jewish Christians generally called themselves ἐκκλησία and not συναγωγή. The exact opposite is found in the case of a Marcionite συναγωγή.[4] When the separation of Jewish Christians from their mother-Church became more clearly marked, they probably called both their meetings and their meeting-places synagogues. It

---

[1] Against Harnack, Mission and Expansion I, 404 ff.

[2] Cf. Zahn, Matthew (1922), p. 546.

[3] Epiphanius, Haer. xxx. 18, 2 : πρεσβυτέρους γὰρ οὗτοι (i.e. the Christians of Transjordan) ἔχουσιν ἀρχισυναγώγους · συναγωγὴν δὲ καλοῦσιν τὴν ἑαυτῶν ἐκκλησίαν καὶ οὐχὶ ἐκκλησίαν.

[4] συναγωγὴ Μαρκιωνιστῶν : le Bas-Waddington, Inscr. Grecques et Letines III (1870), No. 2558, p. 852 ; cf. Harnack, op. cit., 421, 659. [See Schürer, G.V.I. (4), II, 517.]

would seem that at first all Christians, Jewish and Gentile, used both expressions. It must also be remembered that there is evidence for the use of συναγωγή by ancient heathen brotherhoods.[1] But in spite of such analogies, an O.T. origin is even more obvious for συναγωγή than for ἐκκλησία. And the coupling of the two is of primary importance for the discussion of the question, what Aramaic word was used by the early Christians and by Jesus himself? The question is—whether ἐκκλησία owes anything to a Semitic equivalent, and, if so, how its meaning is affected.

[1] Cf. W. Koester, Die Idee der Kirche, etc., n. 12., p. 1.

V. MATTHEW xvi, 18 AND xviii, 17

1. These two sayings raise many difficulties. Neither of them finds its place automatically among the ἐκκλησία passages already discussed. In fact, they demand a thorough-going criticism, especially on the part of those who accept their authenticity. Problems are presented not only by the Greek text, but also by the original Aramaic; and the main question is seriously complicated by the way in which subordinate questions impinge upon one another. Thus the exposition of the Greek text determines the choice of a Semitic word behind ἐκκλησία and *vice versa* the word chosen affects the exposition. Again, the answer to the question of authenticity depends on the nature of the exposition; and *vice versa* the exposition will be influenced if that question has been settled already on other grounds; both positive and negative answers have actually led to more or less convincing expositions. All this bears on the understanding of the Matthean use of the word ἐκκλησία. Furthermore, the linguistic question is bound up with judgments concerning history. This interaction must never be forgotten. Word, idea, and thing in this case are unusually complex—as if a mathematician were to combine imaginary quantities with real ones. But although the complication creates difficulties, it does not necessarily lead to the confusion and bewilderment which have appeared from time to time, as interpretation has swung to and fro, up and down.

2. A peculiar difficulty, which meets us on the threshold, consists in the fact that the two passages, Matt. xvi, 18 and xviii, 17, are not in the same key. If

neither is authentic, the former may mean the universal Church and the latter the individual congregation ; and there can be no doubt that this common—but not therefore correct—differentiation reacts upon the interpretation of both passages, supporting the view that they are unauthentic. But if they are authentic, the interpretation seems to be extremely difficult, taking the first to refer to the *qahal* and the second to the synagogue. How are we to explain the fact that ἐκκλησία is used for both ? We must examine again the relationship between *qahal* and synagogue. Is it certain that the former is the right word in xvi, 18 ?

3. The text of Matt. xviii, 17, and still more that of xvi, 18, are above suspicion. We have no Greek MSS. or ancient translations which do not contain Matt. xvi, 17-19 or at least xvi, 18 ; and it can safely be asserted to-day that no objection to the verses under discussion can be based on their occurrence or non-occurrence in patristic writings from the time of Justin Martyr onwards.[1]

The persistence of a critical attitude to the text is due—apart from " Protestant ", and above all "Modernist ", efforts to get rid of the *locus classicus* for Papal primacy,[2]—to the strong impression made on many

---

[1] See K. L. Schmidt, Die Kirche, 283 ff. It must be specially emphasised that the latest critical attempt to discredit the text, as made by Harnack on the basis of a passage in St. Ephraem, has been rebutted by Catholic scholars. Cf. C. A. Kneller in Zeitschr. f. kath. Theol. (1920) 147 ff. ; J. Sickenberger, " Eine neue Deutung der Primatstelle (Matt. xvi, 18) " in Theol. Revue. (1920), 1 ff. ; S. Euringer in Festgabe f. A. Ehrhard (1922) 141 ff. ; J. Geiselmann in Bibl. Zeitfr. xii, 7 (1927) ; K. Pieper, Jesus und die Kirche, 37 ff. See Joachim Jeremias, Golgotha (1926) 68 ff.

[2] Cf. K. L. Schmidt, Die Kirche, 300 f., in opposition to J. Schnitzer, Hat Jesus das Papsttum gestiftet ? (1910) and F. Heiler, Der Katholizismus (1923) 25 ff., 39 ff.

by the fact that Matt. xvi, 18 forms part of a saying
which is found in neither Mark nor Luke. Two
deductions may be drawn from this : *either* Matt. xvi,
17-19 in an interpolation into the text of Matthew, *or*
Matthew (or his authority) added them to an earlier
text, perhaps going back to Jesus, which was known to
Mark and Luke. The first is too crude to be taken
very seriously. Words of such importance must be
treated with great care. It is not usual in other cases
to regard a passage as unauthentic because it has no
parallels.[1] But even the second, though more careful,
has not the significance often attached to it. The
question may certainly be raised whether these verses
are interpolated by Matthew (or his authority).
But that does not settle the question of the authenticity
of the logion. We have to reckon with the possibility
of an interpolation drawn from an otherwise unknown
genuine tradition, whose value is to be tested quite apart
from its present setting. Even if there are chrono-
logical and psychological questions which we cannot
answer, owing to the nature of the Gospel tradition,
a logion without a context has to be expounded as
such.[2]

4. Literary criticism is in any case so uncertain that
the wise student must direct his attention to matters
of fact. All objections to the ἐκκλησία sayings in
Matthew lead directly to the discussion of factual
problems. The first clear point is, that Matt. xvi, 17-19

[1] Linton, in his survey (see Bibliography), p. 158, rightly
says of critical objection to the text, " This by itself is not enough ;
other material peculiar to individual Gospels is not judged in this
rigorous way ".

[2] Cf. K. L. Schmidt, Der Rahmen der Geschichte Jesu (1919)
217 ff. Bultmann, Die Geschichte der synoptischen Tradition
(1931), 277, dealing with Mark viii, 27-30, gives a different
analysis. Against this, which appeared in the 1921 edition, cf. K.
L. Schmidt, Die Kirche (1927) 282 n.1.

is thoroughly Semitic in character : its native place
must be within the early Christian community in
Palestine.[1]   But this does not prove it to be a genuine
saying of Jesus.   Further inquiries have still to be
made, in two directions : *first* as to Jesus and the Church
and *secondly* concerning the position of Peter in the
early Church.   Each of these includes two questions,
so that we have four subjects [2] to deal with : (*a*)
statistics relating to the fact that the word ἐκκλησία
only occurs twice in the Gospels ; (*b*) eschatology and
the question whether Jesus, as the preacher of the
Kingdom of God, could have founded a Church ;
(*c*) does Church History show Peter to have held the
position of authority ascribed to him in Matt. xvi, 18 ?
(*d*) from the point of view of psychology, did Peter
really make good as the " Rock " ?

(*a*) Mere statistics prove as little in the present case
as in I Peter, where the actual word ἐκκλησία does not
occur, but that for which it stands is indicated by an
abundance of other terms, mostly drawn from the
Old Testament.   Similar synonyms [3] are found in the
Gospel tradition.   Matt. xxvi, 31 and John x, 1
speak of the ποίμνη (flock), which at I Cor. ix, 7
quite clearly means the Church.   With this we may
compare ποίμνιον (little flock) Luke xii, 32 ; Acts
xx, 28 ; I Pet. v, 2 f. ; αὐλὴ τῶν προβάτων (sheep-
fold) John x, 1 ; ἀρνία μου (my lambs) John xxi, 15 ;
τὰ προβάτια μου (my sheep) John xxi, 16 f.   Note that
the sheep are " mine ", as the Church is at Matt. xvi,
18.   Just as the Good Shepherd is the same as the Lord

---

[1] Cf. Strack-Billerbeck ad loc. ; Bultmann, Die Gesch. d. syn.
Trad., 277 ; Jeremias, Golgotha, 68 ff.

[2] Well characterised by Linton, op. cit., pp. 175 ff.

[3] Cf. Linton, 176.   The problem of the Church in the fourth
Gospel is dealt with by E. Gaugler in Intern. Kirchl. Zeitschr.
(1924), pp. 97 ff., 181, and (1925), pp. 27 ff.   The latter, on p. 28,
treats specially of synonyms of ἐκκλησία.

so his flock is the same as his Church. This group or
company is, to begin with, the college of the twelve
disciples appointed by Jesus. He separated a small
band from the rest of the Jews, sharply opposed to the
Pharisaic scribes and ultimately to the whole impeni-
tent nation, to constitute the true ἐκκλησία or people
of God. Thus Matt. xvi, 18 gives us more than an
item in the life of Jesus : this is an event in the history
of the Christ. The existence of this inner circle of
disciples in the lifetime of Jesus is not rendered doubtful
by differences in the lists of names or by the lack of
individual characterisation. The concrete personal
note was certainly missing at the time when these lists
were compiled, viz. in the period of the early Church.
Details were supplied later in the apocryphal Acts of
the Apostles, which were embroidered in the usual
style of Hellenistic romance.[1]   For the early Church,
on the other hand, it was more important that
Jesus had the Twelve with him than that something definite should be known about each of them.
This being so, there is no reason why we should
not accept the traditional picture of the historical
Jesus with his disciples.[2]   A deeper and broader
foundation is reached when the discussion is extended
so as to include the questions whether, and in what
sense, Jesus regarded himself as the Son of Man, and
whether, and in what manner, he instituted the Lord's

[1] Cf. K. L. Schmidt, " Die Stellung der Evangelien in der
allgemeinen Literaturegeschichte ", in Gunkel-Festschrift (1923),
II, 80.

[2] R. Schütz in Apostel und Jünger, 1921, says on the one hand,
following Wellhausen and Bultmann, " The historical college
of the Twelve cannot be earlier than the beginning of Paul's
Apostleship " (p. 75), but, on the other hand, is compelled to
agree that " the possibility that Jesus himself had already referred
to the symbolic meaning of the number, Twelve, cannot be ruled
out " (72). [See Ed. Meyer, Urspr. u. Anf. (1924), I. 291–9.]

Supper. If Jesus understood his Messiah-ship in the
sense of Daniel vii, this will open up new vistas when we
are considering the nature and the importance of his
founding of the Church. For the Son of Man in
Daniel is not a mere individual : he is the representative of " the people of the saints of the Most High "
and has set himself the task of making this people of
God, the ἐκκλησία, a reality.[1]   From this point of view
the so-called institution of the Lord's Supper can be
shown to be the formal founding of the Church.[2]   Thus

[1] Three modern scholars seem to have drawn attention independently to this aspect of the founding of the Church by Jesus
Christ. T. Schmidt, in Der Leib Christi (1919), has a section
entitled " Analogie von Messias und Gemeinde " (pp. 217 ff.).
A. Schlatter, Die Geschichte des Christus (1923), p. 375, says,
" The title, Christ, demanded of him that he should bring the
perfect community into being." Finally, the deepest insight is
shown by Kattenbusch in the Harnack Festgabe (1921), 143-172 :
" Christ has an independent existence, just as much as each of those
who are his, but is only himself in the σῶμα ; without this he
would not be what his name indicates " (145) ; " he must so shape
his personal life that he really is, and can claim to be, the type of a
people of the saints of the Most High ; and he must create and
build up this people among men " (160). These are followed
by Gloege, Reich Gottes und Kirche im N.T. (1929), 218, 228 :
" The saviour is only saviour as the creator of a new, redeemed
and justified people ; . . . the Χριστός can no more be Christ
without the ἐκκλησία than the ποιμήν can be shepherd without
the ποίμνιον." See also Linton, op. cit., 148 : " The Messiah
is no private person ; a community belongs to him ; to the
shepherd belongs the flock ".
  [Reference may also be made to T. W. Manson, The Teaching
of Jesus (1931), 211-236 ; J. R. Coates, The Coming of the Church
(1929), 23-54 ; R. Newton Flew, Jesus and his Church (1938).]
  [2] Again it is to Kattenbusch that we owe our deepest insight.
In the Harnack Festgabe (p. 171) he writes : " When he founds
the ἐκκλησία, a community in his name, through the Last
Supper, he does not forget the title he chose for himself out of
Daniel, but puts it in the foreground [Mark xiv, 21], indicating
the nature of the Son of Man by means of a reference to Isaiah

we not only become more and more certain that, so
far as facts are concerned, Matt. xvi, 18 does not stand
alone, but also realise—an important point—that this
conception of the complex of ideas (Jesus, Messiah,
Son of Man, Disciples, Community, Lord's Supper)
leads directly to the Pauline and sub-Pauline doctrine
of the ἐκκλησία, which on the one hand is " from
above " and on the other is " the Body of Christ ",
just as Christ is at the same time highly exalted and
present in the midst of the community. The question
whether Jesus himself founded the Church is really the
question concerning his Messiah-ship.[1] Problems of
detail concerning time and place, which the Gospels
do not enable us to solve, are of secondary importance
when compared with this, which is the main problem.[2]

(b) How does all this fit in with the eschatology of
Jesus' proclamation of the Kingdom of God ? After
what has been said, we can deal with this question more
briefly. The eschatological presuppositions of Jesus'
self-designation as Son of Man, and of the institution
of the Lord's Supper, prove that the idea of the
Church also is eschatological. But this does not mean
that Church and Kingdom of God are the same
thing. They are not the same in the early Church,
which certainly regarded itself as the ἐκκλησία while
continuing the proclamation of the Kingdom. Nor
are they the same in the preaching of Jesus, for he
promised the Kingdom of God to his Church, i.e. the

liii ". This would perhaps be more impressive if the analysis of
the text were more convincing. Cf. K. L. Schmidt on " Abend-
mahl im N.T." in Rel. Gesch. Geg., 2nd ed., I, 6 ff.

[1] Cf. the concise presentation of the affirmative view, against
Wellhausen, Wrede and Bultmann, by K. L. Schmidt in R.G.G.,
2nd ed., III, 149 f.

[2] That is what throws doubt on Wendland's otherwise attractive
picture of stages in Die Eschatologie des Reiches Gottes bei
Jesus (1931).

Church which he founded. The ἐκκλησία after Easter
regarded itself as eschatological in this sense. Similarly
the individual Christian may be called eschatological,
because he is a justified sinner.[1]

[1] Bultmann's construction misses the points upon which we
have here briefly touched, in his Gesch. syn. Trad. and also in his
review of Wendland in Deutsche Literaturzeitung (1934), 2019 ff.
When he says that the real problem of the ἐκκλησία is presented
by the fact that it takes the place of the Kingdom of God, for
the speedy coming of which Jesus had been looking, he is viewing
the matter in the light of his earlier formulation of the question,
i.e. from an evolutionary standpoint, which is not adequate for
the understanding of the transition from Jesus to the community,
whether of Peter or of Paul. If Bultmann agrees that the early
Christians regarded themselves as the ἐκκλησία, and gave this
word "a radically eschatological meaning", it is incumbent
upon him to answer the question how the early Christians distinguished between the Kingdom of God and the Church.
Cf. the Preface to the 2nd impression of K. L. Schmidt, Die
Kirche ; Linton, op. cit., 179 f.

J. Haller, in Das Papsttum I (1934), p. 4, lays it down that "a
sober criticism, bearing in mind the whole of the Saviour's
teaching, can never believe that Jesus spoke the words ascribed
to him in Matthew. . . . This is a prediction introduced after
the event had taken place." In a comment on this (p. 442) we
read : "It is not yet settled whether the saying is authentic.
In my judgment the verdict must be negative, unless we are to
depart from the rules of criticism that prevail everywhere else.
Many, it is true, still do this, e.g., Kattenbusch. . . . The same
judgment must be passed on K. L. Schmidt's verbose and pretentious essay, in spite of its learning and ingenuity." As for
"the rules of criticism that prevail everywhere else ", to which
Haller appeals in the interests of "a sober criticism ", it is
enough to point out that an entirely different verdict, in whole and
in part, is given by the jurist, G. Holstein, in Die Grundlagen des
ev. Kirchenrechts (1928) and by the historian, E. Caspar, in
Geschichte des Papsttums (1930-33). Of the latter Haller (p. 441)
merely remarks, "Our ways in general are so far apart, and our
divergence in the assessment and treatment of sources is of so
fundamental a nature, that I think it is right for me to avoid
critical discussion, apart from a few cases. There are different
ways of writing history, and every man must go his own way

(c) From the point of view of Church History, the argument against Matt. xvi, 18 is that Peter did not occupy the authoritative position in the early Church that has been ascribed to him. This objection, supported by reference to I Cor. iii, 11 ; x, 4 ; Eph. ii, 20 (see note on p. 15), [1] may be met by two considerations. On the one hand, Peter played a bigger part on the occasion of his condemnation by Paul than is admitted by Protestants in their controversy with Rome. Since there are no obvious historical or psychological reasons for his being singled out, the simplest solution of the problem is that he had been designated by Jesus himself. On the other hand, if Peter was faced with opposition in the early Church, in Johannine as well as Pauline circles (note the rivalry

(' sehe jeder wie er's treibe ') ". This makes it unnecessary to say any more about Haller just now. Cf. K. Pieper, Die angebliche Einsetzung des Petrus? (1935) ; Jesus und die Kirche (1932).

The latest writer who deals with this subject, W. G. Kümmel, in " Die Eschatologie der Evangelien " (Theol. Blätt., 1936, 225 ff.) fails to explain the special eschatological character of the ἐκκλησία over against the Kingdom of God, and writes as follows (p. 231). " K. L. Schmidt seeks the support of linguistic research for the view that Jesus intended to found a special community, and employs Matt. xvi, 18 as evidence, regarding it as authentic. It is characteristic how in this whole discussion systematic construction takes the place of an exegetical formulation of the question. But a true Biblical theology must start from a strict exegesis." To such a " critical " pronouncement it can only be replied that the present re-statement and enlargement of our interpretation of the locus classicus ecclesiae does not start from a " systematic construction ", but from " an exegetical formulation of the question ", and therefore what the writer is concerned with is precisely a " true Biblical theology ", consistent with a " strict exegesis ". [See G. D. Kilpatrick, The Origins of the Gospel acc. to St. Matthew (1946), pp. 39 f. : " . . . these sections may well have a basis in unwritten tradition " ; G. Johnston, The Church in the N.T. (1943), 48-51, is negative.]

[1] According to H. Windisch in Theol. Rundsch. (1933), p. 251, " to-day it is only the third objection which has any real weight ".

between Peter and the other disciple, John xx, 2 ff.),
it is not easy to see how Matt. xvi, 18 could have arisen
out of such a situation. The theory of a prediction
after the event comes to grief on the fact that the
" event " for Peter is very different from what might
have been expected from Matt. xvi, 18. We may therefore accept the disputed text as genuine on the principle of preferring the harder reading.[1]

(d) As for the psychological objection that Peter did
not turn out to be a rock—to admit that would mean
giving up the fundamental idea of the ἐκκλησία. The
setting apart of Peter is an enigma, and must be accepted as such. Psychological theories of all sorts may
throw a certain amount of light on the subject, but
they cannot remove the final mystery. We cannot and
dare not give an answer to the question why God made
Israel his people and his Church. Peter is specially
chosen and is disobedient, but remains chosen, for
he has become the *fundamentum ecclesiae*. Israel also is
chosen and is disobedient, but remains chosen, for
there is a remnant that returns.[2]

[1] In connection with the many attempts to depreciate Peter
more than is permissible, here again one must not follow Luther's
exegesis, seeing in Matt. xvi, 18 nothing more than in Matt. v, 3.
Cf. K. L. Schmidt, Die Kirche, 289 ff. Strack-Billerbeck's
effort (I, 732) to put Matt. xvi, 18 back into Hebrew is vitiated
by the desire to depreciate Peter. Bultmann finds the effort
" absurd " (Gesch. d. syn. Tr., 148), but Linton says it " deserves
attention " (op. cit. 170).

[2] Cf. W. Leonhard in Una Sancta, 1927, p. 485 : " . . . the
shaky man of rock, the confessor prone to denial, the upholder who
needs upholding—that this should be the first Christian man is
indeed one of the most startling paradoxes of the Gospel ; it is a
piece of the Passion Story, and has its reflex in every Christian
life. Peter must not be depreciated. So says K. L. Schmidt
convincingly." Otherwise Leonhard disagrees with K. L. S., who
" cannot refrain from expressing the judgment that it is just the
singling-out of the personality of Simon Peter that confounds the
claims of the Roman hierarchy " ; he calls that " a Protestant

A note may be added on the difficulty, often emphasised, that " Church " is not a suitable object after
the verb " to build ".[1] The figure of building is
common in Judaism and early Christianity, specially
for the creation of the world.[2] It might be suggested
that the word " house " lies behind the word " Church"
in Matt. xvi, 18.[3]

overplus " ; but that is another matter. Karl Heim makes a
good point on the other side in Das Wesen des ev. Christentums
(1929), p. 36 : " It is a strange irony of world history, that just
these words of Christ should be displayed in gigantic letters on the
dome of the Pope's great basilica—just these words of Christ which,
understood in their original sense, exclude and forbid the Papacy
in every form, seeing that they are practically unique in assigning
to the apostle a peerless and absolutely unrepeatable position in
God's spiritual temple ".

W. G. Kümmel (op. cit.), p. 232, can only say here, " It
is entirely inconceivable that Jesus should have conferred on a man
the control of admission into the Kingdom of God ". To this it
may be replied that, as indicated in the text above, everything
becomes inconceivable if Matt. xvi, 18 is regarded as an in-
vention of the community.

K. Pieper starts from Catholic premises in his controversy with
K. L. S. and Karl Heim, in Jesus und die Kirche, pp. 60 ff. It is
characteristic that according to him J. Geiselmann (see p. 36, n.
1) declares that " we must bear in mind that there are limits to
what the Bible alone can tell us of what the Lord's promise
involves in detail concerning the Petrine primacy " ; and that
J. Sickenberger, in Bibl. Zeitfragen (1929), pp. 16 ff., dealing with
the confession at Caesarea Philippi, does not make the slightest
reference to the bearing of Matt. xvi, 17 ff. on Peter's successors ;
while Karl Adam, in Das Wesen des Katholizismus (1934), p. 118,
expresses the opinion that the reference to Peter's successors can
be denied by those who confine their attention to the Biblical
text, and do not link it up with the Incarnation and its object.

[1] This is the ground on which Holtzmann (N.T. übers. I, 165 f.)
decides against authenticity : " If Jesus were speaking, we should
expect οἰκοδομεῖν to be followed by a concrete object, such as
τὴν οἰκίαν μου".

[2] Cf. Strack-Billerbeck, I, 732 f. ; Zahn, Matt., 547 ; Schlatter,
Matt., 506 f.

[3] Cf. Hermann's careful and weighty contribution in Th. Blätt.

5. The arguments so far advanced are valid if ἐκκλησία at Matthew xvi, 18 and xviii, 17 corresponds to the Hebrew *qahal*, as it does elsewhere in the New Testament. But it is still an open question whether we ought to think of Hebrew or of Aramaic. And, further, it is not settled whether we should confine ourselves to *qahal* or its Aramaic equivalent *qᵉhala'* (a loan-word from Biblical Hebrew).

If Jesus and his disciples spoke Aramaic, it does not necessarily follow that this was the only language they used for religious purposes.[1] We must assume that they had a certain familiarity with Hebrew as the language of their ancestral Church life.[2] But this does not point conclusively to *qahal*. We need not concern ourselves with *qᵉhillah*, the word used by Franz Delitzsch at Matt. xvi, 18 in his Hebrew translation of the New Testament (1880), since it occurs so rarely in the Old Testament and Rabbinic writings. A word to be taken more seriously is *'edhah*,[3] which in the Old Testament differs very little from *qahal*.

Neither of these expressions is much employed by the Rabbis. They prefer *çibbur*, which occurs once in the Old Testament (II Kings x, 8), meaning " heap ", and may be said to be the proper word for the community, whether national or local, in later Judaism.[4]

(1926), pp. 203 ff. Bultmann (Trad., 149) is mistaken in calling it " quite superfluous ", for it has the distinction of recognising the special affinity of ἐκκλησία and οἰκία in both O.T. and N.T. Pieper (op. cit.) has no evidence for the charge that Hermann's suggestion would reduce the meaning of ἐκκλησία to a religious fellowship of any kind.

[1] Cf. Dalman, Jesus-Jeshua (English Trans., Levertoff, 1929).

[2] Dalman, op. cit., refers to Luke iv, 16 as showing Jesus' familiarity with Hebrew.

[3] See O. Procksch in Deutsche Theologie (1928), p. 23, with answer by K. L. S. on p. 26.

[4] So Strack-Billerbeck, I, 734. See Dalman, Wörterbuch, sub voc.

Another common expression is *kᵉneṣeth Yisra'el* ; only the verb (*kanaṣ*) is found in the O.T., meaning " to gather ", " to assemble ". This word is used to emphasise the personification of the believing community of Israel.[1] Actually it is impossible to establish any real differentiation between the four terms, *qahal*, *'edhah*, *çibbur*, *kᵉneṣeth*, and so no conclusions can be drawn from Hebrew usage.

Assuming the existence of an Aramaic equivalent of ἐκκλησία, we might think of *qᵉhala'*, which is not pure Aramaic but borrowed from Biblical Hebrew. While this occurs in the Targums, they contain no example of an Aramaic *'edhta'* for the Hebrew *'edhah*.[2] We shall therefore do well to rule out *'edhta'*. There are examples of *çibbura'* ; but the commonest expression is *kᵉnishta'*.[3] Special importance attaches to this word, because it is used for ἐκκλησία and for συναγωγή in Syriac versions, whose language is closely akin to the Palestinian Aramaic of Jesus.

Of the Syriac versions, the Curetonian (3rd cent.), the Peshitta (beginning of 5th cent.) and the Philoxenian (beginning of 6th cent.) use *'edhta'* for ἐκκλησία as the Christian Church, and *kᵉnushta'* for συναγωγή as the Jewish synagogue ; but the Sinaitic (3rd cent., earlier than the Curetonian) uses *kᵉnushta'* for both. (The Sinaitic omits Matt. xvi, 18 but retains xviii, 17.) Connected with the Sinaitic is the Palestinian-Syriac version, chiefly known to us through the lectionary called *Evangeliarium Hierosolymitanum*.[4] No precise date

[1] Cf. Str.-Bill, I, 734 ; Schürer, G. J. V., II, 504 : " When considered as a religious community, it is called *kᵉneṣeth* ".

[2] Dalman, however, gives it as an Aramaic word. It is not in Levy. Wellhausen, Matt., p. 84, says it is not Palestinian but Syriac.

[3] Cf. Levy s.v. Dalman also gives the form *kᵉniṣta'* (cf. *kᵉneṣeth*), as meaning synagogue, viz., the building.

[4] Edited by Lagarde in Bibl. Syr. (1892). See Schwally,

can be assigned to this, but it certainly creates the
impression that it is older than the others. The dialect
in which it is written differs considerably from ordinary
Syriac, and may bear a relatively close resemblance to
the language of Jesus and his disciples.[1] It actually
uses the Aramaic word *k^enushta'* (= *k^enishta'*) for both
the Christian ἐκκλησία and the Jewish συναγωγή.[2]

After what has been said, it seems highly probable
that Jesus used the word *k^enishta'*.[3] Now if the application of the word *qahal* (Aram. *q^ehala'*) to the Christian
Church implies its claim to be the true Church of the
Old Testament, it is also possible that *k^enishta'* is
meant to indicate the whole body of that Church. At
the same time we must remember that this Aramaic
word, like its usual Greek equivalent, συναγωγή,
means a fellowship in the narrower sense, as defined
by reference to locality, membership or constitution.
This points to the idea of a separatist *k^enishta'*. Are
we then to think of the early Christian Church as a
sect within Judaism ? Actually it was often treated as
such by the Jewish authorities. Its own conviction
was that it was the only synagogue entitled to claim

Idioticon des christlich-palästinischen Aram. (1893), and Schulthess,
Lexicon Syro-palaestinum (1903). For all other Syr. cf. O. Klein
Syrisch-griech. Wörterbuch zu den vier kanonischen Ev. (1916).

[1] So E. Nestle, Einführung in das Gr. N.T. (1909), 115 ; Schulthess, Gramm. des christlich-palästinischen Aram. (herausgeg.
E. Littmann) 1924, p. 3.

[2] Cf. Schürer, II, 504 : " in Christian Palestinian Aramaic
k^enishta', corresponding to the Greek συναγωγή, seems to have been
the usual word for Church ". Wellhausen, Matt., p. 84 : " The
original Aramaic word *k^enishta'* stands for both the Jewish and the
Christian fellowship. The Palestinian Christians continued its
use for both Church and Synagogue."

[3] Cf. Zahn, Matt., 546, and Merx, " Die vier kanonischen Ev.
nach der syrischen im Sinai-kloster gefundenen Palimps.", Matt.
(1902), 268. Joach. Jeremias, in Golgotha, p. 69, pleads for
" probably *çibbura'*—otherwise *k^enishta* ".

that it embodied true Judaism, the true Israel. This
was not the first time such a thing had happened.
The evidence is not plentiful, but it is enough to prove
the point. Reference may be made to I Maccabees
ii, 42 (συναγωγὴ Ἀσιδαίων) and vii, 12 (συναγωγὴ
γραμματέων) ; these might have made the same
claim, though separating themselves for more scholastic
reasons.[1] Here belongs also the Jewish community
of " The New Covenant at Damascus ", known
through the document found in the Genizah (lumber-
room) of the Cairo synagogue : its members called
themselves 'edhah (vii, 20 ; x, 4, 8 ; xiii, 13) or qahal
(vii, 17 ; xi, 22), and felt themselves to be the
" Remnant ".[2] The idea of the q[e]hal Yahwe was not
only not given up ; it acquired a special significance,
for such a group constituted the " Remnant ", on
which Israel's standing as the people of God depended.
Thus the Church of God was embodied in the synagogue
of Jesus the Messiah. In this seeming paradox of a
part representing the whole lies the secret of the

[1] That such a synagogue should have claimed to represent the
q[e]hal Yahwe Bultmann considers " scarcely credible ". His
objections, involving as they do an exaggeration of the teaching
function of the synagogue, are not convincing.

[2] The text is given by Schechter in Documents of Jewish
Sectaries (1910), to which our figures refer. L. Rost, in Die
Damaskus-schrift (Kleine Texte 167 (1933), gives Schechter's
arrangement along with another, and amends the text, reviewing
all the work done on the subject up to 1933. Attempts to assign
a date differ by centuries. Bertholet, in Rel. Gesch. Geg., 2nd ed.,
I, 1775 f. (Damaskusschrift), suggests the Maccabean or the
Roman period, perhaps 1st century B.C. G. Hölscher, Gesch. der
isr. u. jüd. Rel. (1922), and others (see Rost, p. 4) think the documents come from precursors of the Karaites referred to by Kirki-
sani (10th cent.) as " sons of Zadok ".

[See Foakes Jackson and Kirsopp Lake, The Beginnings of
Christianity, Vol. I, pp. 97-101 ; R. H. Charles, Between the Old
and New Testaments, pp. 234-236, and Apocr. and Pseudepigr.,
II, 785 ff.]

genuine synagogue and of the genuine congregation of Jesus Christ. The famous founding of the ἐκκλησία by Jesus simply means this combined separation and concentration of his band of disciples (Matt. xvi, 18). All that we know of the attitude of Jesus towards the q^ehal Yahwe gains breadth and depth, and colour too, when we recognise his concern with the k^enishta'.[1]

Finally this view makes the connection clear between Matt. xvi, 18 and Matt. xviii, 17. In the latter passage, the command to report an erring brother's fault to the ἐκκλησία should not be explained as obviously an item from an early Christian catechism,[2] but understood as referring to the synagogue, the Old Testament congregation. Jesus' attitude to that institution is not negative but positive. Indeed it is he, and only he, who brings it to perfection, taking his stand as Messiah, here as elsewhere, under the Law.[3]

---

[1] Bultmann (Trad. 149 f.) shows a complete misunderstanding when he asserts that it makes no difference for Matt. xvi, 18 f. whether ἐκκλησία represents qahal or 'edhah or k^enishta'.

[2] Evidence for this common " critical " view need not be given.

[3] Cf. K. L. Schmidt, " Die Verkündigung des N.T. in ihrer Einheit und Besonderheit " (Th. Blätt. (1931), Sp. 120) ; " Das Christuszeugnis der synoptischen Ev." (Kirchenbl. f. d. ref. Schweiz (1933), 403), which also appears as " Jesus Christus im Zeugnis der Heiligen Schrift und der Kirche " (Sammelband (1936), 22). [See G. Johnston, The Church in the N.T., 140.]

VI. OLD TESTAMENT AND JUDAISM

1. *Greek Judaism.* (a) The word ἐκκλησία occurs about 100 times in the LXX, and occasionally in Aquila, Symmachus and Theodotion. The Hebrew equivalent is almost always *qahal*. The only exceptions to be noted in the LXX are as follows : I Sam. xix, 20 (*lahᵃqah*) ; Neh. v, 7 (*qᵉhillah*) ; Ps. xxv (Heb. xxvi), 12 (*maqhelim*) ; Ps. lxvii (Heb. lxviii), 27 (*maqheloth*). The usage is thus uniform and clear. The Hebrew words just mentioned all come from the root *qahal*. In the case of *lahᵃqah* the radical letters are found in a different order : this may point to some derivative of *qahal*, or may be due to dittography, coming so soon after *laqahath*.[1]

In the LXX ἐκκλησία has no ecclesiastical significance ; it simply means " gathering ", and denotes either coming together, as at Deut. ix, 10 ; xviii, 16 (*yom haqqahal* : Luther " Versammlung " ; R.V. " assembly ") or being together, as at I Kings viii, 65 (*qahal gadhol* : Luther " Versammlung " ; R.V. " congregation "). The nature of the gathering depends entirely upon the nature of those who compose it. Thus at I Sam. xix, 20 we have " the company (ἐκκλησίαν) of the prophets ", and at Ecclus. xxvi, 5 the context justifies " a concourse of the rabble " [Oesterley] as the translation of ἐκκλησίαν ὄχλου.[2] The

---

[1] So Gesenius-Buhl s. v.

[2] V. Ryssel, in Kautzsch's Apokr. und Pseudepigr., renders " Zusammenrottung des Pöbels ", arguing for *qᵉhalah* as the Hebr. original, against Fritzsche, who suggests *qᵉlalah*, and regards LXX as a mistranslation. But perhaps Fritzsche is right, since elsewhere in Ecclus. ἐκκλησία is always a technical term for the congregation of Israel.

meaning, " People of God ", is first indicated by the
addition to ἐκκλησία of the word κυρίου (Lord, i.e.
Υahwe) : Deut. xxiii, 2 ff ; I Chron. xxviii, 8 ; Neh.
xiii, 1 ; Micah ii, 5 ; cf. ἐκκλησίαν σου (qahal lakh,
" thy congregation ") at Lam. i, 10 ; ἐ. τοῦ ὑψίστου
at Ecclus. xxiv, 2 ; τοῦ λαοῦ τοῦ θεοῦ at Judges xx, 2.
The word " Israel " is often added : I Kings viii, 14, 22,
55 ; I Chron. xiii, 2 ; II Chron. vi, 3, 12 f. ; Ecclus.
l, 13 ; I Macc. iv, 59.   Less frequent are the attributes
" of the children of Israel " (Ecclus, l, 20) ; " of
Judah " (II Chron. xx, 5, xxx, 25) ; " of the holy
ones " (Ps. lxxxviii, 6 [R.V. lxxxix, 5]) ; " of the
saints " (Ps. cxlix, 1) ; " in Jerusalem " (I Macc. xiv,
19) ; " of the captivity " [Ezra x, 8].   There are
also passages in which ἐκκλησία, standing by itself,
means the congregation of God.   The context often
makes this quite clear.   Examples are so numerous,
especially in Chronicles, Psalms and certain Apocryphal
books, that the word must be regarded as a technical
term.   Now and then, of course, the matter is doubtful.
In any case, such additional words as " of God "
must be either expressed or understood.   The importance of the community in its gathered form is shown
by the frequency with which it is described as " the
whole community ".   The plural occurs at Ps. xxv, 12
(R.V. xxvi, 12) ; lxvii, 27 (R.V. lxviii, 26) ; the MSS.
of Ps. cvi (cvii), 32 vary between singular and plural.
The coupling of ἐκκλησία and συναγωγή at Prov. v,
14 shows how far the former is from having an established technical sense.   The translator is puzzled to
know how to render two expressions which obviously
mean the same thing : [thus A.V. and R.V. have
" congregation and assembly ", J. Moffatt " community ", A. R. Gordon " assembled community "].

The verb ἐκκλησιάζω (ἐξεκκλησιάζω) occurs at Lev.
viii, 3 ; Numb. xx, 8 ; Deut. iv, 10, xxxi, 12, 28 ;

I Kings viii, 1, xii, 21 ; I Chron. xiii, 5, xv, 3, xxviii, 1 ;
II Chron. v, 2 and elsewhere for the Hiph'il of *qahal*,
which is also rendered by συναθροίζω (Exod. xxxv,
1), συνάγω (Numb. i, 18, viii, 9, x, 7), and ἐπισυνίστημι
(Numb. xvi, 19)—all meaning " assemble " (transi-
tive). Ἐξεκκλησιάζομαι occurs at Josh. xviii, 1 ;
Judges xx, 1 ; II Sam. xx, 14 and elsewhere, meaning
" assemble " (reflexive), and representing the Niph'al
of *qahal*, which is also rendered by συνίσταμαι (Aq.,
Theod., ἐκκλησιάζομαι), Exod. xxxii, 1, and συναθροί-
ζομαι Josh. xxii, 12.

The situation is the same with regard to the more or
less technical use of the word συναγωγή. It is often
defined by a following Genitive : " company of
peoples ", Gen. xxviii, 3, xlviii, 4 ; " company of
nations ", Gen. xxxv, 11 ; " assembly of evil-doers ",
Ps. xxii, 16 (LXX xxi, 17) ; " multitude of the bulls ",
Ps. lxviii, 30 (LXX lxvii, 31) ; " congregation of
violent men ", Ps. lxxxvi, 14 (LXX lxxxv, 14) ; cf.
Jer. xliv, 15 (LXX li, 15), l, 9 (LXX xxvii, 9). On
the other hand, like ἐκκλησία, it is sometimes followed
by " of the Lord ", corresponding to *qᵉhal Yahwe* or
'adath Yahwe : Numb. xx, 4, xxvii, 17, xxxi, 16 ;
cf. Ps. lxxiv, 2 (LXX lxxiii, 2).

The result of this comparative study of ἐκκλησία
and συναγωγή is that (1) both words have more or
less the same meaning and often represent the Hebrew
word *qahal* ; (2) both have sometimes a technical and
sometimes a general meaning, as is shown in the
differing translations, " assembly ", " congregation ",
" company ", etc.

(*b*) The situation is the same in Philo and Josephus,
though they make more use of the words in the
technical sense which they have in secular Greek ;
the reference is often to public meetings for political
or other purposes.

Philo combines ἐκκλησίαι with ἀγοραί (Spec. Leg. II, 44) and with βουλαί (Omn. Prob. Lib. 138) ; cf. also Abr. 20. He speaks of the ἐκκλησία " of God " or " of the Lord " in connection with Deut. xxiii (Leg. All. III, 8, 81 ; Ebr. 213) ; cf. Poster. C. 143. At Mut. Nom. 204 he puts " of the Ruler of all " for " of God ". His Hellenism shows itself very clearly in his addition of the word θεία (divine) to ἐκκλησία (Conf. Ling. 144) ; cf. Leg. All. III, 81. Nowhere in LXX or N.T. is the Church spoken of as divine, or as sacred (ἱερά)—though Philo uses the latter epithet at Somn. II, 184, 187 ; Deus Imm. 111 ; Migr. Abr. 69 ; cf. Aet. Mund. 13.[1]

Josephus, who likes to avoid ἅγιος, using θεῖος or ἱερός instead, might well have spoken of the ἐκκλησία as Philo did ; but he only applies it to secular gatherings, dissociating it from religion, as he does in the case of βασιλεία [2] : see Ant. xix, 332, xvi, 62, xvii, 161, xiv, 150 ; Vit. 37 ; Bell. iv, 255, vii, 412.

2. *Hebrew Text.* The term *qahal* and words of similar meaning, such as *'edhah*, have already received adequate treatment, with a view to explaining their Greek equivalents. It remains to reverse the process, and use the Greek words to explain the Hebrew. While *qahal* usually becomes ἐκκλησία, this is not always the case. It is so in Joshua, Judges, Samuel (except I Sam. xix, 20), Kings, Chronicles, Ezra, Nehemiah, and in Deuteronomy (except v, 22) ; in the rest of the Pentateuch *qahal* is translated συναγωγή, which elsewhere represents *'edhah*. (G. Bertram points out that Origen's parallel texts sometimes have ἐκκλησία for the LXX συναγωγή : Ἄλλος at Lev. iv, 14, 21 ; Jer. xxxiii, 17 ; Aquila at Jer. li, 15 ; Ezek. xxvi, 7 ; Theodotion at Ezek. xxvi, 7 ; xxvii, 27 ;

---

[1] Cf. θεῖος and ἱερός in Cremer-Kögel.
[2] Cf. Schlatter, Matt., 508 ; Theol. des Judentums, 90 f.

xxxii, 22.) '*edhah* occurs more frequently than *qahal* in Exod., Lev., Numb., and is almost always translated συναγωγή—never ἐκκλησία. Joshua and Judges have '*edhah* more often than *qahal*, but subsequent books show an increasing preference for the latter. The Psalter always uses ἐκκλησία for *qahal*, except at Ps. xl, 10 (xxxix, 11), where Aq. and Theod. have ἐκκλησία, but LXX συναγωγή. The absence of a consistent usage in translation shows that neither of these Hebrew words is in itself a technical term. It only becomes one when it is coupled with Yahwe or with Israel as the people of Yahwe, whether in the text or to be understood. This is shown even more clearly by those cases in which other Greek words are used for *qahal* : ὄχλος at Jer. xxxi, 8 (LXX xxxviii, 8) ; Ezek. xvi, 40 ; xxiii, 46 f. (Aq. and Theod. ἐκκλησία) ; πλῆθος at Exod. xii, 6 ; II Chron. xxxi, 18 ; σύστασις at Gen. xlix, 6 ; συνέδριον at Prov. xxvi, 26.[1]

---

[1] M. Noth expresses a different view in Das System der zwölf Stämme Israels (1930), 102 f., n. 2 : " We need not hesitate to derive the words '*edhah* and *qahal* from the terminology of the amphictyony of ancient Israel ; and it is not surprising that words bound up with a sacral institution—apart from the few places in the O.T. which come directly from the amphictyony tradition itself— should first reappear in the Priestly writings. . . . *Qahal* obviously indicates the gathering, and '*edhah* the people united in such a gathering. The latter is called '*am ha'*elohim* at Judges xx, 2, because the bond of union was the same Covenant-God and his cult."

After the present essay was finished, L. Rost, who saw the proofs, put the following statement at my disposal. " It is usual to find the roots of the ἐκκλησία in the O.T. '*edhah* and *qahal*. Of course the former belongs to the early history of the synagogue, and here we are only concerned with the latter. *Qahal* (a noun related to *qol* [voice], of which verbal forms, causative and reflexive, are in frequent use) means in the oldest passages the ' call-up ' of the people, viz., its men, for counsel or war. It is so in Genesis xlix, 6 and Numbers xxii, 4. It looks as if *qahal* means the community at Numbers xvi, 33, with a meaning on which light is thrown by Micah ii, 5. The prophet speaks there of the qᵉhal Yahwe, the united people (Volksgesamtheit) of Yahwe, the call to unity coming from Yahwe. Deut. (xxiii, 2 ff.), uses the same phrase in the same way when it lays down conditions for the admission of the maimed or of foreigners. Deut. also justifies the coupling together of the two words ; see v, 22 (Heb. 19) ; ix, 10 ; x, 4 ; xviii, 16. The *qahal* which first established the connection between Yahwe and his people is the Sinai gathering ; the day on which this great event took place is ' the day of the *qahal* '. This is why the word *qahal* is used for the worshipping community when Solomon dedicates the Temple (I Kings viii, 14 ff.), and later for the gathering at the Feast of Tabernacles in the year 444,[1] when Ezra read the Law in the presence of men, women and children. While the *qahal* makes its appearance on special occasions of cultic importance, the old secular usage continues alongside ; *qahal* is still the call-up of a people for war ; e.g. I Sam. xvii, 47 and Ezek. xxiii, 24, 46, etc. A call-up of a different kind is the summoning of an extraordinary gathering of the people, such as Jer. xxvi, 17 and xliv, 15 mention—the former of men only, the second including women and children. To sum up, *qahal* may be defined as a gathering summoned in extra-ordinary circumstances, whether of men only, as in the case of war, or of a suddenly convened judicial assembly, or of the whole people, as specially in the case of Ezra. As signifying a meeting constituted by means of a call-up, the term thus comes to indicate those who are qualified to take part, as in Deut. xxiii. The development of the idea in the direction of the N.T. ἐκκλησία is bound up with the fact that the word was used for those who shared in the covenant at Sinai, and also for those who renewed their devotion to the Law under Ezra. Thus *qahal* is seen to connote those to whom belong the covenant and the promises. A second important point is that at least from the time of Ezra (cf. also Jer. xliv, 15) women and children were included. Thus, in its LXX form ἐκκλησία it commends itself to Christians, whose community welcomes women and children, in preference to συναγωγή whose responsibilities were confined to men. (See my forth-coming book, Die A.T. Vorstufen von Kirche und Synagoge.)" [On ἐκκλησία in LXX cf. J. Y. Campbell in J.T.S., 1948, pp. 130–142.]

[1] [Or 397.]

VII. ETYMOLOGY?

WE have left the etymology of the word ἐκκλησία
to the end, because its history is more important.
If the N.T. ἐκκλησία, coming by way of the LXX,
is the fulfilment of the O.T. *qahal*, and if we associate it
with *kᵉnishta'* as representing *qahal*, then there is
nothing to be gained by stressing the derivation of the
noun ἐκκλησία from the verb ἐκκαλεῖν and connecting
it with the adjective ἔκκλητος. It is obviously significant that neither of these two words occurs in the N.T.
The LXX only uses the verb at Gen. xix, 5 and Deut.
xx, 10 (Heb. *qara'*), and the adjective at Ecclus.
xlii, 11. Both are fairly common in classical Greek,
ἔκκλητος being a technical term in connection with
the ἐκκλησία as the political assembly ; cf. Xenophon,
Hist. Gr., II, iv, 38, where the ἔκκλητοι are the members
of the national council which takes the place of the
ἐκκλησία in aristocratic states like Sparta ; cf. also
Euripides, Orestes, 612, 949.

We do not know whether Paul and others were
thinking of the doctrine of election when they used the
word ἐκκλησία ; it is possible, but unlikely. If it
were so, one might have expected to find it in passages
like Eph. v, 25 ff ; I Tim. iii, 15 ; Heb. xii, 23.[1] The

[1] A. Jehle rightly calls attention to this passage, in his short
article " *EKKΛHΣIA*, a humble request to the exegetes "
(Württemberg ev. Kirchenblatt (1934), p. 78), and stresses, on the
whole rightly, the questionableness—if not the irrelevance—of the
etymology of ἐκκλησία. But when he says he has written " in
the hope of getting the final answer through Prof. Kittel's work "
(meaning the present essay), it must be laid down that the answer
has already been given in the recent publications of Kattenbusch,
K. L. Schmidt and others.

It is significant that those Christians who still speak Greek
obviously have no need to explain etymologically how their

truth in matters of verbal usage is not to be reached by adventurous ingenuity, but by a careful study of the actual use and abuse of words. There are theologians who like to connect " Sünde " (sin) with " Sonderung " (being sundered, i.e., from God), which looks quite reasonable in German. There are philosophers who interpret " Zufall " (chance) literally as " Zu-fall " (that which befalls in an existential sense), which also looks quite artistic in German. But all that is pseudo-philology, even though it may be associated with true ideas, as in the case of Paul's queer allegorising. Ἐκκλησία is in fact that group of human beings which is called out of the world by God, even without any conscious emphasis on the preposition, like the original qᵉhal Yahwe, in which no preposition is expressed.

The importance of the history of a word, with its

own word *ekklesia* has come to have its historic meaning. P. Bratsiotis, of Athens, has sent the following communication to the present writer, by request : " Ἐκκλησία in modern Greek, though properly denoting a place of worship (ναός), also has all the meanings of your word, ' Church '. For your word ' congregation ' we say either ἐκκλησία or ἐνορία, though the latter properly means ' parish '. [I. Kykkotis' Modern Greek Dictionary (1942) gives ἐκκλησίασμα for " congregation ".] There is no work on ἐκκλησία in modern Greek, except what is to be found in theological hand-books, in which there is no special philological treatment of the subject." Just as Israelites and Greek Christians appropriated a political terminology long ago, so to-day new converts outside Christendom find suitable expressions for their standing as Christians in their own language and culture. An illustration may be taken from a letter of the missionary, E. Peyer, of St. Gall : " Among the Duala people [West Africa] Christians are called *bona-Kristo*—clansmen of Christ. The word *bona* means family, kin, clan. For the word ' congregation ', *mwemba* has been chosen. This means originally an age-group, e.g., of those born in the same year or half-year, who have certain common rites to perform in youth, and specially in adolescence. The term thus indicates a clearly defined group, with restricted admission."

use and abuse, is shown by the fact that, if we were aiming at an exact reproduction of Biblical usage in the case of ἐκκλησία we ought always to say " assembly (of God) ". But we cannot do so, because language is not amenable to a dictatorial standard, and in the present instance, owing to the wide reach of the expression, we need both the word " Church " and the word " congregation ". There is something to be said both for and against both of these. The former indicates the one great world-wide Christian community but on the other hand may suggest the Catholic hierarchy ; the latter draws attention to the small fellowship which is also Church, but may seem to imply Congregationalism or sectarianism. Having regard to its etymology, we should prefer to say " Church " which is derived from κύριος and means " belonging to the Lord ". But the word has so many meanings that it will not do by itself. Perhaps the " Assembly of God " might be called the " Church community ".[1]

[1] Luther's aversion to the word " Kirche " is well-known. It is less widely-known that the word does not occur in the revised text of Luther's Bible, or in a corresponding concordance, but was actually used by Luther, mostly to denote heathen shrines in the O.T., while it is only found at John x, 22 in the N.T., in the compound " Church-dedication ". Cf. W. Rotscheidt's attractive presentation of this subject in Deutsches Pfarrerblatt (1930), pp. 506 f.

The derivation from κύριος is not absolutely certain. Cf. R. Hildebrand in Deutsches Wörterbuch V, 790 s.v. : " the source is much disputed ; in any case it is foreign, introduced along with Christianity. J. Grimm (Gramm. 3, 156), like Lipsius and others, favoured derivation from the Latin circus, in early forms such as chirih, chirch, etc. ; evidence for this was found in the gloss in Kero [8th cent. Benedictine]—uzzana chirih, foris oratorio—but this was corrected by Hattemer (Denkmale des Mittelalters (1844), p. 94) to uzzana chirihhun." This reference to circus, which is unanimously repudiated by German philologists, may have something to do with the fact that Karl Barth writes in

Credo (1935) : " Ecclesia is a gathering brought together by means of a call-up. The Germanic equivalent, *Kirche*, *Kerk*, *Church*, is not, in my opinion, as is commonly said, a mutilated form of the Greek adjective κυριακή (ἐκκλησία), but points back to the root seen, e.g., in the Latin words, *circa*, *circum*, *circare*, *circulus*, etc. Thus it signifies a particular room or space marked off and to that extent given prominence." How completely unessential etymology is for the understanding of the thing itself may be shown by the fact that the word for Church in the language of the Engadine and S. Tyrol is *baselgia*, in Rumanian *biserica*, in Albanian *bijeske*—all from *basilica*, making their contribution to the history of building ; (see W. Meyer-Lübke, Roman. Etymolog. Wörteb. (1935), s.v. basilica ; J. Jud, Zur Geschichte der bündner-roman. Kirchenspr. (1919), passim) ; the thing itself is there without the etymology ! Finally, Luther's Larger Catechism contains an etymological curiosity (II, 3 : see J. T. Müller, Die symb. Bücher der ev.-luth. Kirche (1860), p. 457) : " The little word, Church, then, means nothing else but a general gathering, and is really not German but Greek, like *ecclesia*, the original word being *Kyria*, which becomes *curia* in Latin." Luther turns Tertullian's interpretation into etymology. After consulting the relevant modern German dictionaries (Weigand, neu bearb. Hirt, 1909 ; Kluge, bearb. Götze, 1934 ; Paul, herausg. Euling, 1935) and on the advice of W. Altwegg (Basel) and A. Debrunner (Bern), I applied to A. Götze, of Giessen, as the greatest authority on the subject, and he has sent me the following communication : " We German philologists are beginning to understand the word ' Kirche ' a little better. We have abandoned both Luther's derivation from the Latin *curia*— obviously a bright idea suggested by his visit to Rome—and Grimm's suggestion of the Latin *circus*. It is now clear that it must come from κυρικόν which is the common form, current in the 4th century, of the older κυριακόν, and means a place of worship (Gotteshaus). Words taken over from Latin in the ecclesiastical sphere, like ' Papst ' and ' Propst,' have the final consonants unshifted, which means that they were not current in Germany about 600 A.D. (' Kelch ' came in with vine-growing ; ' Kreuz ' has its ' z ', not through shifting, but from the Latin *crucem*, retaining the ' ts ' sound of the second ' c '.) ' Kirche ', on the other hand, has the ordinary German ch for k (Swiss-German still keeps the second ch), was therefore already here before 600, and accordingly must have been brought by an earlier wave of missionary activity than that which gave us words like ' Papst ', etc. Which wave it was, is under dispute. Kluge pointed to the Gothic *kyriko*, connecting it with an early Gothic-Arian wave, which must have reached S.E. Germany while Theodoric the Great's kingdom was contiguous with the duchy of Bavaria—and he died in 526. I retained this in the 11th edition of Kluge, in which the ' Kirche ' article was completed in 1934 ; his reasons are fully given in ' Gotische Lehnworte im Althochdeutschen ' (Beitr. z. Gesch. der deutschen Spr. u. Lit. (1909), pp. 124 ff.), which is still worth reading. Modern philologists are agreed that Arian missionaries carried a number of ecclesiastical words up the Danube and down the Rhine ; the question whether ' Kirche ' was one of them has been raised by Th. Fring in Teuthonista (1932), 24, 31, 37 f., 46, 50, 120. He supposes that κυρικόν, assuming a Feminine form under the influence of *basilica*, arrived by way of Marseilles, Lyon and Trèves, and puts ' Kirche ' into a group of Rhineland Christian words, for which he gives good grounds, but I am still in the dark as to where ' Kirche ' comes in, as no evidence is given for it. It is quite true that there is no literary evidence for the Gothic *kyriko*, since Ulfilas died before it arrived, but the Old Slavonic *cruky* and the Russian *cerkovi* may serve as witnesses. So the question of route is still unsettled ; W. Betz, who is responsible for the word ' Kirche ' in the Trübner Deutsch. Wörterb., which I am now editing, will have to make up his mind about it."

VIII. APOSTOLIC FATHERS AND EARLY CATHOLICISM

THE idea of the ἐκκλησία underwent a shifting of emphasis among the Apostolic Fathers and in early Catholicism, even before the N.T. was completed.[1] Titular definition by means of adjectives became frequent though this is not found in the N.T. Whereas in the latter we only touch the fringe of speculation concerning the nature of the Church, this was now the general rule, finding expression in the use of a variety of predicates.

The oldest Christian literature, outside the N.T., makes comparatively little use of the term ἐκκλησία. The one exception is The Shepherd of Hermas. Here it denotes an individual, of whom the author becomes aware in his visions—the " Lady " (κυρία) who belongs to the " Lord " (κύριος) and is dignified with the epithet ἁγία (holy) : Vis. I. i, 6 ;[2] I. iii, 4 ; IV. i, 3. The " Lady ", characterised as πρεσβυτέρα (aged) because of her appearance, is described as the form (μορφή) of a " Holy Spirit ", who again is identical with the " Son of God ". The Pauline and sub-Pauline thought of the Church as the one body is pictured in the Parables as " a tower made as it were of one stone " (Sim. IX. xviii, 3).

The First Epistle of Clement only mentions the ἐκκλησία in three passages all reminiscent of the N.T. :

[1] The fullest statistics and information are in Kattenbusch, Harnack Festgabe (1921), 146 ff., developing his thesis in Das apostolische Symbol II (1900), 683 ff.

[2] The idea that the world was created for the sake of the Church corresponds to the Jewish idea that Israel is the goal of creation ; see Dibelius, Der Hirt des Hermas (1923) ad loc.

in the introduction, " the church of God sojourning at Rome " greets " the Church of God sojourning at Corinth " ; at xliv, 3, reference is made to " the consent of the whole Church ", and at xlvii, 6, to the " ancient Church of the Corinthians ".

Ignatius not only addresses the Churches as being in certain places, Ephesus, etc., but also gives them impressive epithets : " worthy of all felicitation " (Eph.) ; " blessed through the grace of God " (Magn.); " holy, elect and worthy of God " (Trall.) ; " which hath found mercy in the bountifulness ($\mu\epsilon\gamma\alpha\lambda\epsilon\iota\acute{o}\tau\eta\tau\iota$) of the Father " (Rom.—with about a dozen other predicates) ; " which has found mercy and is firmly established " (Phil.) ; " filled with faith and love " (Smyrn.). The language is really excessive. Much of it is dogmatic in character, and of general application, while much is only relevant to the particular situation. One remarkable passage (Eph. v) speaks of believers as being closely joined with the bishop " as the Church is with Jesus Christ and as Jesus Christ is with the Father, that all things may be harmonious in unity ". God, Christ, and the Church form a single entity, as in the N.T. The rise of the monarchical bishop must be understood in this connection. The predicate " catholic " makes its first appearance at Smyrn. viii, where it may mean simply " one and only " (una sancta), though later it came to mean " universal ".[1] It is worth noting that the Roman Church has adopted both the Greek words $\dot{\epsilon}\kappa\kappa\lambda\eta\sigma\acute{\iota}\alpha$ and $\kappa\alpha\theta\omega\lambda\iota\kappa\acute{\eta}$.

Polycarp greets the Philippians as a " sojourning Church " ($\dot{\epsilon}\kappa\kappa\lambda\eta\sigma\acute{\iota}\alpha$ $\pi\alpha\rho\omega\iota\kappa\omega\hat{\upsilon}\sigma\alpha$), like Clement addressing the Corinthians, and similarly, in Mart. Pol., the Smyrnaean Christians say, " The Church of God sojourning ($\pi\alpha\rho\omega\iota\kappa\omega\hat{\upsilon}\sigma\alpha$) at Smyrna to the Church of God sojourning ($\pi\alpha\rho\omega\iota\kappa\omega\acute{\upsilon}\sigma\eta$) in Philomelium and to

[1] So Kattenbusch, op. cit., 148. [See J. B. Lightfoot, ad loc.]

all the sojourning communities of the holy and catholic Church (πάσαις ταῖς . . . τῆς ἁγίας καὶ καθολικῆς ἐκκλησίας παροικίαις) everywhere." [LXX πάροικος is for Heb. *ger*, "resident alien". Hence comes Eng. "parish", through Lat. *paroecia*.] Each of these local congregations regards itself as something unique and holy, and ascribes the same dignity to its sister-congregations. On the one hand the Church belongs to the world in which it lives, without being of it, and on the other hand it belongs to God.[1]

Four passages in the Didache mention the ἐκκλησία : iv, 14 is reminiscent of Matt. xviii, 17 ; ix, 4 and x, 5 correspond to what the N.T. says about the relation of the Church to the Kingdom ; the difficult phrase μυστήριον κοσμικὸν ἐκκλησίας, xi, 11, recalls Colossians and Ephesians, but seems to go beyond them in the direction of esoteric knowledge on the part of believers.

The so-called "Second Epistle of Clement" develops this last tendency still further when it describes the Church as "the first, the spiritual, which was created before the sun and the moon", and goes on to adduce verses of Scripture in support of its doctrine.

The idea of the pre-existence of the Church, according to which it comes before the Synagogue, was based on Pauline (Rom. iv, 9 ff.) and sub-Pauline (Eph. i, 3 ff.) teaching, and was developed among the Valentinian Gnostics into speculation concerning Ἐκκλησία as one of the Aeons [constituting the divine *Pleroma*]. Similarly the doctrine that the Church is from above (ἄνωθεν) became a far-reaching

---

[1] Barnabas shows that, as in the N.T., the word ἐκκλησία does not settle everything, for he never speaks of Christians as ἐκκλησία but frequently refers to them as λαός, i.e., the people entrusted by God to his beloved Son (v, 7 ; vii, 5). Elsewhere he speaks of the Temple of God (iv, 11), or the City (xvi, 5).

[On πάροικοι see E. G. Selwyn on I Pet. ii, 11.]

speculation, which afforded consolation to the representatives of a " theologia gloriae " when they were concerned about the contrast between the empirical Church and the ideal.[1]   So there arose the conception of the twofold nature of the Church, as militant and triumphant.   These speculations were the cause of a surprising lack of clarity in what was said about the Church, among the Greek and Latin Church Fathers. Augustine, the greatest of them, whose comprehensive mind was responsible for putting the Church at the centre of Roman Catholic thinking, is precisely the one who fails to make clear the distinction between the empirical Church and the ideal.   Gnosticism having largely failed, Platonism held the field in matters of speculation, though it also left room for widely differing views, determined by the amount of emphasis given to the gulf between reality and idea.   Protestantism is also under the influence of this unrealistic Platonism when it differentiates between the Church visible and the Church invisible.

---

[1] As Kattenbusch well puts it (op. cit., 155), " It is true that, after a certain time, the idea that the community comes ἄνωθεν became speculative ; it was not so at first."

IX. CONCLUSIONS

WHERE, when, and how does Catholicism begin, as distinct from early Christianity? The switch-over is not nearly so easy to understand as the original meaning of ἐκκλησία. The early Christian writings outside the N.T. show that it has already taken place. Speculation moved increasingly in a Gnostic direction. The Church, which ought to have maintained its unity as *corpus mixtum*, is split up by a latent and often extreme Platonism.

The Church is never triumphant; it is only militant, i.e., under hostile pressure. A triumphant Church would be the kingdom of God, and no longer ἐκκλησία. Nor is the Assembly of God in Christ to be described as on the one hand visible and on the other invisible. The Christian community in any particular place represents the whole body, and is precisely as visible and temporal as the Christian man. Righteousness and holiness are imputed to the community and to the individual without implying that either of them actually possesses these qualities; the Church, like the man who is " called ", receives justification and sanctification. If Luther distinguished—above all in his polemic against Rome—between the Church invisible and the Church visible, he was not thereby subscribing to the Platonism of those who came after him. In his translation of the Bible, he does not speak of the Church, but of the congregation of the saints, as the people of God (*qᵉhal Yahwe*); and this proves that it is the visible ἐκκλησία, and no essentially invisible Platonic community, which is the object of faith. When Luther goes back to the Old Testament, he is following the example of Paul.[1] The significance of the primitive Christian community was recognised by Paul, and can never lose its importance as the invincible bulwark against all irresponsible speculations concerning the Church.[2]

[1] R. Sohm's assertion and inference are characteristic, in Kirchenrecht II (1923), p. 135 : " The early Church had not yet attained to the knowledge that the people of God is invisible. In this way it became catholic. But Luther's discovery that the Church is invisible spelt the end of Catholicism." The judgment of Kattenbusch, in the K. Müller Festgabe (1922), must be upheld against these false notions, when he says that Paul " remains far superior to all who teach about the Church, including Luther ".

On the controversy over the Church " visible " and " invisible ", cf. K. L. Schmidt, " Kirchenleitung und Kirchenlehre im N.T. " in Christentum und Wissenschaft, 8 (1932), 241 ff., esp. 254 ff. against E. Foerster, " Kirche wider Kirche ", Theol. Rundsch. (1932), 155 f. C. H. Dodd, in Essays Congregational and Catholic (1931), deals with the whole question of the Church from the beginning in relation to the present ecclesiastical situation, and rightly avoids the distinction between " visible " and " invisible ", which has spread so widely and done so much harm among the Churches of the Reformation. It should be noted that Luther himself equated the *ecclesia invisibilis* with the *ecclesia (spiritualis) sola fide perceptibilis* (see Weimar Ausg. VII, 710—the oldest passage). J. Boni's treatment of the subject is quite different in Der Kampf um die Kirche, Studien zum Kirchenbegriff des christlichen Altertums (1934), p. 130 : " When one reads about the Church in the N.T., one gets the impression that it is speaking only of an invisible Church ". (Boni's book—326 pages long—is the latest and most comprehensive treatment of the idea of the Church, and is the work of a former Swiss Catholic priest, who is now an evangelical minister. He is not so much concerned with furthering the scientific study of the problems involved as with presenting a statement of accounts and showing how, as the result of many years' reading, he developed from a traditionalist conservative into a modernist liberal.)

[2] Cf. A. Schlatter, " Die Kirche Jerusalems vom Jahre 70-130 ", in Beitr. Ford. Chr. Th. (1898), 90 : " When Israel died, the primitive Church also died, and her death became a disaster to the whole Church ; for the gap was filled by the Christianity of sects—there Mohammed, here bishop, monk and pope." In spite

As the Church of the N.T. cannot be explained by playing off idea against reality, so also it cannot be explained by playing off the Church as the whole body of believers against the individual congregation. The theological and sociological questions involved are secondary. Every true congregation of the primi-

of its queerness, that is a true saying—true and important in spite of E. Peterson ! The latter rightly observes, in Die Kirche (1929), p. 69, " If anyone sees the relation of the Church to the Synagogue as merely a historical, and not as a theological problem, he is bound to revive the Gnostic standpoint, and seek the elimination of the O.T. and of the Messiah according to the flesh. Thus it is no accident that Harnack the historian was sympathetic to the theology of Marcion the Gnostic." But it is not quite clear what he sees when he says, speaking as a theologian, that the Church Fathers, in contrast to the Synagogue, understood *ecclesia* to mean ἐκκαλεῖν, *evocatio*, a calling out of the world, with its natural ordinances and natural sociological creations (pp. 24 ff.), and when he writes as follows : " Cf. also C. Passaglia, De Ecclesia Christi, I (1853), p. 10—I hold this patristic interpretation of the word ἐκκλησία, which helps to differentiate between the constitutional forms of Ekklesia and Synagoge to be more significant than modern demonstrations that ἐκκλησία and συναγωγή are used promiscuously in the LXX. The true meaning of a word is not settled by a quotation, but by the concrete situation in which it is uttered " (p. 70). But more than mere " quotation " is involved in the relation between O.T. and N.T. And to talk about the " concrete situation " smacks more of history than of theology. Peterson has combined his three Salzburg lectures on " die Kirche aus Juden und Heiden " in Schweiz. Rundsch. (Jan. 1936), 875 ff., and while the article is helpful in its survey of the relations between Church and Synagogue, its conclusions are not altogether clear. In the N.T., at any rate, ἐκκλησία and συναγωγή are not so sharply differentiated as Peterson urges. The Church Fathers whom he follows, in conscious agreement with old Christian and mediaeval methods of Biblical interpretation, relying on Romans ix-xi, regarded ἐκκλησία as the true (spiritual) Israel, and συναγωγή as the false (after the flesh), and this has finally become stereotyped, though it could not be the intention of the N.T. as a whole. (See p. 33.)

tive Church represented the whole body as really as the congregation at Jerusalem. The gradual drawing together of many congregations in one organisation naturally suggests a development from individual to corporate. But this impression is misleading, since the only criterion of genuineness is to be found in the congregation's conviction that it represents the whole body. The much discussed controversial question about what is called the development of a system of Church government should be tackled from this point of view. Self-evident matters of constitution are hardly worth our attention. The N.T. shows very clearly that in the beginning there was more leadership by men of the Spirit (Pneumatikertum und Charismatikertum) than in later days, and that their place was afterwards taken by presbyters and bishops. But the way in which Paul thinks and speaks about the gifts of the spirit (χαρίσματα), and particularly the way in which he maintains connection with the original group of believers, shows that it is not legitimate to speak of an essential constitutional change from a " pneumatic " to a " juristic " form. When the time did come, in which matters of human law were given the status of matters of divine law—a change that was largely made possible by the " high " speculations about the ἐκκλησία—then the step was taken from original Christianity to early Catholicism, a step which, rightly understood, marks the cleavage between Protestantism and Catholicism.

INDEX OF WORDS AND REFERENCES

71

III

SIN

BY

GOTTFRIED QUELL
GEORG BERTRAM
GUSTAV STÄHLIN AND
WALTER GRUNDMANN

Translated from the German
first edition, Stuttgart, 1933
with additions by Walter
Grundmann and J. R. Coates

PREFACE

" THE whole nature of the Christian religion stands upon these two great pillars, namely, the greatness of our fall and the greatness of our redemption." These words of William Law are echoed by modern theologians. William Temple, e.g., says in his Gifford Lectures (1934), " The centre of trouble is the personality as a whole, which is self-centred and can only be wholesome and healthy if it is God-centred. . . . Man cannot meet his own deepest need, nor find for himself release from his profoundest trouble. What he needs is not progress, but redemption." * Leonard Hodgson, critical of Temple, says " Sin, then, is the heart of the problem ; what account are we to give of it ? In one sense, no account can be given of it beyond saying that it is the choice of what is wrong because of some desirable quality in it. It is an irrational act, and is therefore incapable of explanation, a surd in the order of reality, opaque to thought, unintelligible. All attempts to give an intelligible account of it explain it away and describe it as something other than what it really is, as is invariably done by philosophers of the school of absolute idealism. . . . A revelation of enlightenment might be adequate to a universe in which evil was at bottom an unreality which could be thought away ; but in this universe in which evil is the grim reality we know it to be, the divine Word must be an act of redemptive power. The heart of the Christian gospel is the proclamation of this act of redemption as a fact of history, or rather, as the central fact of all history." †

* *Nature, Man and God*, pp. 367 and 513.
† *Towards a Christian Philosophy*, pp. 184 and 186.

This is an age of anodynes. Feelings are blunted by much sophistication ; and an urgent problem is how to resensitise modern man. What will break up the cynical determinism that prevails so widely ? Some may think that the panic fear of war will banish man's fear of facing the spectre within, so that the long repression may be ended, and the truth bring freedom. But what will unveil the truth ?

The Greeks and the psychologists can bring us to a deep level of analysis, when we try to be honest with ourselves—when we cease from our multitudinous escapist activities and look inwards—but they do not bring us to the bottom of things. Only the Word of God can do that, penetrating the last screens of self-deceit and making us ashamed of ourselves ; and the Word is spoken in the Bible. The present volume helps us to understand that Word.

Gottfried Quell's exposition of the story of the Fall is a notable contribution to Bible study, and will help the preacher as well as the theologian—and the sinner. Georg Bertram's examination of the theology of the Septuagint is a valuable piece of pioneer work, and may well stimulate others to study what Swete called the " dogmatic interest " of the Greek translators. Gustav Stählin laid the foundation for the rest of the article before he went to India, and the work was completed by Walter Grundmann, of Jena, with contributions from Hermann Kleinknecht and Karl Georg Kuhn. The section dealing with ἁμαρτωλός and ἀναμάρτητος was made into a separate article by Karl Heinrich Rengstorf, and we much regret that we are not able to include it in the present volume.

When the article was published in 1933, Dr. Grundmann was a Pastor in Saxony. During the war he was made prisoner by the Russians, and after his release at the end of 1945 gave himself to social and theological work. Eventually he was appointed to an evangelical Pastorate in Waltershausen, a town of 12,000 inhabitants in the Thüringer Wald. In addition to his work for the Kittel Dictionary, Dr. Grundmann's most important writings are *Die Gotteskindschaft in der Geschichte Jesu und ihre religionsgeschichtlichen Voraussetzungen* (1938) ; "Aufnahme und Deutung der Botschaft Jesu im Urchristentum" (*Gotteskindschaft*, Vol. II, 1941) ; *Jesus der Galiläer und das Judentum* (1941) ; "Die Bergrede Jesu" (*Akad. Antrittsrede*, 1939) ; "Das Problem des hellenistischen Christentums innerhalb der Jerusalemer Urgemeinde (*Z.N.W.* XXXVIII, 45-73, 1939) ; "Die Apostel zwischen Jerusalem und Antiochia" (*Z.N.W.* XXXIX, 110-137, 1940). We are grateful to him for a number of additions to his chapter on "Sin in the New Testament", specially written for this translation, viz. pp. 66, line 12—68, 9 ; 67, notes ; 69, 3-70, 8 ; 70, 19-26 ; 76, 17-77, 7 ; 77, note 1 ; 81, 8-21 ; 83, 6-16 and note 1 ; 84, 6-12 ; 85, 35-86, 10.

J. R. COATES.

CONTENTS

BIBLIOGRAPHY

Chapter I

K. Umbreit : Die Sünde, ein Beitrag z. Theol. d. A.T., 1853.

J. C. Mathes : Theologisch Tijdschrift XXIV, 225 ff., 1890.

J. Köberle : Sünde u. Gnade im relig. Leben d. Volkes Israel, 1905.

W. Staerk : Sünde u. Gnade nach d. Vorstellung d. älteren Judentums, 1905.

F. Bennewitz : Die Sünde im alten Israel, 1907.

H. Seeger : Die Triebkräfte d. rel. Lebens in Israel u. Babylon, 1923.

S. Mowinckel : Psalmenstudien I, 39 ff., 1921.

J. Pedersen : Israel, its Life and Culture, 411 ff., 1926.

J. Hempel : Zeitschr. f. syst. Theol. X, 163-199, 1932.

Chapter II

[C. H. Dodd : The Bible and the Greeks, 76-81, 1935.]

Chapter III

F. Weber : Jüdische Theologie, 2nd edn., 1897.

F. C. Porter : The Yeçer Hara' (Yale), 1902.

W. Bousset—H. Gressmann : Die Rel. d. Jud., 3rd ed., 399-409, 1926.

G. F. Moore : Judaism, 1927 ff.

A. Büchler : Studies in Sin, etc. in Rabb. Lit. of 1st century, 1928.

Chapters IV—VI

H. Cremer—J. Kögel : Bibl.-theol. Wörterb. d. N.T. Gr., 11th ed., 1923.

R. C. Trench : Synonyms of the N.T., 8th ed., 1876.

E. D. Burton : Galatians (I.C.C.), 436 ff., 1921.

H. Lietzmann : Römer, 3rd ed., 75 ff., 1928.

M. Dibelius : Die Geisterwelt im Gl. d. Paulus, 119 ff., 1909.

R. Otto : Sünde und Urschuld, 1932.
  (See also works on N.T. Theology.)

CHAPTER V

K. LATTE : Schuld u. Sünde in der greich. Rel. (A.R.W., XX, 254-298, 1920-21).

L. HEY : 'Αμαρτία (Philologus LXXXIII, 1-17, 137-163, 1927).

J. STENZEL : Metaphysik d. Altertums (Hdbch. d. Philosophie, 17 ff., 1929-31).

H. WEINSTOCK : Sophokles, 1931.

F. X. STEINLEITNER : Die Beicht, etc. in d. Antike (München Diss., 1913).

GENERAL

[G. AULEN : Christus Victor (Eng. Trans.), 1931.

E. BRUNNER : Man in Revolt, esp. VI and VII.

J. MÜLLER : The Christian doctrine of Sin (Eng. Trans.), 1876.

R. NIEBUHR : The Nature and Destiny of Man, I, vii-x.

W. E. ORCHARD : Modern Theories of Sin, 1909.

H. W. ROBINSON : Recent Reconstruction of the Concept of Sin (E.T.), 1925-26.

C. SCHWEITZER (Editor) : Krankheit und Sünde.

F..R. TENNANT : The Concept of Sin.
              The Origin and Propagation of Sin.
              Sources of the doctr. of the Fall and Original Sin.

N. P. WILLIAMS : The ideas of the Fall and of Original Sin, 1927.]

Note.—Square brackets indicate additions by the translator.

ABBREVIATIONS

A.R.W.	Archiv f. Religionswissenschaft.
C.B.	Cambridge Bible for Schools and Colleges.
Ditt. Syll.	W. Dittenberger, Sylloge Inscript. Graec.
E.T.	Expository Times.
G.V.I.	R. Kittel, Geschichte d. Volkes Israel.
I.C.C.	International Critical Commentary.
LXX.	Septuagint.
R.G.G.	Religion in Geschichte u. Gegenwart, 2nd ed.
Str-Bill.	Strack-Billerbeck, Komm. z. N.T. aus Talmud u. Midrasch.
Winer.	G. B. Winer, Gramm. d. n.t. Spr., 2nd ed. by P. Schmiedel.
Z.A.W.	Zeitschrift f. A.T. Wissenschaft.
Z.N.W.	Zeitschrift f. N.T. Wissenschaft.
Z.S.T.	Zeitschrift f. systematische Theologie.

I. SIN IN THE OLD TESTAMENT

1. LINGUISTIC

(*a*) The idea of sin is expressed in the Old Testament by a great variety of terms, whose differing shades of meaning are not adequately conveyed, either by our word, "sin", or by the Septuagint ἁμαρτία, ἀδικία, ἀνομία, ἀσέβεια, κακία and their derivatives. One of the most striking and instructive illustrations of this may be seen in the fact that we generally use the word, "guilt", as the translation of the Hebrew *'asham*, *'awon*, etc., whereas in the Greek Bible the latter is almost always represented by one of the words just mentioned,[1] and the former either by one of them or by some other inappropriate expression.[2] The following statistics show the most important facts concerning LXX usage, and also display the wealth of the Hebrew vocabulary.

ἁμαρτία predominantly for *ḥaṭṭa'th* (238 times) and *'awon* (70). It also represents the derivatives, *ḥeṭ'* (28), *ḥaṭa'ah* (8), *ḥaṭṭa'ah* (1), *ḥaṭṭayah* (1), *ḥaṭṭaya'* (1), and the Inf. *ḥaṭo'* (1). Other Hebrew equivalents are *pesha'* (19), the verb *pasha'* (2), *'asham* (4), *'ashmah* (2), *'ashem* (1), *resha'* (2),

---

[1] Only at Gen. iv, 13, by αἰτία, the most suitable term.

[2] Mostly πλημμέλεια, -λεῖν, "mistake in music" [metaph. in Plato, etc., for "offence"] (22 times) ; also ἄγνοια (5), βάσανος (4), ἱλασμός (Amos viii, 14 *'ashmath*), καθαρισμός (Prov. xiv, 9). Ἁμαρτία only Lev. v, 7 ; Numb. xviii, 9 (Plur.) ; II Kings xii, 16 (Heb. 17) ; Is. liii, 10 ; ἀδικία Jer. li (LXX xxviii), 5.

to'ebhah (2), and the clearly theological *ḥⁱoli* (Is.
liii, 4), *maḥshabhah* (Is. lxv, 2), *mᵉshubhah* (Jer.
xiv, 7), *'ᵃlilah* (Ezek. xxxvi, 19), Aramaic *'illah*
(Dan. vi, 5), *ra'ah* (Prov. xxvi, 26), *ṭum'ah* (Lev.
xiv, 19), *derekh* (I Kings xxii, 53), Aram. *ḥᵃbhulah*
(Dan. vi, 23), and *rasha'* in the Hiph'il [but LXX
translator probably read *bᵉrish'e*] (Dan. xi, 32).

ἁμάρτημα most frequently for *ḥaṭṭa'th*, four
times each for *'awon* and *pesha'*, once each for
ḥeṭ', *resha'*, *derekh* (Hos. x, 13) and *qeçeph* (Numb.
i, 53 by mistake).

ἁμαρτωλός 72 times for *rasha'* and twice for
resha' ; 11 times for *ḥaṭṭa'*, once each for *ḥaṭṭa'ah*
and *hoṭe'*, and twice for the verb *ḥaṭa'* ; once each
for *ḥaneph*, *ra'*, *ḥoresh* (Ps. cxxviii (cxxix), 3,
theological).

ἁμαρτάνω 162 times for *ḥaṭa'* Qal and twice for
the Hiph'il ; also for the verbs *pasha'* (Lam.
iii, 42), *'asham* (3 times), *ma'al*, *shaḥath* Pi'el
(once), *'asah* (e.g. Numb. v, 7) and *rasha'* Hiph.
(each 3 times) ; and, by mistake or as intentionally free translation, for the nouns *ḥaṭṭa'th* (e.g.
Gen. iv, 7 ; I Sam. xx, 1), *ḥaṭṭa'*, *ḥeṭ'*, and *pesha'*
(each 3 times), *'ashem*, *'ashmah*, *rasha'* (each twice),
and once for *'awon*.

ἀδικία : of the 36 Hebrew equivalents, the
commonest is *'awon* (50 times), whereas *pesha'*
only occurs 7 times, *ḥaṭṭa'th* (Dan. ix, 24) and
'asham (Jer. li (xxviii), 5) each once.   Others are
'awlah (14), *'awal* (9), *'awen* (8), *ḥamaṣ* (8), *sheqer*
(7, only in Ps.), *ra'ah* (4), *'osheq* (4),   Though
only found once or twice each, the following are
also relevant : *resha'*, *ma'al*, *ḥawwah*, *'awwah*
(Ezek. xxi, 32), *'awwal*, Aram. *'ᵃwaya'* (Dan. iv,
24), *ra'*, *muṭṭeh*, *mirmah*, *ma'aseh*, *'eseq* (Gen.
xxvi, 20), *meri* (Ezek. xii, 2).

ἀδίκημα 5 times for ʿawon, 4 for peshaʿ, twice for ʿosheq, once each for ḥamaṣ, ʿawlah, raʿ, raʿah, mishpaṭ.

ἄδικος 33 times for sheqer (as nomen rectum [or Genitive]), 10 times for ḥamaṣ, 8 times for ʿawlah. It also represents ʿawel (4), rashaʿ (4), ʿawwal (3), ʿawen, mirmah, ʿosheq, raʿ each twice, and tahpukhah, nᵉbhalah, rᵉmiyyah, tohu each once.

ἀδικέω 3 times for ḥṭʾ, once each for pshʿ, rʿʿ, rshʿ Hiphʿil. On the other hand, 14 times for ʿshq, and 3 times for mʿl (Dan. ix, 5 Theod. (A) for mrd). The relevant nouns are ḥamaṣ (2) and mᵉshubhah (1).

ἀνομία represents 24 Hebrew words : ʿawon (63), ʾawen (26), toʿebhah (26, all in Ezek. except 1 at Jer. xvi, 18), peshaʿ (20, and also the verb at Is. liii, 12), rishʿah (8), reshaʿ (5), zimmah, ḥamaṣ, ʿawlah, ḥaṭṭaʾth (each 7) ; less frequently bᵉliyyaʿal, beçaʿ, derekh, hawwah, maʿal, maʿᵃlal, ʿᵃlilah, nᵉbhalah, mispaḥ (Is. v, 7), ṣarah, ʿawel, ʿoçebh (Ps. cxxxix, 24, perhaps for dᵉbhar-ʿeçebh, as Gunkel suggests), ʿathaq, qalon, sheqer, and once the verb shḥth Hiphʿil.

ἄνομος 31 times for rashaʿ, but only once for ḥaṭṭaʾ (Is. xxxiii, 14) ; elsewhere for ʾawen (5), ḥaneph, ʿawwal, holel, ʿawon (2), etc.

ἀνόμημα is less frequent, standing for ʿawon (3), peshaʿ (3), zimmah (2), ḥaṭṭaʾth (2), and nᵉbhalah, toʿebhah, tiphlah once each.

ἀνομεῖν for rshʿ (Qal and Hiphʿil 8 times), pshʿ (3), shḥth (Piʿel and Hiph. 3) ; also for ʿwh, mʿl, ḥṭ (Theod. Dan. ix, 5 ?) and some nouns.

ἀσέβεια next to ἁμαρτία the most definitely religious term, generally represents peshaʿ (27 times), but also reshaʿ and rishʿah (4), and less frequently hawwah, zadhon, zimmah, ḥamaṣ, mirmah, ṣarah, *ᵃlilah, ra'ah, to'ebhah*, etc. There are only two cases each of *ḥaṭṭa'th* and *'awon*, and these are not well attested.

ἀσεβής stands almost exclusively for *rasha'* (14).

ἀσεβεῖν generally for *pasha'*, never for *ḥṭ'*. *marah* (Lam. iii, 42) should be noted.

κακία usually for the derivatives of *ra'a'*, but also, in some MSS. for *'awon* (I Chron. xxi, 8 ; Jer. xvi, 18 ; xiii, 22 (A) ; *'awen* (Is. xxix, 20) ; *ḥaṭṭa'th* (Jer. xv, 13 A).

κακός. Besides the regular *ra'*, the following are noteworthy : *'awen* (3), *zimmah* (Prov. x, 23), *'amal* (Job xvi, 2), *resha'* (Prov. xvi, 12), *'awlah* (Job xxii, 23).

κακοῦν (Is. l, 9) is the rendering of *rasha'* Hiph'il, and κακοποιεῖν (II Sam. xxiv, 17 A) of *'awah* Hiph.

Equivalents for *maradh* or *marah* in a religious context are ἀθετεῖν and ἀφιστάναι (both also for *pasha'*), ἀμελεῖν (Jer. iv, 17), ἐρίζειν (I Kings xii, 14 f.), παραβάινειν, παροξύνειν (Numb. xx, 24 : *mᵉrithem 'eth pi*), μὴ εἰσακούειν (Is. i, 20), and above all παραπικραίνειν (Ezek. ii, 3 for *maradh* and 18 times for *marah* ; Ezek. also has παραπικραίνων for *beyth meri* 9 times).

The limitation of the LXX vocabulary here exposed is not due to the translators' method. The reason for it is to be found in a peculiar difficulty in the Hebrew, which obviously has no single word suitable for religious or theological purposes, like our word, " sin ". All the terms employed in this connexion can also be used for secular purposes, so that we have to be on our guard against over-emphasising their religious connotation. Close examination shows, more or less clearly, that they all involve a rational

interpretation of religious phenomena. They do not
arise spontaneously from experience, but are the
coinage of theology and have different associations.
Thus the translator has more scope for the exercise
of subjectivity than might have been desired. In
some cases a religious flavour is introduced where it
is lacking in the Hebrew,[1] and in others the use of a
secular word spoils the religious meaning.[2] It is
abundantly clear, from the rich variety of terms used,
that the Old Testament offers no neat uniform doctrine
of sin ; qualifications are always necessary, and all
sorts of subsidiary questions are involved in the general
problem of sin.

(*b*) Our word, "sin", represents four different
Hebrew roots, each with its own nuance, which it is
difficult for us to reproduce.

ḥṭ'. The verb occurs 177 times in the Qal, including
infinitive and participial forms, 32 times in the Hiph'il
and 9 in the Hithpa'el. In addition 15 Pi'el forms
are found, all denominative, in the privative sense of
putting sin away.[3] Some of the Hithpa'el forms
accordingly mean absolving oneself. Most of these
223 forms are used in a religious sense.[4]

The commonest noun formed from this root is
ḥaṭṭā'th (masculine only at Gen. iv, 7—see p. 15, n. 3),
which occurs 289 times and is preferred to words
coming from other roots. In a large number of
cases[5] the meaning corresponds to the privative use
of the verb so that it denotes the means of putting
away sin or its consequences, and indicates a

---

[1] Cf. e.g. Prov. i, 31, ἀσέβεια for *mo'eçah*, etc.

[2] Cf. e.g. Job ix, 22, δυνάστης for *rasha'*, etc.

[3] Cf. Bauer-Leander, Hist. Gram. d. hebr. Spr. I (1922),
291 ; G. Bergstrasser, Hebr. Gram. II (1929), 94 ; [S. R.
Driver, Exod. (C.B. 1911), 324].

[4] For exceptions, see p. 7.

[5] B. Baentsch (on Exod. xxix, 14) enumerates 101 cases.

particular kind of sacrifice, described in Leviticus iv,
1–v, 13.[1] Otherwise it simply means sin, though in
certain cases it may be rendered by a legal term such
as crime or negligence. All the extended forms of the
word, in the plural or with suffixes, could equally
well come from *ḥaṭṭa'ah*, but this only appears twice
(Exod. xxxiv, 7 and Is. v, 18). *ḥᵃṭa'ah* occurs 8
times,[2] and the masculine *ḥeṭ'* 35 times.[3] *ḥaṭṭa'* (sinner)
occurs 18 times in the plural, but only in the singular
at Amos ix, 8, where it is feminine.

psh' (rebel) as verb 41 times, including Qal participle (10) ; as noun 92 times (sing. and plur.).

'wh occurs in 17 verbal forms, of which, however,
perhaps 6 (Niph. and Pi.) have the secular meaning,
" twist ", either literally or metaphorically (see p. 20).
The noun *'awon* [4] has a much stronger religious tone,
stressing the idea of guilt. It occurs 227 times.[5]

shghh (err) as verb 19 times, with the parallel

---

[1] This meaning, as in the case of *'asham*, is perhaps to be
accounted for by the fact that these were key-words in the
sacerdotal theology, and therefore suitable as headings for groups
of sacrifices. The earliest evidence seems to be that of Ezekiel
(cf. R. Smend [and G. A. Cooke] on Ezek. xl, 39). Baentsch
(Lev. 321) assumes a connexion with the pre-exilic fines
(II Kings xii, 16 ; cf. Amos ii, 8) ; but these are only analogies,
—they do not represent a stage in the development of ritual
ideology.

[2] Ps. xl, 7, where *ḥᵃṭa'ah* seems to mean sin-offering, as *ḥaṭṭa'th*
and *ḥaṭṭa'ah* do elsewhere, must have been pointed by someone
with a phrase like *'awen wa 'ᵃçarah* (Is. i, 13) in mind.

[3] *ḥeṭ'* often indicates guilt : Lev. xix, 17 ; xx, 20 ; xxii, 9 ;
xxiv, 15 ; Numb. ix, 13 ; xviii, 22 ; Is. liii, 12 ; Ezek. xxiii, 49.
(See pp. 21 ff.)

[4] Formed from the root, which ends in a vowel, by the addition of the suffix *-an*. Cf. J. Barth, Die Nominalbildung in
d. sem. Spr., 1889, 326.

[5] Other derivatives from the same root, such as *'iy*, *'iw'im*
and *mᵉ'i*, are far removed from the language of religion, with
the possible exception of *'iw'im* in Is. xix, 14.

shghgh (4) and the noun *sh^eghaghah* (19), expresses the idea of sin as creaturely going astray.[1]

These four roots, though closely related to one another in their religious and theological use, differ from one another so fundamentally in their essential quality that a study of them will enable us to trace the main lines of Hebrew thought on the subject of sin. (Of the words listed above under (*a*), *mrdh* and *mrh* go with *psh^'*; *rsh^'*, *'wl*, *'shm* should also be considered.)

2. LEGAL AND THEOLOGICAL

(*a*) The statistics show that *ht'* and its derivatives play the principal part in expressing the idea of sin, no doubt because this root conveyed a clear objective picture to the mind, with no reference to motive or to the inner quality of sinful behaviour. Its pictorial character must have been obvious to all who used it. There are a few places in the Old Testament where the word means literally missing the mark, and this must be the clue to its religious, legal and ethical significance. Thus Prov. xix, 2 : " misseth his way " (R.V.m.) ; Prov. viii, 36 : " misseth me " (R.V.m.) contrasted with " findeth me " in ver. 35 ; Job v, 24 : " shalt miss nothing " (R.V.), i.e. " shalt find what thou seekest " ; Judg. xx, 16 : " every one could sling stones at an hair breadth, and not miss ".[2] Ps. xxv, 8 provides an instructive example : the author obviously wrote *hoṭe'im* [Moffatt, " going astray "], meaning those who, with the best will in the world, yet miss the mark (LXX ἁμαρτάνοντας ἐν ὁδῷ), but the Massoretic editors pointed this as *hatta'im* (sinners), in order to convey the idea that

[1] Also *sh^eghey'ah* (Ps. xix, 13), *mishgeh* (Gen. xliii, 12) and *m^eshughah* (Job xix, 4).   [2] LXX οὐκ ἐξαμαρτάνοντες.

even those who look to Yahwe for guidance feel
themselves to be sinners.　What made it possible to
read this fine idea into the text was the fact that the
author had already used the word metaphorically.
It follows from these examples, even though they are
not very numerous,[1] that *ḥṭ'* never quite lost the sense
of making a mistake ; the commonest expression for
sin in Hebrew lacks the deep religious quality of our
word.

This conclusion is supported by many passages in
the O.T., in which *ḥṭ'* expresses a legal idea, either in
the wording of a law or in the context.　Originally
denoting a faulty action, it came to be applied to
all kinds of wrong-doing.　This can be seen wherever
it indicates failure to comply with the normal laws of
human intercourse.　In the law concerning witnesses,
Deut. xix, 15-21, *ḥaṭṭa'th*, like *'awon*, means any
breach of the civil law : there is no reference to religion or the cult ; the case is tried in a secular court.[2]
Similarly, at Deut. xxi, 22, *ḥeṭ'* means an ordinary
criminal case (*mishpaṭ*).[3]　There is a special reference
to legal proceedings in the threat (Is. xxix, 21) against

---

[1] In Is. lxv, 20, *haḥoṭe'* means " he that falls short " of a full
life,—a parallel to " an old man that hath not filled his days ".
He is only a sinner from the point of view of the dogma that
untimely death is evidence of sin.

[2] Most modern commentators regard the verse as awkwardly
expanded by the introduction of Yahwe and the priests.　[" But
it is quite as probable that *before the LORD* was all that the
original text of the law contained " (G. A. Smith *ad loc.*, C.B.
1918).]

[3] Like Deut. xxii, 26.　[G. A. Smith : " This compound
phrase seems a fusion of *a sin of death*, a capital sin, xxii, 26, and
a sentence of death, a capital charge, xix, 6.　Or *mishpaṭ* is a gloss."]
On the other hand a religious tone is given to *ḥeṭ'* by the mention
of an appeal to Yahwe at Deut. xv, 9 ; xxiii, 22 ; xxiv, 15.
As the protector of right, he is affected by any departure from
the norm.

those who compel people to make false statements :
mah⁽ᵃ⁾ṭi'e 'adham b⁽ᵉ⁾dhabhar ; and Hezekiah is obviously
using legal terminology when he says *ḥaṭa'thi* to the
king of Assyria (II Kings xviii, 14).[1] It is with the
same word that Jephthah meets the Moabite king :
" I have done no wrong to you " [Moffatt] ; the
reference is to the common practice in international
relations (Judg. xi, 27). Breaches of the civil law are
indicated on the part of Joseph's fellow-prisoners by
the employment of the verb at Gen. xl, 1 (E? J?) and
the noun at xli, 9.[2] The verb also occurs in the account of David's loyalty to Saul, and the latter's dis-
loyalty (I Sam. xix, 4 ; xxiv, 12 ; xxvi, 21), referring
to the ordinary laws of personal relationship.

Other examples border very closely on the forensic,
even though they speak of deviation from an ethical,
rather than a legal norm. When Reuben (Gen.
xlii, 22 E)[3] and Jonathan (I Sam. xix, 5) use the
word, they are speaking of murder. On the lips of
Jacob (Gen. xxxi, 36) and Abimelech (Gen. xx, 9)
it means things that " are not done ". It can even
denote a continuing state of guilt or moral boycott, as
in the case of Judah (Gen. xliii, 9 J ; cf. xliv, 32),
who is obviously describing the unfortunate consequences for himself if he fails to fulfil his promise.

(b) Our brief study of the usage of *ḥṭ'* [4] lays the

[1] Exod. v, 16 (pointing *w⁽ᵉ⁾ḥaṭṭa'th 'immakh* with Symmachus)
voices an appeal against unjust treatment.

[2] Obviously there can be no reference on the part of the Hebrew
writer to the divinity of the Pharaoh.

[3] Cf. the self-accusation of the brothers in ver. 21 : *'⁽ᵃ⁾shemim
'⁽ᵃ⁾nahnu.*

[4] A similar picture is presented by *rasha'*, which is more definitely legal in character. In law it means the one who is in
the wrong : e.g. Exod. xxiii, 1. That gives rise to all its other
shades of meaning. Cf. G. Marschall, Die " Gottlosen " des
erstens Psalmenbuches, 1929, 49 ff.

foundation for an understanding of its religious significance, and indeed of the O.T. doctrine of sin as a whole. In the case of the other roots mentioned above, we cannot trace with the same historical accuracy the development from colloquial and legal to theological and religious usage ; whereas this one clearly involves the presupposition that the religious life is subject, or ought to be subject, to legal norms or at least to generally recognised rules. If the religious life is regarded predominantly as being under rules and regulations, intercourse with God being possible only under prescribed conditions, then we have here a specifically theological consideration. It would be possible, if it were so desired, to regard theology as the clue to the whole process of the transference of meaning, and this could not be disproved by the quotation of any passage in the O.T. But we cannot help feeling a certain fundamental hesitation about making theology responsible for the coining of ideas so deeply rooted in the flesh and blood of those who express them, especially in view of the fact that roots like *psh'* are not merely, like *ḥṭ'* and *'wh*, formal in character, but also include the idea of human motive.

psh' represents sin under its most active, and therefore least formal aspect. E. König suitably equates it with practising rebellion (Rebellion üben).[1] In secular, non-legal speech it means the wilful breaking of a relationship of loyalty and peace, as when Israel broke away from the house of David (I Kings xii, 19), or Edom from the " hand " of Judah (II Kings viii, 20). When Isaiah (i, 2) depicts the opposition of Israel to Yahwe as the rebellion of sons against their father, or Jeremiah (ii, 29) draws a parallel between their rebellion and the initiation of legal proceedings against Yahwe, human responsibility for the situation, i.e.

[1] E. König, Wörterbuch, s.v.

for sin, is unmistakable.[1] Amos has no need to explain his cry, " transgress " : that one word, *pishe‘u*
(iv, 4) is all that is required to indicate Israel's almost
instinctive self-assertion and defiance of God. Expressions like these imply a numinous element underlying sin ; rebellion is a consciously willed " offence
not against a mere whim, but against a numinous
object of worth—whatever it may be ".[2] Sin is then
a spontaneous human reaction to the holy and the
godlike.

The same thought is involved in the idea of " erring
and straying " in our relations with God, which brings
out the tragic element in human experience. Though
often unobserved, the essentially theological problem
of sin comes into view here, compelling our attention.
Unfortunately *shaghah* (err) appears in the O.T.
mostly in a rather feeble way in the terminology of
ritual, as though it had lost its original force ; or
perhaps we should put the matter the other way
round, and say that at first its true value was developed by a few religious thinkers from its relatively
harmless connexion with ritual. It is this connexion
which has made it appear to be the weakest of the
words for sin, indicating as it does, not culpable
negligence but ignorance (Ezek. xlv, 20 ; Lev. iv, 2, 13,
etc.). Similarly, in the law concerning cities of refuge,
the noun *sheghaghah* is used for " unintentional "
manslaughter (Numb. xxxv, 11 ; Josh. xx, 3). In

[1] For further examples see Hos. vii, 13 ; viii, 1 (rebellion
against Yahwe's Torah) ; Jer. ii, 29 ; iii, 13 ; Ezek. xviii, 31 ;
xx, 38 ; Is. xliii, 27 (parallel to *het*'). Ps. v, 10 (Heb. 11) shows
how closely *pesha'* and *marah* are related to each other, and how
both bring out the part played by the will. The enemies' plans,
which prove to be their downfall, are parallel to their acts of
rebellion, and both are summed up in the final *maru bhakh*,
" they bid thee defiance ".

[2] Cf. R. Otto, Sünde und Urschuld, 1932, 4.

all these cases the hidden force of the word is lost. *Shaghah* is by no means a mild expression. It is really much more weighty than the terms which indicate a formal missing of the mark or an emotional rebellion, since it implies a right intention on the part of the one who goes astray ; his going wrong is to be attributed to circumstances, i.e. from the religious point of view, to God. An element of demonic horror comes upon the scene the moment error is viewed religiously apart from ritual, and indeed is not entirely absent from the latter, in spite of the possibility of accommodation, so far as the cult is concerned. Job's remark, that he who is misled and he who misleads both belong to God, is not just a harmless truism (Job xii, 16) : he is voicing the alarm and agony of the thought that man, struggling towards God, cannot reach the goal because God denies him the ability to do so. The bitter poet, relentlessly analysing his own spiritual life, lays resolutely upon God the responsibility for man's fatal incapacity. Job holds himself justified in disputing the matter with God.

Isaiah's mind seems to have moved in the same direction, though he never reached such a titanic outburst of despair. He launches out (xxviii, 7 f.) against those whose business it is to lay down the law about going astray, on the ground that they themselves have gone astray in drunken folly. His painful realism brings out the double meaning of *shaghah*—reeling under the influence of drink and getting off the track in religion—thus laying the blame for their behaviour half upon themselves and half upon God, whose messengers they are. What he thinks of, when he uses the word, is the contemplation of God with minds beclouded and incompetent. God will speak to those who " err ", with " stammering lips and another tongue " which they cannot understand. They will know the suffering of Job, who finds no escape from his error, in spite of every human effort to comfort him, but must endure the torture of the mystery of God (Job xix, 4 ; vi, 24). Doubtless many failed to perceive, or were unwilling to perceive, the dread import of this word, *shaghah*. It is certainly missed by the quiet man of simple faith to whom we owe Psalm cxix, as it was by Job's friends : all he knows is that formerly he went astray, but the Law has been his teacher and he has learned a lesson from his affliction (Ps. cxix, 67).

Although recognition of the irrational factor in sin is not lacking in Hebrew, as may be seen in *pasha'*, *marah*, and *shaghah*, it must be admitted that, apart from *pasha'*, it does not play a predominant part. It seems to have been largely displaced in the O.T. by the idea of ceremonial impurity. This is a less primitive conception, being fundamentally theological in character, owing to its connexion with a more or less established doctrine of God. It is, of course, hardly possible apart from explicitly theological texts like the codes of law in the Pentateuch, to say how far O.T. writers had theological considerations in mind —or whether they had any at all. Logical structure is usually in inverse ratio to lively feeling. Yet even in such cases one can recognise the underlying idea of missing the mark or offending against the norm, and it is easy to reconstruct the relevant doctrine. We must certainly beware against what Gunkel called "over-heightening" in the exegesis of O.T. passages dealing with sin. But the O.T. itself obviously feels the need of further definition from time to time, when it adds a phrase like "with a high hand" (Numb. xv, 30). The so-called "sin" of Sodom and Gomorrah (Gen. xviii, 20) was not sin in the eyes of the inhabitants of those cities : it was

first recognised as such by the Israelite narrator on
the ground of a theological judgment. Many other
statements about sin are more naturally associated
with the authors' theories than with numinous feelings. This has to be remembered even in the interpretation of prayers in which sins are confessed.
Thus, e.g., in Ps. xxxii suffering leads to reflexion,
and this again to the confession of sin. One cannot
help suspecting that many an action comes in this way
to be branded as sin, which was never directed against
God, and that God is regarded as keeping a sharp
watch over the performance of ceremonies and the
technique of ritual.

(c) Scepticism as to the specifically religious character of the prevailing idea of sin in the O.T. is
strengthened by the fact that the Wisdom movement
in Israel fostered an emphatically intellectual conception of it. There were no doubt good peda-
gogical reasons for this, but one cannot resist the
impression that such doctrine was popular, and that
it was the sort of thing that Isaiah was making fun
of, with his " precept upon precept, line upon line "
(Is. xxviii, 10). A fool (nabhal),[1] according to the
wise men, is a man who does not know his duty towards God, or, if he does know it, fails to realise that
his success in life depends upon his performing that
duty (Ps. xiv, 2 etc.). The pious man's feeling of
superiority as thus expressed, is always objectionable,
even though the same kind of argument is occasion-

[1] Cf. also k*sil, Prov. iii, 35, etc. ; he is stupid like the beasts
(ba'ar) Ps. xcii, 6 (Heb.7), cf. xlix, 10 (11) ; nabhubh, Job xi, 12.
It is significant that the simpleton (pethi) can become religiously
sensible if he comes under the influence of the Law : Ps. xix, 8
(7) ; cxix, 130. When on the other hand, as is more often the
case, such persons are described by words like " cunning ", that
is either to be understood as the language of controversy or
regarded as an example of primitive thinking.

ally used by Jeremiah (Jer. iv, 22 ; v, 21) and finds a place in Moses' exhortation (Deut. xxxii, 6). There may be a touch of pastoral sympathy with the "foolish people" in such utterances, but they completely fail to give proper expression to the idea of motive, which is the real characteristic of sin.

Sin's true nature is much more clearly recognised when the enlarged Decalogue (Exod. xx, 5 ; Deut. v, 9) designates offenders against the instructions of Yahwe as "those that hate me". Nothing could make it clearer that there is something finally inexplicable in sin, for the dynamic of hatred lies beyond human understanding. R*sha'im (wicked)[1] and leçim (scorners) too, seem to be full of hatred towards God, like many other kinds of godless men, whose designation is for the most part quite obscure as to etymology and meaning.[2] It can hardly be claimed that typical scholastic views of sin are conveyed by terms like to'ebhah (abomination), zimmah (device), 'awen (trouble), ḥamaṣ (violence), r*miyyah and mirmah (deceit), b*liyya'al,[3] hol*lim, etc.

The words just mentioned lack the peculiar pregnancy of terms like ḥeṭ', pesha', 'awon—that quality which has given them their place in the language of piety as simple metaphors, unencumbered with theological speculation. If this seems to mean that the complete and unmistakable idea of sin was a comparatively late growth on Israelite soil, such a

---

[1] The Book of the Covenant (cf. Exod. xxiii, 7) emphasises Yahwe's antipathy to the rasha', which may be the reply to his antipathy to Yahwe (cf. also Exod. ix, 27).

[2] Cf. esp. Mowinckel and Pedersen (see p. xi), and Marschall, op. cit., esp. 125.

[3] Cf. esp. Ps. xviii, 4 (5), where the reference is to a demon dwelling in Sheol. Similarly, at Gen. iv, 7, ḥaṭṭa'th represents a demonic being. Cf. H. Duhm, Die bösen Geister im A.T., 1904, 8 f.

conclusion can hardly invalidate our thesis.[1] It rather attests the full maturity of a form of religious expression, based on immovable categories, the validity of which no-one, at that stage of culture, was in a position to dispute. Nothing could show the simple man more simply and clearly why his heart was restless in the presence of the holy than the use of words which meant missing the mark, rebelling against the normal, or going astray and needing to find the right way again. By the employment of these pregnant terms conduct was judged, responsibility was fixed, and above all the demand of God's will was sternly recognised, so that they came to have the value of formulae, giving forceful expression to man's sense of creaturehood amid the trials of life. If the religion of Israel recognised the will of God as the supreme and universal law, then it must try to bring home to men the fact of their separation from God, and hostility towards him, by means of ideas which had binding force because they indicated the direction in which human life ought to move. Now this is exactly what we find : in *ḥaṭa'* as a verb of motion, or in *'iwwah*, in the thought of going astray, and in the legal implications of *pasha'*—all thoroughly typical of Hebrew idiom. No doubt it took many generations of theological thinking to work all this out, at least theoretically, and it cannot be denied that the whole development was closely bound up with the idea of the Covenant, which forms the basis of Israelite religion.[2] In both cases the feeling of fear is repressed by a sense of responsibility which

[1] The absence of the idea of sin from our earliest specimens of O.T. literature may be accidental, and has no evidential value.

[2] Cf. Dan. xi, 32 : *marshi'e b*e*rith* (who bring guilt upon the covenant), and Pedersen, op. cit., 415 : " The breach of the covenant is the kernel of sin ". [Cf. p. 2.]

increases with a growing apprehension of the greatness of God, and covers the whole of life when it surrenders all to him in the confession (Ps. li, 4) : " Against thee only have I sinned " (literally, " in relation to thee only have I missed the mark ").

This shows clearly how sin differs from other kinds of failure. In order to ascertain what sin really is, we must exclude all human opinion as to the meaning of what has happened. Whether man's judgment be severe or lenient, for the suppliant himself only the thought of God and what he has willed can reveal the true character of his failure. He is accountable to no judge but God himself. That is his " wisdom in the hidden part " (Ps. li, 6). He has broken God's rule : that is what he recognises as his sin. He has done what every sinner does, and his action constitutes sinful behaviour as such. To make that stand out sharply, he rounds off his confession with the almost blasphemously disarming words : " I sinned in order that thou mightest be just and clear ", representing as the sinner's aim what was actually the effect of his sinful action on his apprehension of God. He sees now—and this is the climax—how the objective fact of his sinning appears to serve the purpose of leading him to acknowledge the absoluteness of God's law. It may seem strange that he should put this into the form of a rather unhappy negative piece of flattery (the positive follows in the sixth verse) : " I sinned to the glory of God " ; but his assertion is very important from a theological point of view, for it represents a determined effort to find a place for human failure within the divine order, without giving up its religious characterisation as sin.

Hermann Gunkel [1] can hardly be right in suggesting

[1] H. Gunkel, Psalmen, 1926, 226, following B. Duhm. [Oesterley, The Psalms, 1939, 271, 274, seems to hold both views !]

that David could not say he had sinned against God
alone, when he has seduced a woman and arranged
the murder of her husband. No, David may have
committed a crime against Uriah, but it was only
in relation to God that this act of oriental despotism
was a sin. Ps. li, 4 gives no clue as to what the
Psalmist has actually done, and therefore cannot be
used to disprove the statement made in the title.
Unless this is ruled out for other reasons, it may well
be correct, so far as ver. 4 is concerned, for that deals
with the resulting religious situation and not with the
act itself. To weaken the close of the daring self-
accusation by connecting the second half of ver. 4
with ver. 3 [1] is a vague exegetical device which con-
vinces nobody, since it fails to take the author seriously,
and casts unnecessary doubt on a textual tradition
which there is no reason to suspect. Those who
" rejoice in the spiritual depth " [2] of this Psalmist
ought to ask themselves whether he really could have
expressed himself in such a confused way as is required by this hypothesis. The theory of an " ellip-
tical mode of expression " [3] is afraid to acknowledge
the blasphemy involved in the element of flattery ;
but this sort of manipulation of the passage remains
objectionable, even though it can point to precedents
in ancient Israel or the Jewish Church. If the writer
had meant this, he would have expressed himself
more clearly. The simplest explanation, and therefore surely the right one, is given by W. Staerk.[4]
How Paul understood the words under discussion is
shown by Rom. iii, 5a.

(d) The O.T. as a whole teaches that sin denotes

---

[1] Duhm and Gunkel.   [2] Gunkel, 225.
[3] R. Kittel, Psalmen, 1922, 190.
[4] W. Staerk, Schr. d. A.T., 1920, 231. [See also A. F.
Kirkpatrick, C.B., Psalms, 1902, 286, 289.]

abnormal behaviour, from the point of view of both law and theology. Although the words concerned are mainly used in a theological sense, the fact that they are also found in other connexions is highly significant. It should also be observed that the idea, rationally conceived, belongs much less to religion, the actual intercourse between God and man, than to theology, the theoretical elucidation of that intercourse. Such an idea is coined by the latter in an attempt to define, and so to interpret, a quite distinct religious situation, or a psychical event. In the nature of the case, therefore, the O.T. has to use a large variety of expressions for sin. These are best interpreted as formulae representing different theological views. They are efforts to exhibit religious phenomena, whose background lies beyond human understanding.

The resultant idea of sin, which justifies and necessitates the bringing together of all these terms, is certainly many-sided, but nevertheless has a real unity. This is indeed emphasised by the way in which the O.T. itself brings the words together—as poetical synonyms (Ps. xxxii, 5), or for impressiveness (Exod. xxxiv, 7),[1] or sometimes, whether intentionally or not, with the effect of bringing to the fore certain shades of meaning : e.g. Job xxxiv, 37 points to a gradation ("he adds *pesha'* to his *ḥaṭṭa'th* "), and at Lev. xvi, 21 (cf. ver. 16) the addition of the word *ḥaṭṭa'th* gives a special character to *'awen* and *pesha'*.[2] It is obvious that all variations mean fundamentally one and the same thing, viz., deviation from a prescribed norm, which is what the predominant root *ḥṭ'* means. The number

[1] Here also belong Ezek. xxi, 19, and Dan. ix, 24. On all these passages see L. Köhler, Z.A.W., 1928, 214.

[2] Hos. xii, 9, is less significant, since the punctuation is out of order.

of different roots available provides amply for the presentation of all sorts of views and judgments on the subject. Sometimes the emphasis is on the psychical aspect, sometimes on the sinful act itself, and sometimes on the resultant situation. But usually it is not the root itself, but the context, which brings out precisely the thought and feeling behind the words, and determines their religious significance, which is not always immediately obvious.

Careful examination of the relevant passages makes it possible to differentiate a whole series of stages, from simple objectivity to the unmistakable encounter with God. Even in the case of a religious utterance which seems to be almost entirely free from theology, the idea never completely loses its theoretical colouring, just because it remains an idea, and, as such, easily leads to a rational and juristic view of the subject ; and this, however valuable from an educational point of view, always tends to rob religious phenomena of the very variety indicated by the use of different terms. Those roots especially which connote deviation from a norm (*ḥṭ'*, *'wh*, *shghh*, *t'h*, etc.) have a pictorial quality which is hardly suitable for the religious situation to which they point. All they can do is to establish the fact that something is out of order. On the other hand, a root like *psh'* (rebel) gets much nearer to the real problem of the origin and meaning of sin as a religious phenomenon, because it leaves no doubt as to the sinner's dominant motive. But actually, even when one of the other terms is used, the irrational event to which it refers imparts to it something, more or less, of its own quality. This is seen, e.g. in prayers, where confession or lamentation takes the place of theological terminology. The story of the "Fall" is specially instructive, as the only extended treatment in the O.T. of

the religious problem of sin : here are none of the
regular technical terms, apart from the quite general
idea of evil ; the true nature of sin is shown in quite
a different way.

3. SIN AND GUILT

Before analysing the story of the " Fall " and stating
its theological import, we must look again at the fact
that a considerable number of the Hebrew words for
sin frequently seem to justify, or actually demand, the
English word " guilt " for their translation. This is
always the case when the writer is thinking, not of the
sinful action itself, but of the results of an irregularity,
the situation created by sin, or the underlying state
of mind. It is evident, from their promiscuous use
of terms, that the Hebrews attached little importance
to the distinction between sin and guilt, the causal
connexion being obvious between abnormal behaviour
and an abnormal situation.

There is only one root in Hebrew (*'shm*) which
expresses quite definitely the ideas of guiltiness and
guilt, and its use is almost confined to matters of
ritual law,[1] so that its quality is material and objective,
meaning uncleanness. Thus " guilt " does not necessarily involve sin in the sense of wilful rebellion against
God's ordinance. It is incurred unintentionally, by
mistake, and loses much of its force in the sphere of
casuistry (see p. 11). At the same time the consequences of such error are regarded almost as seriously
as those of other sins. Going wrong by mistake

[1] Gen. xxvi, 10, uses it in connexion with the marriage law :
guiltiness may be " brought upon " a man by inducing him to
commit adultery with the wife of a stranger ; so also at Judg.
xxi, 22. The law of property employs terms which are never
associated with the religious idea of guilt, e.g. *mashsha'*, *mashsheh*,
nᵉshi, *ḥobh*.

(*bish^eghaghah*), i.e. without premeditation—whether
through negligence (Lev. iv, 13, 22) or from some other
cause (Lev. iv, 2 ; v, 15, 18 ; Numb. xv, 22, etc.)
—incurs guilt just as much as premeditated crime,
committed " with an high hand " (Numb. xv, 30, cf.
the verbs in ver. 31). Even though a man be completely unaware of his error, he still becomes " un-
clean and guilty " (Lev. v, 2). The ritual for the
removal of guilt is the same as that for the restoration
of cleanness.[1]

This dynamistic circle of ideas does not provide
the background for those statements about guilt which
avoid the use of the technical term '*shm*. A favourite
expression is '*awon*, the meaning of which is perfectly
clear when it is said to be " borne " or " removed "
(the verb is *nasa*' in both cases).[2] Ps. xxxii, 1 f. is
specially instructive : " Blessed is he whose transgression is forgiven (*n^esuy pesha*'), whose sin is covered
(*k^esuy h^ata*'*ah*). Blessed is the man unto whom the
LORD imputeth not iniquity ('*awon*)." Here we have
the same triad as before (see p. 19), and the emphasis
on the element of guilt is unmistakable. The guilt
is " an heavy burden " (Ps. xxxviii, 4), which cannot
be borne. It is the accumulated guiltiness of a series
of sins. It is substantially identical with the suffering
that may torment a man, and shows itself through
this suffering. When Cain says, " My '*awon* is
greater than I can bear " (Gen. iv, 13), the Hebrew
word must be understood as meaning two things, as
it does in many Psalms of lamentation, viz., misfortune
inflicted as punishment, and a state of affairs contra-
dictory to God's standard. Suffering evokes a sense
of guilt, or is one with it. The theological and

[1] Cf. A. Bertholet, Das Dynamistische im A.T., 1926, 36 f.
[2] This is strangely overlooked by the LXX, which far too
often has ἀδικία (80 times), ἁμαρτία (69), or ἀνομία (64) for
'*awon*. Cf. p. 5, n. 1.

rational character of the idea of guilt in the O.T. is very clearly brought out by the way in which theories of atonement and retribution, starting from this identification, are worked out from a legal point of view. It was through the application of legal ideas to the relationship between God and sinners, in respect of righteousness divine and human, that the religious conception of guilt was developed from its numinous root. Its full effect upon the thinking of O.T. writers is therefore purposely discussed in connexion with those complexes.

4. THE STORY OF THE FALL (GENESIS III)

(*a*) The handling of the problem of sin in Gen. iii, in the setting of the Garden of Eden, is notably free from all theories with a legal tendency, and has no bearing on them. The Yahwist author makes fearless and masterly use of primeval mythological material,[1] to show with absolutely convincing simplicity, which a child could understand, how sin happens, what it is, and what it leads to. It is remarkable that in this myth of the so-called " Fall " the usual technical concepts are all lacking, with the exception of the term *ra'*, which is beset with difficulties. The reader is only aware that this is a story about sin.[2]

[1] For the analysis of motives see, in addition to commentaries, H. Gressmann in the Harnack Festgabe, 1921, 24 ff. ; R. Kittel, G.V.I., 1923, 220 f. ; J. Feldmann, Paradies und Sündenfall, 1913. [See J. Skinner, Genesis (1910), 90-97.]

[2] It is hardly correct to say that this view was first taken by the so-called Deuteronomists, as H. Schmidt does in Die Erzählung von Paradies und Sündenfall, 1931, 49 f. The Israelite author knew, as well as all his readers, that sin is the main point of the story. Cf. K. Budde, Die Biblische Urgeschichte, 1883, 72 : " It seems to me that, if the author were to ask the reader what spiritual power the story made him see, the answer could only be, sin." For a discussion of all the problems involved, see now also Budde's Die biblische Paradiesgeschichte, 1932.

The storyteller is giving an object-lesson by means of a typical scene from life itself, and therefore has to avoid unsuitable scholastic terms. He leaves theology to the reader who may be interested in it, merely hinting at the direction in which he himself thinks it would be fruitful. His main purpose is to concentrate attention solely upon what took place, the occurrence itself which provides the material for theorising. This is calculated to bring home the fact that our destiny as men is largely determined by that event. What is commonly called sin is for this reason presented as one of a series of happenings, all marked by tension ; which serves better than theorising to exhibit the disastrous living reality with which theology, cult and piety deal so lamely whenever they turn their attention to sin.

Apart from all conjectures—and a few generally accepted theories—concerning its provenance, the story presents the following fundamental ideas. Yahwe's will for men has been unambiguously expressed in a prohibition, the severity of which is heightened by the announcement of the dire results of disregarding it. At first it is not disputed, since God's authority is beyond dispute. It is only the clever serpent that is struck by the disproportionate gravity of the penalty, which is death, in view of the triviality of the offence. He introduces a discussion of the subject by asking the woman a question, ostensibly about the scope of the prohibition, to which a negative answer would be expected. Her naïve reply betrays no trace of scepticism, but opens the door to it, and gives the serpent the opportunity he wants for an audacious criticism of the prohibition. He regards the warning as mere bluff. According to him the whole business is intended to serve God's own interest and not that of man, who has to be frightened off from something which he could easily and safely appropriate by transgressing the prohibition. "Ye shall be as God, knowing good and evil." The woman, already intrigued by the beauty of the forbidden fruit, listens like a fool to the words about being clever, though she hardly understands them— and commits the act of disobedience. The man takes part in the misdeed without a word. He must have heard what the serpent said, since he was with the woman.

The first result of the act of disobedience is that the pair become aware of their nakedness and try to cover it ; the second, that they hide from Yahwe when he draws near ; the third, that the man, when cross-examined, first makes an evasive reply and then tries to explain his conduct ; the fourth, that all concerned fall under Yahwe's condemnation.

It is clear that, in this disastrous chain of consequences, the chief importance belongs to what happens in the spiritual sphere, as suggested by the enigmatic words about being as God and knowing good and evil. Adam and Eve are as God, in that they disregarded his prohibition. This is the immediate result of their being led to doubt, first, whether God's arrangement is in their interest, and, secondly, whether God's will for them is unconditionally binding. We shall not here pursue the point that the story seems to distribute these considerations unequally between the man and the woman. What matters is that it occurs to both of them that they have only to exercise their wills in order to infringe God's regulation. But this can only happen when the self-determining person reaches a positive, binding conviction, such as the serpent has helped to produce by his relentless exposure of obedient faith as mere stupidity. If sin is a breach of God's order, we have here the recognition and characterisation of its driving force. Practical reason, the power to make judgments and act on them, which exalts man to a divine sovereignty in the sphere of his own affairs—that is the germ of sinful behaviour. Reason is able to set aside all correctives, including that of religion, and to launch men upon courses of action which ignore the judgment of God. Nevertheless as a matter of fact, they stand under that judgment.

Beside this picture of bold self-assertion on the part of man, as he becomes conscious of the power of his will, stands the other, which shows how man's assertion of self against God creates a situation in which he dreads the divine scrutiny, how his will, instead of rejecting the call to render an account, collapses miserably, and finally the Godlike one is caught out like a naughty schoolboy, shuffling and sulky.

Adam and Eve are shown up with a rare sarcasm as "knowing good and evil". This phrase is in apposition to the words about being "as God"— the syntax is no doubt intentionally vague—and means the same thing, though what that is remains entirely uncertain, since both are sarcastic rather than didactic, intended to conceal rather than to reveal. The conjecture that the reference is to puberty seems to rely mainly on the fact that the first result of transgression is the "discovery" [Heb. "knowledge"] of nakedness, and not so much on the fact that "knowledge" is a sexual term [cf. Gen. iv, 1].[1] It is utterly impossible to drag the terms "good" and "evil" into the sexual sphere. It can hardly be suggested that they conveyed that sort of nuance to Hebrew ears; such a theory is not proved by Prov. xxxi, 12, or Deut. i, 39, and least of all by II Sam. xix, 35 (36). Accordingly, to entitle

---

[1] Gressmann, 46. Cf. E. König, Genesis ad loc.

the story, " Origin of physical love ", does not throw much light on the problem.[1] To say " delightful and painful " instead of " good and evil " smacks too much of sentimentality, and does not sound like the Yahwist writer ; it is more like a paraphrase suggested by Clara in Goethe's *Egmont*. When all is said, failing anything better, we may as well accept Wellhausen's robust interpretation of " good and evil " as what we generally call civilisation.[2]

The impression is irresistible that, though the Prometheus motif is unmistakable, it is finally reduced *ad absurdum* by being coupled with the picture of misery. The unsurpassable greatness of the story comes out in the treatment of the ambition to be as God : it is clearly recognised as a grotesque aberration, and yet not held up to contempt and ridicule, but appreciated with the sympathy of one who has himself passed through this humiliating experience. Man's tragic plight, as he struggles in his own strength to overcome his limitations, is so convincingly portrayed in the phrases, " Ye shall be as God " and " To be desired to make one wise ", that it stirs a longing in the breast of every man, from the simplest to the most mature, and presents him with an apology for sin that is alarmingly persuasive. In this way we are brought with the utmost precision to the religious heart of the problem of sin, which is beyond the reach of abstract thought, and consists in man's incontestable inherent right to defy and reject God. A psychological justification of sin is the only way of establishing its reality, and the Yahwist excels all other Biblical writers in the pregnant way in which he achieves this. Man's determination to be civilised, all the work of the creative mind, obeying its

[1] H. Schmidt, op. cit., 22.
[2] Prolegomena 305 ff. (Gesch. Isr. I, 1878, 344 ff.).

own inherent laws, yes, and the impudent insistence of the lusts of the flesh as well, trying to justify themselves theoretically, he grasps them all quite firmly and drags them into the pitiless light of the thought of God. Two worlds confront each other, and the reader can have no doubt that in every act of disobedience to God the same encounter takes place, with its unfathomable distress. Man ventures bravely with varying success, upon the quest of greatness, but in the end he has to seek a hiding-place from the eyes of God ; that is the path laid down for him by the possibilities of his nature. His likeness to God goes to pieces when God calls him.

(b) The story of the " Fall ", as it stands, affords a vista of man's life as a whole. Naturally it is not free from unevennesses and cultural colourings, since it is shot through with mythology. But a theological interpretation, such as that which we are attempting here, must be determined by the unity of the whole complex. As we have it, the tale is aetiological in form, but not obtrusively so, or to the detriment of its convincing force, e.g., in the curses pronounced upon serpent, woman and man, and the peculiar significance attached to nakedness. The common inescapable ills of every-day life are explained as the consequence of our first parents' misbehaviour. Here is the reason why the serpent is such a queer and repulsive creature, why child-bearing is so painful and dangerous, and why man has to sweat for his bread and return to dust at last.[1] But if Adam and Eve share in the common lot, and make themselves clothes like other people, the alleged reason cannot be some-

[1] When A. Menes, in Z.A.W. 1925, 39, suggests that the creation of woman may have been the result of a sin, i.e. an act of divine anger, he is simply indulging his love of hypothesis. J. Hempel seems to me to go too far when he speaks of the suggestion as " fairly certain ", in Zeitschr. syst. Th., 1931, 223.

thing entirely unique, but necessarily implies that what they did is what every human being is capable of doing and must do. Their experience is typical, in its suffering and its shame, and this becomes clearer to the reader the more he begins to understand that their attitude to God is, *mutatis mutandis*, that of every man. For the aetiology of the passage is not merely concerned with the interpretation of pain, labour and death as penalties inflicted by God, or with shame as the consequence of transgression, but also includes, as its most important theme, an interpretation of sin itself as the prime mover and cause of all man's restlessness and misery.[1]

The objections to this aetiological view, expressed by A. Weiser and supported by Gressmann, fail to do justice to the primitive realism of the story.[2] When we find the ground being cursed for man's sake— an indirect way of speaking of the curse on man himself—we ought not to boggle at the serpent eating dust, which I regard as a townsman's poetic fancy.

The covering of the naked body is also to be understood aetiologically. It suggests that the feeling of helpless perplexity and uncertainty produced by sin is as typical as the sense of shame evoked by nakedness. The statement that " they saw that they were naked " is the story-teller's way of establishing the fact that the guilty pair suddenly felt themselves at a loss. He thinks he can best do this by means of the sense of shame, by raising the question as to its origin and incidentally giving it to be understood that it is a result of sin, something dangerously close to evil, though not identical with it. Without sin, husband and wife would have had nothing to conceal

---

[1] This is not the view of M. Weber, Ges. Aufsätze zur Religionssoziologie, 1921, 242.

[2] A. Weiser, Religion u. Sittlichkeit in d. Genesis, 1928, 36 f.

from each other. Their failure has cost them their
simplicity. It is of course true that this line of argument is bound up with a particular cultural view of
nakedness, viz. that of Israel and the Jews, who had
" a holy horror of stripping the body bare ".[1] This,
however, cannot weaken the impression that the
writer definitely intends to draw attention to something which he considers to be of universal validity,
and that in conclusion he actually touches upon a
problem posed by nature and common to all types
of culture, i.e. the sexual question in its broadest
sense.

(c) The aetiological interpretation of the myth of
the " Fall " undoubtedly justifies our basing upon it
a theory of " original sin " in the sense of man's
universal sinfulness.[2] In any case such a theological
deduction would not run counter to the sense of the
myth. Moreover, when the writer attributes the Fall
to man's passionate longing, shown in a thousand
ways, to get knowledge and be clever, he reveals a
very lively apprehension of the fact that all normal
men in every age, not only fall into the same tempta-
tion, but also act in the same way. He knows that if
the intellect is not under control, it fights against
religion, and sin finds a footing in the freedom of will
and thought. As all men have their share of intellect,
with its fatal possibilities, so all are partners in the
incriminating deed, all caught in the web of universal misery.

The story-teller assigns the part of reckless ques-
tioner to the dramatic figure of the serpent, and thus
purposely emphasises the demonic nature of the

---

[1] " Eine ganz und gar rituelle Angst vor der rein physischen
Entblössung " (Weber, op. cit., 205, cf. 234, 245).
[2] Such as is expressed by the same writer at the beginning
and end of his version of the Flood story : Gen. vi, 5 ; viii, 21.

scepticism that bursts all bonds in its fanatical pursuit of knowledge. He does this in order to stress the unfathomable dualism that is characteristic of all sinful behaviour. The sinner, he would say, falls under a sort of external power, to which he has to submit, against his better judgment, won over by the confidence with which it encourages his self-reliance. The serpent myth is not made to serve any further purpose in Gen. iii. The writer simply uses its hidden dualism in order to set forth the analysis of a very subtle psychical proceeding. The fable is abandoned as soon as it has made its contribution to the presentation of a comprehensible picture of the woman's novel procedure. The reader now has a sympathetic understanding of the way in which physical and spiritual self-reliance are reinforced by callous doubt, personified reason's mighty product, and is not surprised when a sudden impulse overrides uncritical obedience.

No argument from experience can effectively question this account of the way in which one thing leads to another ; it produces an overwhelming impression that man's deviation from God's prescribed norm, in will and deed, is the inevitable outcome of his very nature ; and this demands the recognition, by every type of theology, of the universality of the phenomenon presented in this saga. Undeterred by divine authority, man is determined, and up to a point is able, to gain knowledge, to discover and anticipate God's thoughts ; and this leads to a painful tension between man and God, creating an atmosphere of mistrust, in which man sees the tempting possibility of abandoning his proper attitude as a creature, of criticising his maker, and of thinking and behaving " as God ", free from control and responsible only to himself. Born with reason and the ability to pass judgment upon the world and God, he has the motive for sin, and it is bound to become operative sooner or later, like the rest of his nature.

The more this interpretation is urged from a theological point of view, the more it must be remembered that its starting-point is the realisation that the Yahwist author is not writing a theological treatise, but popularising a fundamental theological idea. He betrays no tendency other than the aetiological, as here set forth. His story, so natural and unscholastic, is rather the expression of a deep and true piety than of a theology. The relentless pursuit of truth makes it unforgettable. Hardly anywhere else in the O.T. do we find a religious question discussed with such a combination of penetration and piety. The way in which the proposition is set forth, that to be human is to be a sinner, betokens, not the spinning of a theory, but the testimony of one who knows the bitterness of inner conflict and is trying to convey to his reader, by means of a very simple story, the momentous nature of the inescapable urge towards self-knowledge. Why then, has it been left to man to decide for or against God? To this final question, though it is fully in line with the insight of such a keen observer, our author gives no answer. In this silence lies his religion.

II. THE DOCTRINE OF SIN
IN THE SEPTUAGINT [1]

THEOLOGICALLY important renderings in the LXX are partly due to misunderstanding and the difficulty of the Hebrew, but partly also to the intention of the translator. In Ps. cxxix (cxxviii), 3, "plowers" (*hor^eshim*) is changed to "wicked" (*har^esha'im*) under the influence of the following verse ; and "furrows" (*ma'^anoth*) to "iniquity" (ἀνομία),[2] as frequently in the LXX, abandoning the metaphor. Another case of the latter is found at Deut. xxix, 19 (18), where the Hebrew says, "to sweep away the moist with the dry". The other Greek versions retain this, but the LXX gives the meaning of the metaphor : "that the sinner may not involve the guiltless in ruin with himself". Similarly, in Ps. cxli (cxl), 5, for Heb. "oil upon the head let not my head refuse", LXX has "let not the oil of a sinner anoint my head " (changing *ro'sh* to *rasha'*), and thus turns it into a warning against fellowship with sinners.[3]

Presumptuousness is a frequent characteristic of the sinner in the LXX. Thus ἁμαρτωλός is the rendering of *zedh* (presumptuous) at Ecclus. xi, 9, and *zadhon* at xv, 7, giving a religious turn to what is secular in the Hebrew (cf. Ps. i, 1). R. Smend's emendation

[1] For a general survey of LXX usage, see pp. 1 ff., 47 f. Here we are concerned with the theology of the Greek O.T. with respect to sin.

[2] Perhaps regarding the Hebrew as a derivative of *'anah* Pi'el (oppress) ?

[3] So A. Bertholet in Kautzsch II, 1923, 269 ; Gunkel emends Heb. after LXX.

of Ecclus. iii, 27 (*mithholel* for *mithḥolel*) would involve the same idea of sin,[1] which also appears at Ecclus. v, 4 f. (cf. x, 12 f.). See also Ecclus. xxxii, 12, where the LXX ("sin not by proud speech ") does not correspond to the Hebrew ("in the fear of God and not without understanding ").[2] The tendency towards uniformity shows itself when ἁμαρτωλός is used for "Belial " (Ecclus. xi, 32), "men of violence " (xv, 12), "injustice " (xvi, 13), and ὁδὸς ἁμαρτίας for "stumbling-block " (xlvii, 23).

Wealth and power are commonly regarded in O.T. and N.T. as marks of a sinner (cf. Eccles. ii, 26 ; Prov. xxiii, 17). This forces its way into Hab. iii, 14, where *ro'sh p⁾razaw* is translated into τοὺς ἀρχηγοὺς τῶν ἁμαρτωλῶν [LXX, 23, 62, 86, 147].

Sin is disease. This familiar O.T. idea leads to the rendering of *hᵒli* by ἁμαρτία in Is. liii, 4, which is thus made to anticipate ver. 12. The remarkable rendering of Symmachus seems to be based on the N.T. programme of Messianic suffering, which is drawn from the LXX : ὄντως τὰς ἁμαρτίας ἡμῶν αὐτὸς ἀνέλαβε καὶ τοὺς πόνους ὑπέμεινεν, ἡμεῖς δὲ ἐλογισάμεθα αὐτὸν ἐν ἀφῇ ὄντα, πεπληγότα ὑπὸ θεοῦ καὶ τεταπεινωμένον. According to Procopius of Gaza, Aquila and Theodotion had the same reading. The equation of sin with disease leads naturally to the healing of sin at Deut. xxx, 3 (" Yahwe, thy God, will turn thy fortune ") : whereas Aquila translates literally, and Symmachus drags in a reference to the history of redemption [as A.V. and R.V.],[3] the LXX quite independently, from the point of view of its special interest in sin, introduces the idea of forgive-

---

[1] Die Weisheit des Jesus Sirach erklärt, 1906, 32.

[2] Smend, 290 f.

[3] So Theod., but without σοι ; Aq., Sym. and Theod. are re-translated by Field after Masius.

ness : "the Lord will heal thy sins" (ἰάσεται κύριος
τὰς ἁμαρτίας σου). Aquila and the LXX here derive
sh^ebhuth from shubh (so also Symmachus at Jer. xxxiii,
26), while Symmachus and Theodotion think of
shabhah as the LXX usually does. The LXX's
negative understanding of sh^ebhuth is important for
the development of the idea of sin. The same thing
occurs at Ezek. xvi, 53, where the rendering is
ἀποστροφή (" apostasy "). This last word represents
m^eshubhah four times in Jer. (v, 6 ; viii, 5 ; at vi, 19,
and xviii, 12, misread for maḥsh^ebhoth). The context
at Jer. xiv, 7 justifies ἁμαρτία for m^eshubhah. The LXX
thus frequently takes sh^ebhuth and m^eshubhah in the
negative sense of apostasy, which, according to Deut.
xxx, 3 and Jer. xiv, 7 is the fundamental sin, for which
redemption and healing are expected and prayed for
above all else. More frequently, however, the LXX
seems to avoid translating the formula, shubh sh^ebhuth.
This happens at Job xlii, 10, partly perhaps because
attention is directed less to the restoration of Job's
former wealth than to the friends' sin in bringing
false charges against him (ver. 8 : κατά ; cf. Ps. cix
(cviii), 6 and see p. 37). The LXX is here emphasising the forgiveness of sin, which is only hinted at in
the Hebrew. [See note on p. 38.]

Anthropomorphism finds expression in the Hebrew of
Job xlii, 7 (" my wrath is kindled against thee "),
but the LXX avoids this (ἥμαρτες σύ), as it does by
its paraphrase in ver. 9, and by its addition at the
end of ver. 10. (Ἔλυσεν τὴν ἁμαρτίαν in ver. 9 could
be justified by fact that nasa' is a technical term for the
forgiveness of sin. Cf. Is. i, 14 for another example.) [1]
Similarly, at Numb. i, 53, ἁμάρτημα stands for " wrath "

---

[1] Aq. and Sym., followed by Jerome in the Vulg., had a
literal translation. Cf. also the LXX addition, τὰς ἁμαρτίας
ὑμῶν, at Is. lv, 7.

(*qeçeph*). Instead of speaking theologically (Rom. i, 18), but still anthropomorphically—of the wrath of God which the community might incur, the LXX speaks psychologically of the sin which it should avoid. According to the Syro-Hexaplar, Symmachus has ὀργή and Theodotion θυμός, translating literally. The same kind of change is seen at Is. lvii, 17, where *qaçaphti* becomes ἐλύπησα αὐτόν. As a punishment for sin, God sends "sorrow unto repentance" (II Cor. vii, 9 f.). It is interesting to compare this with I Esdr. vi, 15 (14), where the Greek avoids the attribution of the emotion of anger to God (παραπικραίνω without object is intransitive), and introduces the word "sin", although II Esdr. v, 12, follows the Aramaic of Ezra [see R.V.m. on Ezra iv, 8].

Idolatry. The verb *ma'al* ("act unfaithfully") becomes ἁμαρτάνειν at II Chron. xii, 2, and ἀφίστημι at 7, the latter in accordance with the Chronicler's view of the sin of apostasy (cf. Judg. x, 10). I Esd. viii, 89, also has ἁμαρτάνειν for *ma'al*, though the corresponding passage, II Esdr. x, 2, has ἀσυνθετεῖν, which occurs six times for *ma'al*, meaning breach of the covenant with God (cf. ver. 3). The same thought is expressed at Nahum iii, 6, where for Heb. "and make thee vile" LXX has κατὰ τὰς ἁμαρτίας σου, connecting it with the word *nabhluth*. B here reads ἀκαθαρσίας, which is LXX for *nabhluth* at Hos. ii, 12 (the only place where it occurs), and is a technical term in the LXX for the sin of idolatry; in Prov. it is used more in a psychological and ethical sense to translate *to'ebhah*, a cultic term commonly applied to idols. A's reading of ἁμαρτία for *to'ebhah* at Ezek. viii, 6, and xvi, 51, is preferable to B's conventional ἀνομία. In both cases the sin of idolatry is meant —deserting Yahwe to play the harlot (Ezek. xvi, 41 ff.). The Hebrew root *tame'*, generally translated ἀκαθαρσία

or μιαίνειν, means cultic uncleanness. LXX at Lev.
xiv, 19, which speaks of the uncleanness of a leper,
purposely substitutes the moral and religious idea of
sin for the cultic.[1]

That *folly is sin* and wisdom piety, is a familiar
thought in the O.T. Perhaps that explains the use
of both ἁμαρτία and κακία for the Hebrew 'iwweleth
at Prov. xxvi, 11 ; it often indicates culpable ignorance of God, and so godlessness. The Wisdom literature and the Law generally teach that lack of knowledge means sin ; e.g. Prov. xxiv, 9 : Aquila and
Theodotion follow the Hebrew, but LXX has ἀπο-
θνῄσκει δε ἄφρων ἐν ἁμαρτίαις. (reading *zimmath* as
muth, as it does with *zimmoth* in ver. 8).

Whether purposely or by mistake, LXX (B) puts
ἁμάρτημα for *pegha'* at I Kings v, 4 (Heb. 18), and
ἁμαρτάνειν for *p'gho'* at I Sam. xxii, 17 (AB) for
ἀπάντημα and ἀπαντᾶν ; in the former case the sin is
something which hinders the holy work of building
the Temple, as at I Chron. xxii, 8. LXX also introduces the idea of sin at Is. lxvi, 4, indicating the
reason for punishment (" I will requite their sins "),
whereas the Hebrew only mentions the punishment
(" I will bring their fears upon them "). Here again
the sin is idolatrous apostasy. Similarly at Is. xxiv, 6,
LXX has " because its inhabitants have sinned "
instead of Hebrew " are found guilty ".

A deeper sense of sin is reached by the LXX in Ps.
cxl, 8 (cxxxix, 9), when it turns " Grant not the
desire of the wicked " (cf. Symmachus) into " Deliver
me not up to the sinner through my own lust ".
Cf. Ps. cix (cviii), 6, where ἁμαρτωλός and διάβολος
have a metaphysical reference, not in the Hebrew,
comparable with II Thess. ii, 3. A spiritual emphasis

[1] Cf. the relation of sickness to sin in the N.T. : Mark ii, 5 ;
John v, 14 ; viii, 11.

is seen at Ezek. xxiii, 49, where "thoughts" is substituted for "idols". According to Jer. l (xxvii), 7, the enemies of the Jews excuse themselves on the ground that the Jews have sinned ; LXX μὴ ἀνῶμεν αὐτούς ἀνθ'ὧν ἥμαρτον suggests, on the contrary, that they are carrying out the will of God. "Are the consolations of God too small for thee ? " says Eliphaz at Job xv, 11 ; LXX changes this to "Thou hast received but little chastisement for thy sins", introducing the idea of suffering as education, so dear to Hellenistic Judaism. This implies a very strong sense of sin, necessitating confession. Thus, e.g., at Ecclus. iv, 26, LXX departs from Heb. "turn from sin", and says "confess thy sins".[1] Correspondingly, the hope of divine grace finds expression : where the destruction of heathen altars is called the full fruit of the putting away of sin (Is. xxvii, 9), LXX says, "This is his blessedness, when I remove his sin".

LXX thus presents a consistent linguistic usage, which points to a principle of unity in its doctrine. Instead of splitting up human sinfulness into all sorts of separate sins, after the manner of late Judaism, it shows a tendency to go to the root of the matter, to that fundamental sin which separates man from God and is indomitable (Ecclus. xxi, 2 ; xxvii, 10) until he lets God save him.

[*Note.*—In a communication of 14. 2. 1950 Dr. Bertram says that in his first draft he drew attention to LXX omission of verses applying the promise of *shubh sh^e bhuth* to Gentiles at Jer. xlviii, 47 ; xlix, 6, comparing this with LXX removal of the universalistic tone from Isaiah xix, 25.]

[1] [But see Oesterley, C.B., *ad loc.*]

III. THE JEWISH IDEA OF SIN [1]

1. THE *Law* determines the conception of sin in Judaism. Since all its provisions reveal the will of God, including what we call civil and criminal law, every kind of transgression is sin, and falls within the sphere of religion, as rebellion against God, along with specifically religious offences and cases of ceremonial carelessness. [2]

Taking over the O.T. idea that the constitutive element in sin is offence against God, Judaism shows two opposing tendencies. On the one hand scribal casuistry regards all breaches of the Law, however trivial, as sin ; [3] and on the other hand an effort is made to maintain the O.T. differentiation between "sinning with a high hand" and sinning through ignorance. On the basis of Lev. xvi, 21, three kinds of sin are named at Sifra Lev. xvi, 6 : unashamed misdeeds (*ªwonoth*) ; acts of rebellion (*pish'eyhem*) ; unwitting offences (*ḥaṭṭ'otham* : cf. Tos. Yoma 2, 1 ; Bab. Yoma 36*b*). [4] Knowledge of the Law is here the criterion. Bab. Baba Metzia 33*b* says that, at Is. lviii, 1, "my people" means those familiar with

---

[1] Cf. G. F. Moore, Judaism I, 461. Tos. Shebuoth, iii, 6.

[2] The juristic idea of crime or transgression is not yet separated from the religious idea of sin. This separation is only tentative in later Judaism, the reason for this being that the O.T. is the very Word of God in its legislation as well as in its religious authority.

[3] E.g. Shab. xii, 3 ff. : "He who writes two letters (on the Sabbath), . . . is guilty ; he who writes on his body is guilty. If one writes with a liquid other than ink, or on any thing which does not preserve the writing, he is free" ; cf. Schürer II, 471 ff. ; Shebuoth i, 2-ii, 5.   [4] Cf. Moore I, 464.

the Law, " whose unconscious mistakes are equivalent
to deliberate sins ", and " the house of Jacob " the
unlearned masses, " whose deliberate sins are equivalent to unconscious mistakes ".[1] The tendency to
differentiate leads, as in O.T., to the singling out of
the deadly sins : idolatry, unchastity, bloodshed.
These must never be committed.[2] The worst of all
sins is idolatry (*ªbhodhah zarah*). " It is the very
essence of rebellion, violating not only the first commandment of the Decalogue—Thou shalt have no
other Gods before me—but the fundamental principle
of the divine unity, the profession of faith solemnly
pronounced by the Jew every time he repeated the
Shemaʿ." [3] To commit idolatry means to commit all
sins (Sifre Numb. 111 on xv, 22). Other sins can
be atoned for by [4] purification rites, good works,[5] or
sufferings,[6] but death [7] is the only atonement for the
deadly sins (Bab. Sanh. 74a).

2. Viewing sin from the standpoint of the Law,
Judaism tended to dissociate it from the community
and to fix the burden of it upon the individual. This
tendency begins in Ezekiel with the rejection of the
idea that guilt can be passed on from father to son—
as expressed in the proverb about fathers eating sour

[1] Cf. also Bab. Taanith 11a.

[2] Cf. the discussion of the Rabbis in conference at Lydda
during the persecution of Hadrian, and the decision that life
must not be purchased at the price of committing one of these
sins (Jer. Sanh. 21b ; Bab. Sanh. 74 ; Moore, I, 467). Cf.
also the apostolic decree, Acts xv, 29, and the discussion.

[3] Moore, I, 466.   [4] Cf. Moore, I, 497 ff.

[5] Cf. A. Schlatter, Jochanan ben Zakkai, 1899, 39 ff., esp. 41 :
" Trusting that the gift would earn forgiveness as its reward ".

[6] Cf. W. Wichmann, Die Leidenstheologie, 1930.

[7] See p. 39, n. 2. When a man is condemned to death under
the Jewish law, i.e. under the Torah, that is not only punishment
for the crime which he has committed—idolatry, bloodshed,
unchastity, etc.—but also atonement for his sin.

grapes and their sons' teeth being set on edge—and
the assertion of the fundamental principle : "The
soul that sinneth, it shall die" (Ezek. xviii, 2-4).
Sin is the actual transgression of the Law by the
individual, for whom it has consequences in this
world and in the world to come. The Law, the
theory of rewards and punishments, and the idea of
sin, form an indissoluble unity. This abolition of the
connexion between the sins of fathers and the fate of
their sons finds expression at two places in the Targum,
where the words of the second Commandment,
"visiting the sins of the fathers upon the children,
upon the third and upon the fourth generation",
are changed into "inflicting punishment for the guilt
of wicked fathers upon their disobedient children"
(Exod. xx, 5), and—still more clearly ". . . when
the children follow after their fathers in sinning"
(Deut. v, 9).[1] Yet the idea of universal responsibility for sin is not quite dead. This comes out in
the parable which likens the sinner to a man boring
a hole in a boat at sea. When asked what he was
doing, he replied to his fellow-passengers, "What has
that to do with you ? May I not bore under myself ?"
Their answer was, "It is our business : the water is
pouring in, and we shall all be drowned" (Lev.
Rabba 4 on iv, 1).[2]

Generally speaking, Judaism takes the view that
sin is universal.[3] "All that are born are defiled with
iniquities, and are full of sins and laden with offences :
and if after death we were not to come into judgment,
peradventure it had been better for us" (II Esdr.
vii, 68 R.V.) ; "We that have received the Law
shall perish by sin, and our heart also which received

[1] L. Baeck in R.G.G.[2], V, 883.
[2] Cf. Moore, I, 471.
[3] Cf. Weber, 233 f. ; Str.-Bill. III, 155 ff.

it " (ix, 36). Cf. Exod. Rabba 31 (beginning) on
xxii, 24 ; Lev. Rabba 14 on xii, 2 (on Ps. li, 7) :
" Even in the most pious there must be a trace of
guilt somewhere " ; Philo, Vit. Mos. II, 147 : " sin
is innate in every man " ; Philo, De fug. et inv., 158.
The heathen also fall under this judgment as sinners
before God from the religious point of view, for,
according to Jewish theory, they have the commandments of Adam and Noah concerning robbery, unchastity, idolatry, blasphemy and bloodshed (Sifra Lev.
xviii, 4), and refused the Torah when it was offered
to them. Rabbi Jochanan said, " The meaning of
Deut. xxxiii, 2 and Hab. iii, 3 is that God passed the
Law round among all the nations and tongues, but
none accepted it until he came to Israel ; she accepted it " (Bab. Ab. Zar. 2b).[1] Therefore they are
not guiltless in their sin.

The doctrine of universal guilt was, however, not
carried quite as far as the above statement might seem
to suggest. A few exceptions are allowed at II Esdr.
vii, 48 R.V. Men of outstanding godliness, like
Abraham, Moses or Elijah, are accounted sinless
(Test. Zeb., 1 ; Jos. Ant. vii, 153 ; Pesiqta 76a ed.
Buber).[2] The possibility of sinlessness rests on the
freedom of the individual will and the gift of the Law.
A clean life is made possible by observing the Law.
" God said to the Israelites, My children, I have
created in you the evil inclination ; I have also
created for you the Law as a means of salvation ; so
long as you occupy yourselves with the latter, the
former will have no power over you " (Sifre Deut. 45
on xi, 18). These ideas form the background of
Paul's assertion, " As touching the righteousness

---

[1] Cf. Str.-Bill. III, 38-43. See II Esdr. vii, 20-24 [and
Ecclus. xxiv, 5-8].

[2] Weber, 53 ff., 224.

which is in the Law, found blameless " (Phil. iii, 6).[1]
If sinlessness is attributed to certain godly men, being
made possible by observance of the Law, it follows
that it will be predicated of the Messiah. Already of
the Servant of the Lord it had been said, " He had
done no violence, neither was any deceit in his mouth "
(Is. liii, 9). Ps. Sol. xvii, 41 says of the Messiah,
" He shall be free from sin ", and Test. Jud. ii, 4(A),
" No sin shall be found in him " (cf. Test. Lev. xviii,
9). Along with this goes the Jewish eschatological
expectation that sin will be removed and men will be
sinless in the Messianic Kingdom (cf. En. v, 8 f. ;
Ps. Sol. xvii, 32 ; Test. Lev. xviii).

3. The origin and the consequences of sin likewise
receive attention in post-Biblical Judaism. The question of origin receives a historical answer ; sin derives
from Adam (and Eve) and has extended its power
over the whole of mankind : " The first Adam bearing
a wicked heart transgressed and was overcome ; and
not he only, but all they also that are born of him.
Thus disease was made permanent ; and the Law was
in the heart of the people along with the wickedness
of the root ; so the good departed away, and that
which was wicked abode still " (II Esdr. iii, 21 f.).
Cf. Ecclus. xxv, 24 ; II Esdr. iii, 26 ; vii, 48 ff.,
esp. 118 ; Syr. Bar. xlviii, 42, where sin is derived
from Eve ; and esp. Syr. Bar. liv, 15 : " Though
Adam first sinned, and brought untimely death upon
all, yet of those who were born from him each one
of them hath prepared for his own soul torment to
come ".[2] Sin is here seen, as throughout the N.T.,

[1] See Aboth R. Nathan, 59, where it is said of Jochanan's
son, " He departed this life without sin ". Cf. A. Schlatter,
Jochanan b. Zakkai, 1899, 20 f.

[2] Cf. Tanchuma, Bereschith, 29, Hukkat, 39, ed. S. Buber,
for a clear expression of vexation with Adam for the trouble
he has caused by his sin.

as a power controlling this world at the deepest level. A different account of sin's origin is found in En. x, 4 ff. ; lxiv, 1 ff. ; Mart. Is. v, 3, where it is traced to the fallen angels of Gen. vi. 1 ff. A more philosophical treatment of the question asserts that the root of man's sin is the evil inclination which God has implanted in him : Ecclus. xv, 14 ; xxxvii, 3 ; II Esdr. iii, 20 ; iv, 4 ; vii, 48 (*cor malignum*) ;[1] Pesiqta 38b-39a ed. Buber ; Vit. Ad. 19 (ἐπιθυμία . . . ἐστὶ κεφαλὴ πάσης ἁμαρτίας).

It is the evil inclination that entices man to sin. Man's task is to overcome this by observing the Law. If he fails, he has to bear the consequences of sin, which consist of all kinds of suffering. Paul's theme in Rom. i, 18 ff.—God punishes sin with sinning— is familiar to Judaism in the form, " sin begets sin " ; Ps. Sol. iii, 12 says, " the sinner will add sin to sins ". One sin, whatever it may be, leads on to another, until the deadly sin is reached : " To-day the evil inclination says, Do this, and to-morrow, Do that ; until at last it says, Worship other gods, and he goes and does it " (Bab. Shab. 105b ; cf. Ab. iv, 2 ; Sifre Numb. 112 on xv, 30). Sin also causes separation from God. The worship of the golden calf made it impossible for the Israelites to see the glory of God.[2] Sin rules out intimate intercourse with God, face to face (cf. Exod. xxxiii, 11-23).[3] God's gracious pur-

[1] Moore, I, 479 ff. ; Weber, 221 f., 225 ff. ; F. C. Porter, The Yeçer Hara, Yale Bibl. & Sem. Studies, 1902, 93-156 ; A. Büchler, Studies in Sin and Atonement in the Rabb. Lit. of the first century, 1928 ; K. Stier, Paulus üb. d. Sünde u. d. Judentum s. Zeit, Prot. Mon. II, 1907, 104 ; Bousset-Gressmann, 402 ff.

[2] Cf. the exposition of Exod. xxiv, 17 and xxxiv, 30 by Simeon b. Jochai in Sif. Numb. 1 on v, 3.

[3] Gen. iii, 8 ; Exod. xxxiv, 30 ; II Sam. xvii, 2 ; Song iii, 7 f. ; I Sam. xxviii, 5 ; cf. Pesiqta 44b-45a (ed. Buber) and —with a difference—Rom. iii, 23.

pose for man is thwarted again and again by sin. This is illustrated by stories of Israel in the wilderness (Sifre Deut. 319 ; Pesiqta 166*a-b*, Buber).

Sin is followed by punishment. The connexion between the two is close (Ps. Sol. ii, 17 ; Philo Leg. All. I, 35 ; Vit. Mos. I, 96 ; Sacr. A.C. 131). Sickness is a punishment for sin, and it is a· recognised formula that no man can recover from sickness until one (i.e. God) forgives all his sins (Bab. Ned. 41*a*). Finally, sin is punished with death and eternal damnation : " No death without sin and no chastisement without guilt " (Bab. Shab. 51*a* ; cf. Ecclus. xxv, 24 ; Wis. i, 13 ; ii, 23 f. ; Ap. Bar. xxiii, 4 ; II Esdr. iii, 7 ; Sifre Deut. 305 on xxxi, 14 ; Gen. Rabba xvi, 6, near the end, where death is brought into relation with the Fall) ; " the sinner's destruction for ever " (Ps. Sol. iii, 13).

Nevertheless it is possible for man to repent and return to God. This is stated with special lucidity in the Targum of Eccles. vii, 20, where the categorical declaration that " there is none righteous upon earth, doing good and free from sin ", is followed by the words, " but God shows guilty man the way of conversion before he dies ".[1]

[1] See p. 41, n. 1. With the thought of conversion a new tendency takes its place beside the dominant tendency to identify crime and sin, punishment and atonement, viz., the purely religious idea of sin as something which cannot be removed by legal punishment—only a right relationship with God can take it away (through penitence, good works, suffering, death, or punishment by God in the world to come).

IV. GREEK USAGE

1. ἁμαρτάνειν means to fail, miss, mistake ; its synonym is ἀποτυγχάνειν (Suid.), its opposite τυγχάνειν (cf. Hom. Il., V, 287 ; Herod I, 43). From Homer onwards it is used in a concrete sense (Suid. ἄσκοπα τοξεύειν) : Plato, Hip. Min. 375a, τοῦ σκοποῦ; Aristoph. Plut. 961, τῆς ὁδοῦ. After Herodotus it also has a transferred sense, esp. of intellectual failure : Thuc. I, xxxiii, 3 ; Philo, Omn. Prob. Lib. 133 ; hence also absolutely, of being mistaken : Dio Chrys. Or. liii, 3. The contrast to the ἁμαρτάνων is the σοφός ; the ἁμαρτίνοος is the insane : Hes. Theog. 511. But already in Homer it indicates making a mistake : Hom. Od. xxii, 154 ; Xenoph. Cyrop. V, iv, 19, τὸ γὰρ ἁμαρτάνειν ἀνθρώπους ὄντας οὐδὲν θαυμαστόν (errare humanum est). The connotation of wrong-doing in the moral sense also begins to be found : Hom. Il. IX, 501 ; Od. xiii, 214.

The LXX uses ἁμαρτάνειν occasionally for pasha', 'asham, rasha' Hiph., but mostly literally for ḥaṭa', the meaning of which developed from that of missing the way, literally and metaphorically, until it reached the connotation of going wrong morally, i.e. the dominant religious sense of sin. It was through its use for ḥeṭ' in the LXX that ἁμαρτία acquired its definitely religious content (see pp. 1 ff., 33 ff.).

2. ἁμάρτημα as a verbal noun ending in -μα denotes the occurrence of ἁμαρτάνειν, i.e. failure or blunder, suggesting foolishness or delusion rather than wickedness : Soph Ant. 1261. Aristotle defines ἁμάρτημα (Eth. Nic. V, 10, p. 1135b 18 ; Rhet. I, 13, p. 1374b 5) as coming between ἀδίκημα and ἀτύχημα : it is not

unexpected, but is done without malice. In common parlance, and specially in its legal use, ἁμάρτημα more and more indicates intentional, culpable wrong-doing : Tebtunis Pap. v, 3 ; Antiph. i, 27 : ἑκούσια καὶ ἐκ προνοίας ἀδικήματα καὶ ἁμαρτήματα. In the LXX ἁμάρτημα represents mainly ḥaṭṭa'th, sometimes 'awon, pesha', resha'. It occurs with special frequency in Wis. (ii, 12 ; iv, 20, etc.), always with the moral and religious connotation of a sinful action. It is coupled with ἀδίκημα (Gen. xxxi, 36) ; ἀδικία (Deut. xix, 15 ; Jer. xiv, 20) ; ἀσέβημα (Deut. ix, 27) ; ἀνόμημα (Josh. xxiv, 19) ; ἀνομία (Is. lviii, 1). Further, at Is. xl, 2 it means punishment for sin. In secular Greek it is used more frequently than ἁμαρτία, but in Biblical usage the latter far surpasses it, both in frequency and in importance.

The N.T. seldom uses ἁμάρτημα to denote a sinful action : Mark iii, 28 f. ; iv, 12 Rec. ; Rom. iii, 25 ; v, 16 DG It. Pesh. (Sin. B : ἁμαρτήσαντος) ; I Cor. vi, 18 ; II Pet. i, 9.

ἁμαρτία, used from the time of Aeschylus in the metaphorical sense, like ἁμάρτημα, is often distinguished from the latter as the quality of an action is distinguished from the action itself (Clem. Al. Strom. II, xv, 64, 3).[2] But the distinction early tends to vanish, since the fact of sin can only be recognised in the sinful act. Already in Aeschylus ἁμαρτία means wickedness (Ag, 1197 : παλαιὰς τῶνδ' ἁμαρτίας δομῶν). This word has nothing to do with the question of guilt in the modern sense (cf. ἁμάρτημα, p. 46), and often denotes a punishable offence committed with a good motive, e.g. Soph. Phil. 1225 ; Trach.

---

[1] Cf. R. Taubenschlag, Das Strafrecht im Rechte d. Papyri, 1916, 8 ; L. Wenger, Archiv f. Pap.-forsch., 1902, 483 ; Hey, Ἁμαρτία.

[2] Cremer-Kög., 139 ; Trench, 154 f.

483. Correspondingly, in law and philosophy it has a wider reach ; Pseudo-Plat. Def. 416a : πρᾶξις παρὰ τὸν ὀρθὸν λογισμόν (where ὀρθός can be taken morally, formally, or intellectually). As the antithesis of ὀρθότης (Plato Leg. I, 627d ; II, 668c), of course ἁμαρτία specifies the nature of a wicked act (see above), but more often it covers the whole proceeding, from the evil imagination to the deed itself : Plat. Gorg. 525c ; Aristot. Pol. IV, 16, p. 1336a, 1.

Aristotle defines ἁμαρτία as missing the mark of virtue through lack of strength, skill, or knowledge (Eth. Nic. II, 5, p. 1106b, 25 ff.). That means a wrong perpetrated without malice (III, 13, p. 1118b, 16 ff. etc.), i.e. an intellectual shortcoming, that works out morally according to the intellectual character of Greek ethics (III, 1, p. 1110b, 18 ff.). On the other hand, the thought of guilt, excluded by Aristotle,[1] came later to be connected with ἁμαρτία : Pap. Leipz. 1119, 3 ; Ditt. Syll. 3rd ed., 1042, 15.[2]

In the LXX ἁμαρτία, here practically synonymous with ἁμάρτημα, usually stands for ḥaṭṭa'th or ḥ°ṭa'ah, often for 'awon, sometimes for pesha', 'asham, resha'. It was in the LXX that ἁμαρτία, like ἁμαρτάνειν, first came to have the moral and religious quality which it lacked both in the rapidly changing Greek of common speech and in the " tragic " language of Aristotle, and to indicate guilt as the outcome of an evil will, an evil purpose, i.e. of a conscious rebellion against God and contradiction of him (= ἀδικία).

[1] Hey shows how Ἁμαρτία became the key word in Aristotle's teaching on drama, but was unsuitable as the starting-point for the theory of " tragic guilt ". In view of Aristotle's exclusion of the idea of moral guilt in the modern sense, and of its inclusion in the Bible, Hey says that " the word ἁμαρτία thus reflects the deep and far-reaching difference between two worlds of culture " (163).

[2] Cf. Trench, 152.

The choice of the vaguest and most general profane word for wrong—only partly because of its kindred primary meaning—to bear the main burden of expressing the relentless Biblical idea of sin (ḥēṭ') gave it more weight than all its synonyms, and fitted it to denote the godward side of sin much better than, e.g. ἀδικία and κακία, which were primarily ethical terms.[1]

3. The N.T. follows the LXX[2] in using ἁμαρτία, etc., to denote offence against God, with the emphasis on guilt. Ἁμαρτία may be said to indicate sin in three principal forms : (a) a single act (= ἁμάρτημα) ; (b) a characteristic of human nature ; (c) a personal power. These lay already to hand, but their development in the N.T. (esp. (b) and (c)) betokens a doctrine different from all that went before, viz. that sin is a positive force alienating man from God.

(a) The reference is to sinful acts always in the Synoptic Gospels, Acts, the Pastoral Epistles, and the Apocalypse ; and generally in Heb. and the Catholic Epistles. Matt., Mark, Luke, Acts only use the word when speaking of forgiveness (except Matt. i, 21, and Mark i, 5 par.), and always in the plural (except Matt. xii, 31, and Acts vii, 60). In the case of Paul this usage generally occurs only in quotations or traditional formulae (I Cor. xv, 3 ; Gal. i, 4 ; Col. i, 14) ; exceptions are found at Rom. vii, 5 ; II Cor. xi, 7 ; Eph. ii, 1 ; apart from Rom. iv, 8 and II. Cor. xi, 7 the word is always in the plural. John uses ἁμαρτία in this sense in the Gospel only at viii, 24, twice ; viii, 34a ; ix, 34 (allusion to Ps. li, 5) ; on the other hand there are several examples in I John,

[1] Cf. Cremer-Kög., 137 f.

[2] Steinleitner (see p. 61), 85 : "The contrast between heathenism and Christianity appears nowhere more clearly than in the meanings attached to ἁμαρτία ".

which is thus seen to stand nearer to the world of ordinary Christian thought than the Gospel.[1]

(*b*) Wrongness is what Plato means by ἁμαρτία when he contrasts it with ὀρθότης in a discussion of the laws of musical or poetic art (Leg. I, 627*d* ; II, 668*c*). A complete transformation takes place when in the N.T. it comes to mean man's inveterate hostility toward God, specially as that is expressed in John's synonymous formulæ : ἔχειν ἁμαρτίαν (ix, 41 ; [2] xv, 22, 24 ; xix, 11 ; I John i, 8) and ἁμαρτία ἐν τινί ἐστιν (I John iii, 5, cf. John vii, 18). A similar expression, only reversing the spatial relationship, is found at viii, 21 : ἀποθανεῖν ἐν τῇ ἁμαρτίᾳ.[3] Cf. John viii, 24 (Ezek. xviii, 24) ; ix, 34 ; I Cor, xv, 17 : apart from Christ, man lives and dies in sins. The plural in these passages corresponds to the collective use of the singular in John (cf. ix, 41 ; I John i, 7) and frequently in the Pauline and deuteroPauline literature : Rom. iii, 20 ; v, 13, 20 ; vi, 1, 6*a* ; vii, 7 ; viii, 3 ; Heb. iv, 15 ; ix, 28, 26 ; xi, 25 ; I Pet. iv, 1 ; and II Cor. v, 21, a specially pregnant expression for man's sinful condition as a whole.

(*c*) Personification of sin is found in the Paris Magic Papyrus (Preisendanz, Pap. Gr. Mag. IV, 1448) : Ἁμαρτίαι χθόνιαι, underground demons ; and also in Judaism, in Zech. v, 5 ff., the woman of

---

[1] Here also the Cognate Accusative [see A. T. Robertson, A Grammar of the Gk. N.T.[3], 1919, 477], ἁμαρτάνω ἁμαρτίαν, derived from LXX : Exod. xxxii, 30 f. ; Lev. iv, 23 ; v, 6, 10, 13 ; Ezek. xviii, 24 ; also Philo, De Mut. Nom. 233 ; Hermas V, ii, 2, 4. Secular Greek prefers the more exact ἁμ. ἁμάρτημα : Soph., Phil. 1249 ; Plato, Phaedo 113*e* ; Dio Chrys. Or. xxxii, 3. Cf. M. Johannessohn, Der Gebrauch der Kasus u.d. Präpositionen in d. LXX, Diss. Berlin, 1910, 56 f. ; Winer, 32, 2.

[2] Cf. Pesiqta 5 p. 55*b* Buber, in Schlatter, Johannes 232.

[3] Cf. Jer. xxxi (LXX xxxviii), 30 ; Bab. Shab. 55*b* in Schlatter, Joh. 208.

sin,[1] and Ecclus. xxvii, 10, sin lying in wait for prey like a lion—these being related to the gradually developing idea of a cosmic power of evil.[2] A similar presupposition was originally involved in the personal treatment of ἁμαρτία (mostly with the article)[3] which occurs frequently in the N.T., specially in Rom. v-vii.[4] At first it is simply a matter of appearing on the scene, as a person does (v, 12). Sin was originally dead (vii, 8), but came to life again through the commandment of law (ver. 9), which gave it an impulse (v. 7, 11) to deceive and entrap man (ver. 11, cf. Heb. iii, 13 ; xii, 1). Thus, dwelling in man (Rom. vii, 17, 20) and bringing forth passions (ver. 5) and lust (8), sin obtains mastery over him, as a demonic power. Man is under sin (Rom. iii, 9 ; Gal. iii, 22 ; cf. Rom. xi, 32), as a slave (Rom. vi, 16, 20 ; John viii, 34 ; cf. Gal. ii, 17), sold to it (Rom. vii, 14), in bondage to it (Rom. vi, 6), under its law (vii, 23, 25 ; viii, 3), presenting parts of his body to it as instruments of unrighteousness (vi, 13). Sin's domain is the flesh, and its dominion (vi, 14 ; v, 21 ; vi, 12) is consummated when it gives man death as his wages (vi, 23 ; v, 21 ; vii, 11, cf. James i, 15). But through and with Christ man dies to sin (Rom. vi, 2, 10) and is dead to it (ver. 11), set free from it (vv. 7, 18, 22), while it is condemned (viii, 3). Nevertheless the fight against it must ever be maintained (Heb. xii, 4).

[1] Cf. R. Smend, Lehrbuch d. A.T. Rel. Gesch.², 1899, 402.

[2] Cf. Köberle, 473 f.

[3] Generally speaking, the presence or absence of the article, though used, e.g. in Cremer-Kög., as a principle for the grouping of meanings, is of little significance : cf. Rom. vi, 6 with viii, 3 ; vi. 16 with 17 etc.

[4] Cf. Lietzmann, Röm.², 65 ; M. Dibelius, Die Geisterwelt im Glaube d. Paulus, 1909, 119 ff. ; P. Feine, Theol. d. N.T.⁵, 1931, 200 f.

It is difficult to decide how much of this to regard, with Dibelius, as referring to the demon, Sin, playing the part of Satan in Rom. vi f., and how much, with Feine, as mere poetic imagery. How fluid the boundaries are between these N.T. forms of the conception of sin is well illustrated in the Johannine literature : cf. John viii, 34 ; I John iii, 5 ; John viii, 21 and 24.

V. SIN AND GUILT IN CLASSICAL GREEK AND HELLENISM

1. THE Christian idea of sin is not found in classical Greek literature, which knows nothing of the hostility to God that excludes what is right from thought and will.[1] In this chapter, therefore, we shall do well to avoid that idea, and substitute the Greek conception of failure and guilt, adhering to the fundamental meaning of ἁμαρτάνειν, etc., which is to miss the mark—whether through error or guilt, or error that is guilt.

The field is wide, extending from crime to trivial blundering,[2] and includes moral lapses as well as intellectual or artistic mistakes—even in the writings of a single author.[3] Ἁμαρτάνειν had become a purely negative term for doing what is not ὀρθόν, i.e. customary or conventional, or logically or technically correct.[4]

A full treatment of this Greek idea of guilt is not possible without reference to certain other ideas and terms ; e.g. ἄτη for the early period, combining fate and freedom,[5] and ἀδικία, etc., for post-Homeric

---

[1] Kierkegaard, The Sickness unto Death, trans. W. Lowrie, Princeton, 1941, 153 : "Sin does not consist in the fact that man has not understood what is right, but in the fact that he will not understand it, and in the fact that he will not do it." See the whole chapter (141 ff.), The Socratic definition of sin, which analyses the Greek and Christian ideas of sin. [See also A. W. Mair in E.R.E. XI, 545-554 ; R. Livingstone, The Greek Genius.]　　　　　　　　　　　　　　　[2] Hey, 14.

[3] Cf. the large number of examples in Hey, 7 ff., esp. from Thucydides and the law-courts (14 f.) and from Aristotle (141 ff.).

[4] Hey, 15 f.

[5] Cf. W. Jaeger, Solons Eunomie, Sitz. Akad. Berl., 1926.

times. Hesiod's own personal experience led him to base everything in the " Works " on the conviction that all injustice is sin.[1] Since community life is impossible without justice, ἀδικία came to mean simply departure from the norm of ordinary life. Other terms to be noted are ἄγος and μίασμα, denoting ritual pollution, ὕβρις (insolence), and κακός, κακία, specially in philosophical literature.

2. Greek life in the earliest days was a glad acceptance of whatever came from fate and the gods, without any fully developed self-consciousness or sense of personal freedom, and this determined the conception of guilt (cf. Homer, Il. xix, 83 ff.) [2] It was misfortune that drew attention to the fact that guilt had been incurred. Guilt or failure is a matter of behaviour. In the Homeric age it consists of negligence in worship, false witness, breach of the laws of hospitality, offence against the honour (τιμή) of gods and men. Hesiod widens the circle, so as to include the injuring or dishonouring of parents, adultery, illtreatment of orphans and social injustice in general (Works 327 ff.). Such things call forth the anger of the gods, who are the guardians and guarantors of law and order. Cf. Homer, Od. xiii, 214 : " Zeus . . . watches over all men and punishes the transgressor ". Rohde's remark about the Greek spirit in its spring-time is broadly true : " In those happy centuries they were practically free from that infectious disease, the consciousness of sin ".[3]

3. The Homeric world of the seventh and sixth centuries B.C. was inundated with oriental morbidity, and the Greeks began to see life in terms of guilt and death ; [4] behind the familiar light of day they

---

[1] Latte, 266.   [2] Cf. esp. Stenzel (see Bibliogr.), 17 ff.
[3] Rohde, Psyche [9], [10], 1925, I, 319.
[4] Cf. H. Weinstock, Sophokles 275 ff., esp. 279 f.

began to sense "the dark backward and abysm of time ", [1] to doubt the reality of their existence, to tremble at fate, to feel that guilt is inescapable. Everywhere men sought refuge from their fears in the Mysteries, and specially in Orphism. The new doctrine was that life itself is the consequence of guilt. " The soul is condemned to life in the body for the expiation of guilt ; the wages of sin is life on earth, which is death to the soul." [2]   Man's chief concern is with the " original guilt " which precedes life, and the judgment of the dead which follows it ;[3] and these are elaborated in art and philosophy. The way in which the Greeks met the menace of all this deepened and enriched their spiritual life. " Tragic drama is the visible and abiding proof that the Greek spirit transformed the menace into a blessing." [4]   Whereas formerly the guilt was seen in the deed itself, now it was recognised as a deeply rooted condition of the inner man (see p. 57).

Human guilt is disturbance of the established order, interference with an objective state of affairs, for which man has to pay with the consequent suffering and misery, and sometimes with death. It has not the moral quality of a free choice between good and evil, but is an infatuation concurrent with life itself. [5]   Man is doomed to incur guilt. The idea of ἄγνοια (ignorance), which plays such an important part in the Greek view of life, here reaches its deepest level.

---

[1] Weinstock, 280.   [2] Rohde II, 126.
[3] Cf. Latte, 281 ff., for evidence.   [4] Weinstock, 280.
[5] Cf. the scene in Sophocles, Antigone, in which Creon comes out of the house with Haemon's body :—Chorus : " Evidence he with him bears against himself ; " Creon : " Woe for sin of minds perverse, deadly fraught with mortal curse. . . . Heavy the hand of God, thorny and rough the paths my feet have trod " (1258 ff). Shortly before this Teiresias had said : " To err is common to all men " (1023 f.). [Trans. F. Storr in Loeb ed.]

All guilt springs from ignorance, but this is conceived as the limitation of man's powers without which he would not be human. The deep meaning of the Oedipus tragedy, e.g. is to be found in " the tragic limitation of human knowledge, which as such is necessarily fragmentary ", and which " gives men's actions their tragic quality, since they cannot be actions in the full sense unless they are consciously directed towards an object and arise out of clear knowledge ".[1] Thus " all action involves guilt, since it affects the course of things in the continuum of space and time, the agent, in his ignorance, being neither able to foresee the results nor ultimately responsible for them ".[2] The only thing man can do is to shoulder his guilt,[3] as, e.g. Oedipus does, accepting his guilt and his doom from the hand of the gods,[4] and acknowledging guilt when his suffering comes. This suffering contains the final secret of man's life and of all existence. Like everything else, human guilt is taken up into the will and decree of the gods. By incurring guilt and reaping its bitter fruit, the Greeks felt that they were brought to a deeper understanding of the world (Aeschylus, Agam. 176 f.). That is Greek religion.

The idea of guilt as inseparable from human action made it possible to conceive of voluntary guilt, like that confessed by Prometheus in the famous tragedy of Aeschylus (259 ff.). The Chorus says, " Seest thou not thou hast erred ? Yet to say how thou didst, can bring to me no joy, and to thee pain " ; to which

---

[1] Weinstock, 151 ; cf. 172 ff., 230 ff.　　　[2] *Ibid.* 175.

[3] Cf. further the analysis of Ajax in W. Schadewalt, Sophokles Aias und Antigone, in " Neue Wege zur Antike ", 8, 1929, 70 ff., esp. what is said in the closing section on " greatness and guilt " (100 ff.).

[4] Cf. Oedipus Col. 974 : " And if when born to misery, as born I was ".

the hero replies, " Wilfully I erred, wilfully ; I deny
not ; succouring mortals, I reaped woes myself."
[Trans. by R. C. Trevelyan.]   This is the existential
guilt which conditions the human situation and involves it in suffering.

The tragedians' ideas of existential guilt is closely
connected with a late Homeric development, as seen
in the well-known passage (Od. i, 32 ff.) where Zeus
says, " Lo you now, how vainly mortal men do blame
the gods! For of us they say comes evil, whereas
they even of themselves, through the blindness of
their own hearts, have sorrows beyond that which is
ordained." [Trans. Butcher and Lang.]   In the
midst of that suffering which is the inescapable doom
of a guilt that is also doomed, there is another kind
of misery, self-inflicted, when a man incurs guilt in
spite of divine warning of the fatal consequences of
wrong-doing : " With sheer doom before his eyes,
since he had warned him " (Hom. Od. i, 37 ff.).
This is the first indication of insight into the operation
of immanent laws which are clearly discernible,
" the laws ", as Solon later calls them, " of evolving
reality, according to which justice is done in every
age, so that evil is defeated and good victorious ".[1]
The ignorance which leads to guilt is here the lack of
the knowledge of what is good, i.e. of what leads to
happiness by the very working of these laws.   Philosophy developed these ideas.   Democritus had already
said that " the cause of sin is ignorance ($\dot{\alpha}\mu\alpha\theta\acute{\iota}\eta$) of
the better way " (Fr. 83, Diels II, 78, 13).   Socrates
based his work as an educator on the fundamental
principle that ignorance is the ground of guilt and
evil.   The Greek philosophers took it for granted that
right understanding leads to right action, the reference

[1] Stenzel, 27 after Fr. 3, 30 ff.   (Diehl I, 24) ;   24, 3 (I, 35) ;
10 (I, 28 f.).

being to existential insight and not to mere intellectual knowledge. He who really understands and knows [1] will act rightly. The theory rests on the belief that man is fundamentally good.[2] Greek tragedy starts from this idea of insight as determining action : it is animated " by belief in a comprehensible, unified world-order, in which we may expect wickedness and presumption to meet with their deserts, and so regulate our behaviour according to the obvious relation be- tween guilt and punishment, gaining insight through the great examples of suffering in mythology or through our own experience " ; [3] and it also stands in a vital relation to the idea of the city-state.[4] Along

[1] Cf. Kierkegaard on the inner dialectic of this Socratic theory of ignorance : " When a person doesn't do the right thing ; why then, neither has he understood it ; his understanding is a vain conceit, his assertion that he has understood it is a false indication of the way. . . . But then indeed the definition is correct. If a man does the right thing, then surely he doesn't sin ; a.ıd if he doesn't do the right thing, then neither has he understood it ; if in truth he had understood it, this would at once have moved him to do it, would at once make him an echo of his understanding—*ergo*, sin is ignorance." (Trans. W. Lowrie, 149 f.)

[2] Kierkegaard shows that the Socratic definition of sin is no definition. " If the Socratic definition is correct, sin does not exist " (144). He also brings out the point that the Greeks believed man to be naturally good, when he asks pertinently, " What determinant is it then that Socrates lacks in determining what sin is ? " and replies, " It is will, defiant will." The Greek intellectualism was too happy, too naïve, too aesthetic, too ironical, too witty, [too sinful] to be able to get it into its head that a person knowingly could fail to do the good, or knowingly, with knowledge of what was right, do what was wrong. The Greek spirit proposes an intellectual categorical imperative " (145).   [3] Stenzel, 87.

[4] Stenzel (84-87) analyses Aeschylus, Eumenides, and shows that the ordering of the state is a divine ordering : " The doctrine of the immanence of the supernatural in the natural, at which philosophy arrived after long and painful wrestling, was antici- pated by the poet ".

with this, it is true, goes the idea of existential guilt
(see p. 55), which can over-ride all insight, for guilt
is fore-doomed and ignorance is an infatuation (ἄτη).
But both lines of thought come together in the moral
underlying Tragedy, which reveals the part played by
ignorance and teaches reverence for the divine omnis-
cience.[1] Plato's ideas about guilt find their fullest
expression in what he says about unrighteousness
(ἀδικία), which is identical with sin (ἁμαρτία)—cf.
e.g. Gorg. 525c ; Phaed. 113e ; Laws X, 906c—and
about evil (κακόν). He takes the opposite view of the
connexion between guilt and destiny, echoing Homer,
Od. I, 32 ff. : man chooses his own lot. He alone is
guilty, and God has no responsibility (Rep. X, 617e).
Aristotle makes a sharp new distinction between ἁμαρτία
and ἀδικία.[2] " I mean by an accident (ἀτύχημα)
anything which cannot be foreseen and does not
proceed from vice, by an error (ἁμάρτημα) anything
which might have been foreseen and yet does not
proceed from wickedness, and by a crime (ἀδίκημα)
anything which might have been foreseen and is itself
a result of wickedness " (Rhet. I, 13, p. 1374b, 7 ff.,
Welldon). What sort of " errors " are meant here ?
The word-group to which ἁμαρτία belongs is widely
used, indicating error in the fields of art and thought,[3]
technique and hygiene,[4] law and its administration,[5]
and politics.[6] Finally, in the sphere of ethics, ἁμαρτία
means an error committed in good faith, the result
of ignorance to which no blame attaches. Virtue is

---

[1] Cf. the end of Sophocles, Oedipus Tyr. : " Therefore wait
to see Life's ending ere thou count one mortal blest ; wait till
free from pain and sorrow he has gained his final rest " [Storr].
Note also how the idea of an immanent law appears again in
the revelations of the oracle (see Weinstock's interpretation,
op. cit., 184 ff.).

[2] Cf. esp. Hey, 137 ff.   [3] Hey, 141.

[4] Hey, 141 f.   [5] Hey, 143.   [6] Hey, 145.

for Arisotle the mean between two extremes, and
ἁμαρτία means going astray to right or left : [1] "There
are many ways of going wrong (ἁμαρτάνειν) . . .,
but only one of keeping straight ; . . . it is easy to
miss the mark but hard to reach it " (Eth. Nic. II, 5,
p. 1106b, 28 ff.).   Error in every sphere is the result
of ignorance (for ethics see Eth. Eud. VIII, 1, p. 1246a,
32 ff. ; Pol. III, 11, p. 1231b, 28) ; every trace of
moral responsibility has disappeared ; for Aristotle it
is all a matter of the intellect. [2] This belongs to the
rationalism of Aristotle and his successors.

4. The two lines of thought, which had been held
together by the theories of ignorance and immanence,
now fell apart : on the one hand existential guilt,
foredoomed, and on the other hand error, due to
ignorance and causing suffering. Philosophy continues to be rationalistic. All guilt comes from
ignorance, which is to be removed by education. Man
is naturally good, and realises goodness through the
exercise of reason. "Error (τὸ ἁμαρτάνειν) comes
from not knowing how to decide what ought to be
done " (Clem. Al., Strom. II, 15, 62, 3 ; cf. Epict.
Diss. I, 26, 6). Thus the philosophy of the later
period lost the serious view of guilt which had pre-
vailed in the classical age. [3]

But the thought of doom maintained itself. No

[1] Hey, 147 ff., with full evidence.

[2] Hey, 160 ; cf. 161 : " We have no expression exactly corresponding to the Greek word, ἁμαρτία, with all its varied nuances ;
it is for us an ἀνώνυμον, to use Aristotle's term. We can use
such renderings as mistake, blunder, miscalculation, error, slip,
wrong inference, misunderstanding, perversity, folly—but not
lapse or transgression—according to the nature and gravity of
each instance."

[3] A recovery of the conception of sin is not to be thought of :
sin—" the word really has no place in the Stoic system "
(Bonhöffer).

longer rising to the same height by identifying guilt with fate, it robbed man of responsibility by making him the plaything of chance.[1] The Mystery religions, which invaded the Greek world in increasing numbers in the Hellenistic period, aimed at counteracting the curse of doom and mortality. Similarly the Hellenistic mysticism of the Corpus Hermeticum sees the world as the domain of cosmic evil and man as the victim of vice from which only the free gift of Gnosis can save him. Ignorance and Gnosis are metaphysical opposites. The prevalence of the idea of fate weakened the sense of personal responsibility : " Chance . . . made man sin, in spite of his reason " (Libanius, Ep. 1025). It makes no difference whether a man has knowledge or not ; his guilt is predestined, like the rest of his existence. The terms $\dot{a}\mu a\rho\tau\dot{\iota}a$, etc., consequently have a different connotation : " Euergetes II's peace proclamation shows how far the intellectual colouring of the word $\dot{a}\mu a\rho\tau\dot{a}\nu\epsilon\iota\nu$ had been lost when it makes $\dot{a}\mu a\rho\tau\dot{\eta}\mu a\tau a$ complementary to $\dot{a}\gamma\nu o\dot{\eta}\mu a\tau a$, in order to include all offences in one expression."[2] $\dot{A}\mu a\rho\tau\dot{a}\nu\epsilon\iota\nu$ is now the universal lot of mankind.[3]

5. Steinleitner's collection of Phrygian and Lydian inscriptions lies outside the main stream of Greek and Hellenistic thought.[4] The primitive religions which they represent show the god as the absolute lord of those who worship him, benevolent towards them, and himself punishing every offence. Sin is

[1] [Cf. Polybius i, 4 : " It is my task as an historian to put before my readers a compendious view of the part played by Fortune in bringing about the general catastrophe. . . . She is constantly producing dramas in the life of men."]

[2] Pap. Tebt. I, v, 3 (Latte).

[3] " No man can live without sin " (F. Preisigke, Sammelbuch, 4949, 17 ff ; 5716, 17).

[4] F. S. Steinleitner, Die Beicht im Zusammenhange m.d. sakralen Rechtspflege in d. Antike (Diss. München, 1913).

offence against the deity, whether conscious and intentional or unconscious and unintentional ; its religious character is seen when it is equated with despising the god.[1] Sin includes refusal to give thanks to the god, insulting speech, breach of purity rules, damage to the shrine, neglect of the demand for ritual chastity, mistakes in ritual, and perjury.[2] A number of the sins mentioned are ethical in character. The god reacts against every sin with a particular punishment. Sickness is specially regarded as a punishment for sin, which is actually called a "substance begetting sickness ".[3] Steinleitner aptly characterises the sins that are specified : " Sin and guilt are here related to matters of cult and ritual, not to absolute ethical principles, and so the most important thing is the sinful act itself ; the question of moral responsibility is not raised ".[4] The whole purpose of the atonement procedure is " to make the sinner physically and ceremonially normal again ", being " directed not to his conscience but to his outward appearance ".[5] When a man despises his god, he

---

[1] It must be remembered that in classical Greek also the gods are concerned with sin : e.g. Plato, Phaedrus 242c ; Laws X, 891e ; Aeschylus, Prom. 945 ; Xenophon, Hist. Gr. I, vii, 19 ; later, Musonius, p. 78, 9, 13. Greek humanism is religious. The gods were identified with the immanent laws of nature. They are embodiments of reality. Here we have something different. [2] Cf. Steinleitner, 83 ff.

[3] *Ibid.* 99. [4] *Ibid.* 121.

[5] This view of sin is also found in the examples from the mysteries of Samothrace given by J. Leipoldt in Das Gotterlebnis Jesu, 1927, 35, and Der Sieg d. Christentums über d. antiken Religionen, in Ihmels Festschrift, 1928, 81 f. Cf. Plutarch, Ap. Lac. Antalcidas 1 (II, 217cd), Lysandros 10 (II, 229d), where a confession is required. " It was precisely to sinners that Samothrace was open, and doubtless those concerned were forgiven their sins. But it is uncertain how far sin in this case belongs to the cultic sphere, and how far to the

is not revealing an existential characteristic of human nature, he is simply committing one of the offences already mentioned ; no proper consciousness of sin is indicated.

Plutarch's essay on Superstition contains a passage which is appropriate here : " Let me . . . suffer punishment, unholy and accursed as I am, hated by gods and demons " (II, 168c).[1]

ethical ; those acquainted with Greek religion will understand the difficulty of deciding. The position of Christianity is per-fectly clear. Jesus and Paul are indifferent to cultic matters." (Leipoldt, Sieg, 81 f.   Cf. Steinleitner, 118 f. ; [L. R. Farnell, Kabeiroi, in E.R.E. VII, 628-632]).

[1] Latte, 294.

VI. SIN IN THE NEW TESTAMENT

IT is remarkable how small a part is played by ideas about sin in the Synoptic Gospels, as compared with the rest of the N.T. What they have to say is concerned with two main points : (*a*) Jesus did not talk about the nature and consequences of sin, but he recognised its reality, e.g. in the Sermon on the Mount, and acted accordingly ; (*b*) in word and deed he knew himself to be victorious over sin. These assertions may now be illustrated.

(*a*) The mission of Jesus is to proclaim the Rule of God, which is realised in his words and actions. The historic event brought to pass under this Rule is the conquest of sin. Jesus preaches God as Father, and shows by his works that God is loving, with the result that men recognise that they are far from God in their uncleanness, and long to get back to him. This historic event, brought to pass through the coming of Jesus, is described in the parable of the Prodigal Son, who goes to his father with the confession, "Father, I have sinned against heaven and in thy sight" (Luke xv, 18, 21). Here we see how Jesus understood sin : it is leaving the Father's house, losing touch with him, living without him in the world, with all its pleasure and its sordidness. The historic event, brought to pass by the coming of Jesus, is this recognition of sin and return to God. Jesus here shows, not only what sin is, but also what repentance is, viz. the way to God as the Father who welcomes the sinner with love. "I say to you that even so there

64

shall be joy in heaven over one sinner repenting more than over ninety-nine good people who have no need of repentance " (Luke xv, 7, cf. ver. 10). Having this twofold knowledge, Jesus does not talk about sin, but preaches of God as the Father, and how he rules, confident that this will reach the sin, which is both ungodliness and unneighbourliness,[1] and will bring about repentance. What gives sin its tragic importance is that it is guilt towards God.[2]

The truth comes to light in what Jesus does. " I came not to call the righteous but sinners " (Matt. ix, 13).[3] This mission explains his behaviour, as described in the Gospels : " And it came to pass, as he reclined at meat in the house, behold, many publicans and sinners came and reclined beside Jesus and his disciples " (Matt. ix, 10 ; cf. ver. 11 and par. ; Luke xv, 1 f. ; xix, 7). This sort of thing led to his being called " friend of publicans and sinners " (Matt. xi, 19 ; Luke vii, 34).[4] The oriental regards eating together as the expression of the closest possible fellowship, and in behaving as he does, Jesus is the conqueror of sin, not only because he puts an end to the separation of the righteous from sinners, but also because, by forgiving the sinners, he ends their separation from God, and by drawing them into fellowship with himself, creates a new fellowship with

[1] Cf. Matt. xviii, 23 ff. ; v, 21 ff. ; vi, 14 f.

[2] See Matt. vi, 12 ; xviii, 24.

[3] From the fact that Jesus distinguishes between the righteous and sinners, and yet puts beside the prodigal son the one who stayed at home but grumbled at his brother's return—a thing he had seen happening—it is certain that he regarded sin as universal, and found it in the righteous when confronted by himself. This explains sayings like Mark viii, 38 ; Luke vi, 32 ff. ; xiii, 1-4. Cf. R.G.G.[2], V, 885, 3.

[4] On the formula, " publicans and sinners ", see J. Jeremias in Z.N.W., 1931, 293 ff.

God.[1] That is the effect of his pronouncement of forgiveness, which shows him to be the Christ, standing at God's side and endued with power (cf. Matt. ix, 2 ; Luke vii, 47 ff.). Many stories make it clear that by his own behaviour Jesus actually produced the crisis described in the parable of the Prodigal Son : e.g. Luke v, 8 (Peter) ; Luke vii, 37 ff. (the sinful woman) ; Luke xix, 1 ff. (Zacchaeus). His commendation of the publican who prayed, " Have mercy on me, a sinner ", makes it clear that fellowship with himself is God's answer to repentance (Luke xviii, 13 ff.). This admission into fellowship is specially clear in the case of the Prodigal Son. He wants to become one of his father's hired servants. But the father comes to meet him, interrupts his confession, sends for clothing and shoes, and for the ring which is the badge of sonship, crowning his welcome with the sharing of food. The meaning is plain. Man, created for fellowship with God, has broken the fellowship. That is his sin. The arrival of the Kingdom of God restores the fellowship with God, in which Jesus lives, inviting men to share in it by following him.

The same parable makes another point. Those who are righteous object to the behaviour of Jesus towards sinners. The elder son stands for the earnest but joyless worship of the formally righteous (Luke xv, 29), who fail to realise the full meaning of fellowship with God (ver. 31). He is a warning to the Pharisees of the import of what is happening, viz. that Jesus is finding the lost, bringing the dead to life. But the righteous are deaf to his call, and the end of the story is the Cross, which confirms and seals the authority of his words and deeds.

The forgiveness proclaimed and practised by Jesus is something new and extraordinary : it is the defeat

[1] Cf. esp. Schlatter, Matt. 304.

of sin, the breaking in of the Kingdom of God, an eschatological event. He always speaks and acts with authority : that is the great thing. The description of sin and repentance, of the rupture and restoration of fellowship, e.g. in the parable of the Prodigal Son, would make a fine story, wonderfully conceived, but it would never be the life-giving word of forgiveness, unless it came with the authority of Jesus, which is the authority of the eschatological ambassador from God. This connexion becomes perfectly clear at the Last Supper.

The Last Supper is to be associated, on the one hand, with earlier meals, shared by Jesus and his disciples, in which he bound them together as the fellowship of the Kingdom of God (Mark i, 32, the first example ; [1] ii, 15, Capernaum ; vi, 34 ff., Galilee). He often referred to the Kingdom, both directly and indirectly, as a common meal in the Father's House. On the other hand, the Last Supper is to be distinguished from those that went before it, both because it is the last, and because the parabolic action of Jesus gives it a special meaning. The bread he says, means himself as the bread of life ; [2] and the wine means his blood, which seals the founding and inauguration of the institution which embodies the

[1] Ministry (Mark i, 31) means waiting at table.

[2] The expression, " my body, thy body ", etc., often stands in Aramaic for the reflexive pronoun (cf., e.g. John vii, 38 : $\dot{\epsilon}\kappa$ $\tau\hat{\eta}s$ $\kappa οιλίας$ $a\dot{v}\tau ο\hat{v}$: " from him "). Therefore it may well be possible that for " this is my body " we should read " This am I ". This is supported by our oldest commentary on the words spoken at the Last Supper, viz., John vi (cf. 35, 48, etc.). The first utterance would then indicate the significance of the coming of Jesus : he appears as the bread of life. But his death means the establishment, sealed with blood, of that which is the actual content of his coming, viz. the gift of the Kingdom of God, for the " many ", i.e. for all nations. This is also confirmed by John (cf. xi, 52 ; xii, 32).

Kingdom of God. His mention of the Covenant probably refers to Jer. xxxi, 31-34 : that eschatological promise is now to be fulfilled. The New Covenant is ratified through his coming ; it becomes operative through his death, and will be brought to perfection at the feast in his Father's house, to which he looks forward in his parting words (Mark xiv, 25). Matthew says that his blood, as blood of the Covenant, is "shed for many unto remission of sins ".

The word of forgiveness and the behaviour of Jesus are not simply a matter of course, but something extraordinary ; in them sin is overcome, the Rule of God breaks in ; it is an eschatological event. This is specially clear in the case of the Last Supper, which explains and fulfils the promise of the New Covenant (Jer. xxxi, 31-34) : it is established by the coming of Jesus, and ratified by his death. His blood is covenant blood, "shed for many, for the remission of sins " (Matt. xxvi, 28).[1] This is the fulfilment of Jer. xxxi, 34, and also of Is. liii, 12.[2] Jesus is the Servant of the Lord who takes away the sin of mankind by his suffering and death. This is how he understood his mission. Through his coming, through his death and resurrection, sin is conquered and the foundation is laid for God's new world.

The pronouncement about the unpardonable sin—whether it be a saying of Jesus himself, or a piece of early Christian doctrine, or a genuine saying embroidered by the community—is to be interpreted from this point of view (Matt. xii, 31 f. ; Mark iii, 29) : it means resisting and denouncing the work of Jesus in spite of the conviction that it is the work of the Holy

---

[1] Matt.'s " for the remission, etc." is thoroughly sound interpretation.

[2] Cf. Is. liii, 5 f. The " many " of Matt. and Mark points to Is. liii, 12.

Spirit. The gravity of the situation is revealed : it is the last time ; the Rule of God is breaking in.

To understand fully what sin meant to Jesus, we must observe another point. The Lord's Prayer says, " Forgive us our debts, as we also have forgiven our debtors " (Matt. vi, 12). This noteworthy expression points to man as being in debt. The conception is further illustrated in a number of parables, in which the relation of God to man is likened to those of land-owner to steward, creditor to debtor, employer to employee. The fundamental situation in all these is that, along with life, God has entrusted to man something which belongs to him, in order that he may make profitable use of it. Man is a steward who will be called to account : Matt. xxv, 14 ff. ; Luke xvi, 11 ff. There are two possibilities—faithful-ness and unfaithfulness ; and the latter means being in debt, through misuse, selfish appropriation or squandering of the trust. When this happens, the owner becomes the creditor and the steward the debtor : Luke vii, 41 f. ; Matt. xviii, 23 ff. God loses his property through man's misuse of it ; but loves what he has made and given, and tries to get it back. The function of Jesus is to proclaim this divine activity as forgiving love, and to embody it. Encountering God in this way, and awakening to love and trust, man comes to know God as Father and himself as God's child. Man's breach of crea-turely fellowship with God takes the form of misuse of the gift entrusted to him, and puts him in debt to God. The restoration of fellowship is not only a return, but a new stage of existence : instead of the creaturely relationship, denoted by the symbols, owner-steward and creditor-debtor, there is the real-ised eschatology of Father-son. This is the stage of the forgiveness of debts ; which only operates, however, when restoration to fellowship with God leads to the renewal of happy relationships among men with regard to their debts to one another (Matt. vi, 14 f. ; xviii, 21 ff.). The Kingdom of God is thus presented in its totality : if the debtor will neither accept forgiveness nor grant it to his fellow, God becomes the Judge. The message and mission of Jesus thus include the whole complex of sin, debt and forgiveness.

(b) Jesus victor over sin—that is the Synoptic *kerygma*, based on the facts : " Thou shalt call his name Jesus, for it is he that shall save his people from their sins " (Matt. i, 21).

John the Baptist, as the forerunner of Jesus, makes sin the focus of all his activity (Matt. iii, 6 ; Mark i, 4 ; Luke iii, 3). His task as described in the Benedictus (Luke i, 77), is " to give knowledge of salvation unto his people in the remission of their sins ". He concentrates on sin, repentance and forgiveness, because the Kingdom of God is coming. He must prepare God's people for the New Age, by means of baptism, which has its prototype in the Flood (I Pet. iii, 20 f.), and is to be understood as voluntary submission to the Judgment and deliverance from it. His mind is filled with the idea that the Judgment is close at hand. But when Jesus is baptised, the dove is the sign that God has concluded peace. The emphasis of Jesus is different, as we have seen, because he is the fulfiller, who conquers sin, forgiving it in every word and deed, and brings in the Kingdom of God.

The story of Jesus is continued in the work of the apostles, who preach Christ as the saving gift of God, calling for repentance and baptism in the name of Jesus Christ for the remission of sins,[1] in clear accord

[1] See also Luke xxiv, 47 ; Acts iii, 19 ; xiii, 38 ; xxii, 16 ; xxvi, 18.

with what he himself did (Acts ii, 38). What differentiates them from him is that they call for the acceptance of forgiveness, whereas he actually gives it by taking sinners into fellowship with himself. They are "apostles"; he is the "Lord". Their preaching differs from that of the Baptist precisely because they came after the event, and he before it (see Acts v, 31; x, 43).

It has already been pointed out that in the Synoptic Gospels and Acts ἁμαρτία always means a particular act of sin (p. 49). That is why it is almost always found in the plural. Jesus and the early Church were not concerned with sin as an intellectual problem; they saw it as a reality in men's lives. Christ's business was with this reality. Paul sees sin as an active force conditioning the world, and deals with it as a theological problem (see pp. 49, 75 ff.). John stands nearer to the Synoptists than to Paul.

2. JOHN

Christ's victory over sin, as presented in the earlier Gospels, meets us again in John's *kerygma*, with the unfolding of its meaning.[1] The keynote is struck in I John iii, 5: "He was manifested to take away sins, and in him is no sin". The Christ takes sin upon himself and removes it. The primary reference is to his death, and the defeat of sin is pictured in terms drawn from the Jewish sacrificial system. This is implied in the quotation above, and appears again at John i, 29;[2] I John ii, 2; iv, 10; i, 7. Christ

[1] Cf. R. Seeberg, Die Sünden u.d. Sündenvergebung, n.d. I Joh., in Ihmels Festschrift, 1928, 19 ff.

[2] But cf. C. F. Burney, The Aramaic Origin of the 4th Gospel, 1922, 107 f., where it is suggested that "lamb" is a mistranslation of the Aramaic for "servant".

defeats the sin of the world as the expiator who makes
atonement. This work of his recognises no human
limitations of nation, race or sex (I John ii, 2) ; its
universal scope is the outcome of his sinlessness (iii, 5).
He is the man after God's will, who is one with the
Father, and therefore the Son of God. (See John
viii, 46 and ix, 16.) [1]

Both aspects of Christ's mission, viz. victory over
sin through atonement and the universal significance
of this, correspond to the Johannine conception of
sin, as defined at I John iii, 4 and v, 17. Sin is behaviour which runs counter to the divine ordinance,
which corresponds to what is right ; and so is both
$\dot{a}\nu o\mu\acute{\iota}a$ and $\dot{a}\delta\iota\kappa\acute{\iota}a$, the contradiction both of what
is right and of the will of God. It is in fact the product
of the contradiction of God, the outcome of man's
godlessness, materialised in unfriendly action. This
establishes its universality. Man is not neutral ; he
is guilty, and his sin separates him from God (see
John ix, 31). This separation is absolute : " He that
doeth sin is of the devil, for the devil sinneth from
the beginning " (I John iii, 8). The contradiction of
God reveals the demonic character of sin, which puts
man under the devil's power. " Verily, verily, I say
unto you, Every one that committeth sin is the slave
of sin " (John viii, 34) : that is no platitude—" verily,
verily " shows that—but the truth about man which
comes to light through Christ ; human sin is enslave-

[1] The agreement of John with the Synoptists is as clear as the
difference between them. They are agreed as to the kerygma.
Jesus, as the Christ, is the conqueror of sin. But whereas the
first three Gospels give a vivid picture of his outward life among
the Jews, John shapes the kerygmatic thesis of the atonement
for the sin of the world through the death of the Christ; and
thus gives prominence to the guiding principle which found
expression at the Last Supper.

ment under demonic power,[1] and so means absolute separation from God.

Christ's coming creates an entirely new situation, best indicated by the word, " crisis ", which means division and decision. He shows up sin as hatred of God (John xv, 22-24), forcing decision upon men and dividing among them (ix, 41). If a man rejects Christ, refusing to believe his " I am " (viii, 24), he remains in his sin and dies in his sin, missing all that Christ came to bring. All other sin is blindness, " unrighteousness, . . . sin not unto death " ; but this, which Christ brings to light, is " sin unto death " (I John v, 16 f.).[2] This is the crisis which came into the world with Christ. The last hour could not be more clearly proclaimed—the hour of decision for life or death. The Jews who turn away from Jesus in hatred face the one possibility, those who believe him the other (I John i, 9). He who acknowledges his guilt before God receives the word of forgiveness. The other cannot receive it because there is no truth in him and he makes God a liar—the diabolic character of sin appearing again (I John i, 8, 10 ; cf. John viii, 44).[3] This situation is not a thing of the past : it is " even now " ; for in the Paraclete Christ abides with his people. The Paraclete continues the work of Christ (John xvi, 8 f.).

Christ's mission, to take away sins, achieves its purpose in the community that is delivered from sin. The affirmation of this deliverance is fundamental, the ground of it being the birth that is of God. Members

[1] It should be noted that Jesus demolishes the claim of the Jews to be the seed of Abraham, and demonstrates their connexion with demons.

[2] Against Seeberg (p. 71, n. 1), 23 ff. [See C. H. Dodd *ad loc.*]

[3] Cf. Hempel (p. 28 n.), 183, in connexion with John viii, 44 : " That is how revelation works : it brings the real situation to light, and so begins the destruction of Satan's kingdom ".

of the community are born again of God through his
free gift of faith, by which they know God and his
Christ.   Regeneration is the result of seeing Christ :
" Whosoever abideth in him sinneth not : whosoever
sinneth hath not seen him, neither knoweth him.
Whosoever is begotten of God doeth no sin, because
his seed abideth in him : and he cannot sin, because
he is begotten of God " (I John iii, 6, 9).[1] The new
situation becomes concrete in the community through
the practice of love, which is the exact opposite of
sin.   These fundamental assertions are maintained
throughout the Johannine literature, their practical
importance being illustrated in the work of Jesus
(John v, 14) ;[2] but a serious problem is presented by
the fact that they are not substantiated in historical
reality, the Christian community not being sinless.
The new energy of love encounters opposition in its
fight against sin.   John is not concerned with the
abstract problem, but deals practically with the
matter in two ways, which serve to emphasise the
fundamental importance of the idea of the sinlessness
of the community.   (a) Christ's atonement avails
also for the sin of the community, and the Paraclete
makes it possible to live in a state of tension (I John
ii, 1 f.).   (b) The community has the privilege of
prevailing intercessory prayer (I John v, 16).

The Apocalypse describes Christ's work as a work
of love, whereby Christians are delivered out of the
sinful complex of this world : they are set free by his
atoning blood (Rev. i, 5).   The task of God's people
in the last days is to avoid all contact with the growing
power of sin, for God's judgment is coming upon the
world to destroy sin and sinners (Rev. xviii, 4 f.).
John sees in his vision a final act of God, putting an

[1] Cf. W. Grundmann, Begriff d. Kraft in d. N.T. Gedanken-
welt, 1932, 113, n. 8.   [2] On John v, 14, see p. 75, n. 1.

end to the universal power of sin from which Christians are set free.[1]

3. PAUL

What Paul says about sin is orientated to the revelation of God in Christ; it is not a natural, empirical doctrine, drawn from a special form of pessimism, but a divine judgment on godless man, resulting from that revelation, and seen as stern reality in the Cross. This is the clue to his teaching on sin, which may be summarised in two sentences : (a) the fact of Christ is relevant to man in a particular situation, viz. to man as sinner ; (b) the fact of Christ comes home to man as release and renewal. What was fact in the case of Jesus is here described and unfolded.[2] In this lies the difference between Jesus and Paul in relation to sin.

(a) Paul owes his conception of sin to the impression made on him by his own experience of the revelation of God in Christ. He had regarded himself as blameless according to the ideal of the Law (Phil. iii, 6 ; cf. Gal. i,14, and see p. 42). That was his self-consciousness as a Jew. The Damascus experience led him to confess that he was the least of the apostles, not worthy to be called an apostle, because he had persecuted the Church of God (I Cor. xv, 9 ; cf. I Tim. i, 15). This is his sin (cf. Gal. i, 23 ; Phil. iii, 6)—the final result of his zeal for the Law, his

[1] The worse thing which may befall the healed man is to die as the result of committing the " sin unto death " (cf. Schlatter, Joh. 145). This preserves the link between sin, suffering and death. But an end is made of the hard and fast logic which looks for a sinful cause for every case of suffering (John ix, 2 f.), since it shuts out the working of God in his grace.

[2] Cf. G. Kittel, Die Rel.-gesch. u.d. Urchristentum, 1932, 154 ff., n. 350, for a working out of the general point of view, which is here applied in detail.

endeavour to attain to salvation along the path of self-righteousness by works of the Law. The judgment upon persecution of the Church of God was also judgment upon that zeal for the Law. When that dawned upon him, he realised that all his Jewish practices were a striving against God's will and amounted to active enmity against God. " Man's determination to manage by himself " [1] is really striving against God's will. From the hour in which that became clear to him, he remained convinced that sin is not merely an offence against the divine majesty—the Jew goes that far—but is active hatred towards God, hostile opposition to his will, on the part of man in his determination to live for himself and manage by himself. This thought of hatred became the constitutive element in the Pauline conception of sin. The fact that this enmity against God comes to light in connexion with the Law, and takes the Law into its service, puts Paul in a hopeless position. With its threat of death for the transgressor, the Law guarantees the very opposite of salvation. Something more than the Law is needed, if the Jew is to be saved, and Paul knew this. But man is under the Law as long as he lives (cf. Rom. vii, 1-4), and so the question arises, how to escape from it. The answer is, by death alone! But that rules out the possibility of salvation. This situation is fundamentally transformed by the fact of Christ. Through his death he is the end of the Law. Dying with Christ, man dies to the Law, to receive salvation in a new life with Christ by means of faith. Surrender to Christ in baptism is the real death of the human ego, which is launched upon a

---

[1] R. Bultmann, Römer vii u.d. Anthropologie d. Paulus, in Imago Dei, Festschrift f. G. Krüger, 1932, 53 ff. ; 60 f. : " Sin is man's determination to be master of his fate, to assert himself, to be like God ".

new life in the obedience of faith, no longer pleasing itself and managing by itself, but belonging to Christ and under his direction. Dying and rising again with Christ, this ego is dead to enmity with God, and has received reconciliation with God by faith ; it is a new creature. Justification by faith alone is for Paul inseparable from mystical union with Christ.[1]

How does Paul regard sin in the concrete ? This question brings us to Rom. v-viii, of all passages in the N.T. the richest in terms referring to sin. First the fact of Christ is presented : " God commendeth his own love toward us, in that, while we were yet sinners, Christ died for us " (v, 8). Then the meaning of this is explained, in connexion with what has gone before : [2] " . . . as through one man sin entered into the world, and death through sin ; and so death passed unto all men, for that all sinned " (v, 12). Paul gives the Jewish answer to the question concerning the origin of sin : it came into the world through Adam, who freely chose to act against God. And death came too, as wages paid to the hirelings of sin (vi, 23). Thus death's dominion over the world is derived from sin (cf. I Cor. xv, 56). The world is essentially not only something that is created (Rom. i, 20), but also something with sin in it. Although Paul can speak of doom, like Greek and Hellenistic writers—death and doom stand close to each other [3]

[1] Cf. W. Grundmann, Gesetz, Rechtfertigung und Mystik bei Paulus ; Zum Problem der Einheitlichkeit der paulinischen Verkündigung, in Z.N.W., 32 (1933), 52-65.

[2] Rom. v bases the demand for patience in tribulation, by an *a fortiori* argument, on (1) the Christian experience of salvation (v, 7-11), and (2) the new world-situation (v, 12-21).

[3] It must, of course, be remembered that there is a fundamental difference of feeling about life between Greek and Hellenistic dualism and Christianity : " For the former ", as Rohde puts it (see p. 55), " life is the wages of sin ; for the latter, with its consciousness of sin, the wages of sin is death."

—he differs from them in making sin the secret of
death's power. It is the author of all evil. Sin
" reigned the reign of death " (Rom. v, 21 [Moffatt]) :
that is the Christian view, not the Greek. The third
assertion follows from this, viz. that sin, as hostility
towards God, is universal (Rom. iii, 9, 23 ; v, 9 f. ;
viii, 7 ; Gal. iii, 22). Here Paul departs from Judaism,
with its doctrine of individual freedom of choice ;
" through the one man's disobedience the many were
made sinners " : every man shares the common lot
(v, 19). Adam's fall, human mortality, and the
universal propensity to sin are inseparably bound
together. No doctrine of original sin is developed,
but a judgment is expressed upon man as man—
based, it is true, upon the facts of life, but only possible
after the coming of Christ.

What exactly is this propensity to sin ? " For
until the Law ", continues Paul, " sin was in the
world : but sin is not imputed when there is no
Law " (Rom. v, 13). This sentence, linking together the idea of sin and Law, is typically Jewish.
The propensity to sin, already present " in the world"
(cf. vii, 8), is actualised as transgression through the
commandment of the Law (cf. Gal. iii, 19). The
true nature of sin is thus made clear : it is man's self-
assertion in rebellion against God (cf. the basic sin
of Rom. i, 21). This is where sin in general corresponds to the sin of Adam. But it can only be recognised as such after God's will has been declared in
the commandment. Therefore sin between Adam
and Moses is not sin after the likeness of Adam's
transgression (v, 14) ; it is not imputed (13). So
the function of the Law is to actualise the sinful
propensity as transgression, and unveil the true
character of sin as enmity against God (viii, 7) ; to
use an illustration, it is to transform the potential

energy of a state into the kinetic energy of a sinful act ; and further, to establish guilt and ratify the death penalty. Sin for Paul is guilt before God, and as such is man's outstanding characteristic. He thus absorbs the Jewish conception, deepening and re-orientating it. He agrees with Judaism in the importance which he attaches to the sinful act when he establishes the relation between sin and Law ; but the function of the Law is for him exactly the opposite of what it is in Judaism.

Paul deals fully with the relation between sin and Law in Rom. vii. When he speaks of life in the flesh as a life of sin (vii. 5), he is not identifying sin with the flesh, as if bodily existence itself constituted sinfulness ; he simply means that sin is in possession. This is brought to light by the Law (vii, 7-10), which awakens the slumbering desire and leads to the commission of the sinful act. Desire ($\epsilon\pi\iota\theta\upsilon\mu\iota\alpha$) is not to be limited to the sensual or sexual sphere, but must be understood in a comprehensive sense as the mania for self-assertion over against the claim of God, which bursts into flame when challenged by the commandment. Here is the nerve of every kind of sin, from the primal flouting of God (Rom. i, 21) to the sexual perversions and anti-social crimes and all that further sinning which Paul sees as the divine punishment of sin (Rom. i, 24-31 ; I Thess. ii, 16). It is from this point of view that every single sin committed in this world assumes importance before God, and the sinner is found guilty.[1]

---

[1] The function of the Law is to release desire and disclose its inmost nature (Rom. vii, 7 ; iii, 20). We are not concerned here with the functions ascribed to the Law in the dogmatic teaching about its fourfold meaning [Haggadhah, legal ; Halakhah, practical ; Peshaṭ, literal ; Ṣodh, mystical], but with its cosmic and historical function.

It is remarkable that sin should appear here personified as a demon (see pp. 50 ff.). It is indeed demonic in
character, as may be seen in the way in which it makes
use of God's holy will for its own advancement (Rom.
vii, 13) ; the function of the Law in the divine purpose
for the world, of which we have already spoken,
reaches its culminating point when it shows up sin
in its demonic nature as absolute hostility to God.
The same characteristic marks the universal propensity
to sin since the time of Adam, directed as it is against
God. That is why Paul's account of the human
situation is completely adequate, when he says, " I
am carnal, sold under sin " (Rom. vii, 14). Man is
sold as a slave to sin, and consequently under the
dominion of death, even before he actually dies (cf.
Eph. ii, 1) ; his inner conflict is to be understood in
terms of demonic possession (Rom. vii, 15-20) ;
and the wages of sin is death (vi, 23).[1] Our examination of Paul's views leads to an important conclusion, viz. that, as in the case of death's dominion,
all his references to demons and to Satan are meant
to give actuality to his teaching about sin ; they are
not the outcome of dualistic speculation, but the
testimony of one who sees sin as it really is.

(*b*) This is the situation which is met by the fact of
Christ,[2] who is sent by God to condemn sin and destroy
it (Rom. viii, 3). Here is the meaning of the In-

[1] We share Bultmann's interpretation of Rom. vii (R.G.G.[2],
IV, 1022) : " Paul is describing the position of the Jew (only
the Jew ? W.G.) in its essential meaning, as seen by the believer ".
This also appears in his book, Röm. vii u.d. Anthropologie d.
Paulus, 53, and is taken up by W. G. Kümmel, Röm. vii. u.d.
Bekehrung des P., 1929.

[2] Cf. Hempel, op. cit., 181 : " This recognition of sin in all
its terrible power both prepares the way for the gratitude of
Rom. vii, 25, and makes the right background for the work of
Jesus ".

carnation, so powerfully expressed by Paul in the arresting words of II Cor. v, 21 : "Him who knew no sin he made to be sin on our behalf". The sinlessness of Jesus is the necessary presupposition of his being sent. All human sin rests on him, past as well as present (Rom. iii, 25). Because of Christ and his defeat of sin, God grants a period of grace, and judgment is postponed. The fact that God intends to disclose, judge and destroy the dominion of sin in Christ enables him to be forbearing before the plan is carried out, so that both Jews and Gentiles, whose life and work tend generally in the direction of God's will, are given a share in salvation, although they cannot have faith in what God did in Christ. The recognition of this (Rom. ii, 21-26) rounds off the preceding argument about judgment according to works, obedience among the Gentiles and Jewish disobedience. But now a new way of salvation has appeared through Christ, in which justification does not depend on life and work, but solely on faith in Jesus—and this means a complete re-orientation. Christ's defeat of sin is described as atonement. Here lies the importance of his death. It is at the Cross that sin is defeated once for all (Rom. vi, 10 ; cf. I Cor. xv, 3 ; Gal. i, 4). That is why the Cross is the sign of victory over sin, and consequently over death and demons, and the preaching of the Cross is the power of God and the wisdom of God (I Cor. i, 18 ff.). The Cross is inseparable from the Resurrection, without which it would be ineffective (I Cor. xv, 17). The one historic event, which comprises them both, is "on our behalf" (II Cor. v, 21 ; I Cor. xv, 3 ; Gal. i, 4). This is made possible by the fact that, in Paul's view, men are not isolated individuals, but are bound together in a common destiny of sin and death by Adam's sin. The fact of

Christ gives men victory over sin and the beginning
of the mastery of life. It is the turning point of time
(Rom. v, 21).

When this comes home to man, it literally saves
him from sin and sets his life upon a new foundation.
Here is the Gospel, viz. that through faith and baptism
a man is justified, becomes a new creature, risen with
Christ, reconciled, redeemed—in a word, that he
obtains the forgiveness of sins (cf. Eph. i, 7).[1]
Christians share in Christ's death by faith, and their
union with him is perfected in baptism (Rom. vi, 2 f.).
The theme of Rom. vi is : the Christian and sin.
Throughout the chapter runs the fundamental conviction that the Christian is set free from sin. He is
dead to sin because he has died with Christ (ver. 6) :
the meaning of the fact of Christ is realised in him ;
he exemplifies the old familiar thesis : " he that hath
died is justified " (ver. 7).[2] Further, he is free from
the Law and its function as the releaser of sin (ver. 14) ;
and finally, he is no longer the slave of sin (18-22).
The Christian must bear all this in mind, and draw
the consequences of the principle laid down in ver. 16.
There can be no question of remaining in sin and
sinning as though nothing had happened—in order
that grace may abound (vv. 1, 15)! On the con-

[1] Actually Paul only uses ἄφεσις at Eph. i, 7 [and Col. i, 14],
though he has the verb in a quotation at Rom, iv. 7 [and has
χαρίζεσθαι at Eph. iv, 32 and Col. ii, 13 ; iii, 13]. Many other
words come in for consideration here, e.g. βαπτίζω, δικαιόω,
καταλλάσσω, ἀπολύτρωσις, σύν, etc. We can only deal here
with certain ideas relevant to our subject.

[2] K. G. Kuhn, Z.N.W., 1931, 105 ff. : " The recognition that
Paul in Rom. vi, 7 is quoting a piece of Rabbinical theology
makes the argument clear and simple : our old man is crucified
with Christ, and that does away with the body of sin, so that
we are no longer under the necessity of serving sin—in accordance
with the principle that he who dies is acquitted of sin because
of his death ".

trary, dying to sin means living to God (11 f.), a new possibility described by Paul in various ways in vv. 13-19. Sanctification (19, 22) means a life of holiness, devoted to God, and is the object to be achieved by the fact of Christ (cf. ἵνα in Rom. viii, 3 f. and II Cor. v, 21). This is significantly implied in the τύπος τῆς διδαχῆς of ver. 17. Τύπος is the moulding pattern ; διδαχή the teaching which regulates conduct. These terms cannot refer to a thing ; they must mean a person.[1] For one who has died and risen again with Christ, i.e. for his ego, Christ has become the pattern, shaping his conduct. Τύπος τῆς διδαχῆς is Christ. The fellowship with Christ, which begins with the sharing of death and resurrection, and means ultimately the gift of sonship, grows in this way until it is perfected in the sharing of glory (viii, 15-17). It is a life of faith. Freedom from sin finds its fulfilment in the obedience of faith (Rom. xiv, 23), and the new life of faith, which is lived unto God, shows itself in brotherly love, which is the fulfilling of the Law (cf. I Cor. viii, 12).

The Christian is in a state of tension between two actualities. Fundamentally he is delivered from sin, redeemed, reconciled and sinless ; as a matter of fact he is at war with sin, which is still threatening, aggressive and dangerous. So he must be summoned to sanctification.[2] The true state of affairs is described in Rom. viii, 10 : in his bodily life the Christian is given up to death, in which sin finally works itself out ; but he has a new spiritual life from Christ, with whom he has died and risen again, and is under the

[1] Not " the Christian doctrine " (Zahn), or " the Pauline mode of teaching " (Kühl), or " Christianity " (Lietzmann). Schlatter takes a step in the right direction (Gerechtigkeit Gottes ad loc.), but does not proceed to the proper conclusion.

[2] See Grundmann, Begriff d. Kraft, etc., 79 f., 108 ff.

possession of a new Spirit (viii, 11, in contrast to
vii, 18, 20). This spiritual life has overcome death,
and springs from the mastery of life which began
with Christ, and is to be perfected in the complete
destruction of sin and death at his second coming
(Rom. viii, 11 ; I Cor. xv, 26). The ego, the inward
man, has already died and been delivered from death
through fellowship with Christ ; he is with Christ,
though the body be dead (Phil. i, 23), and at the
resurrection of the dead this ego receives a new body
of glory, no longer hidden but manifested with
Christ. The present state of tension belongs to the
time of waiting " for the glory which shall be revealed
to us-ward " (Rom. viii, 18).

4. HEBREWS, JAMES, I PETER

(a) The Epistle to the Hebrews deals with sin from
the point of view of the part played by the high priest
and sacrifice under the old covenant in the ritual of
atonement (Heb. v, 1). Christ is preached as the
eternal high priest who has wrought atonement and
taken away sins by the offering of himself as a sacrifice.
His sinlessness differentiates him from the human
high priest (iv, 15 ; v, 3 ; vii, 26 f.), and his one
historic self-sacrifice has achieved that removal of
sin which is beyond the power of the whole sacrificial
system (x, 2-4, 11 ; ix, 26). Thus an end is put to
that system, for the fact of Christ has brought salvation
in the remission of sins (x, 18). This inaugurates
the Messianic age, which is moving towards its climax
(ix, 26-28)—the age of forgiveness foretold by the
prophets (viii, 12 ; x, 17 ; cf. i, 3 ; ii, 17 ; x, 12).

The Christian community is exhorted to meet persecution by laying aside the sin that clings so closely,
resisting unto blood, i.e. martyrdom, in the fight

against it (xii, 1-4 ; cf. iii, 13). The warning is emphasised by a reference to the unpardonable sin (x, 26), which involved the whole problem of the struggles over repentance in the early Church. Conscious falling away from faith is unforgivable, though it differs from the sin against the Holy Spirit in the Synoptic Gospels and its Johannine " crisis " formulation. Early Christianity here shows its martyr spirit.

(b) The Epistle of James moves on Jewish lines. The root of sin in man is desire (ἐπιθυμία), which corresponds exactly to the [Rabbinical] evil inclination. The illustration of conception and birth is used to show what happens. A man is tempted by desire, and when he consents, desire conceives and brings forth a sin. But that is not the end of the process, for when the sin is full-grown, it brings forth death (James i, 15). Desire, sin and death are connected with one another by a necessary natural process. The reference is to a definite act of sin, as at ii, 9 and iv, 17—the latter a sin of omission. The end of the Epistle deals with matters connected with repentance : intercession procures God's forgiveness of sins ; confession before a brother is recommended, and in cases of sickness is regarded as a condition of healing ; it is the duty of a Christian to guard his brother against sin, or to save him from it, this availing for atonement (v, 15-20). The aim of the Epistle throughout is practical.

(c) I Peter sets forth the sinless Christ as victorious over sin in terms of the Servant of the Lord of Isaiah xl ff. (I Pet. ii, 22, 24 ; iii, 18). It is further stated that separation from sin shows itself in willing suffering for Christ's sake (iv, 1), because here self-interest submits to the will of God. Finally, genuine love to one another is enjoined, on the ground that " love

covereth a multitude of sins " (iv, 8). Sin is overcome by forgiveness in Jesus Christ and the life of
love.   The thought of love as covering sins and saving
is also found at James v, 19 f., and I John iii, 17 f.,
v, 16 ff. point in the same direction. This early
Christian teaching goes back to the teaching of Jesus.
The forgiveness brought by Jesus and the love that
forgives a brother and takes care of him—these fill
out the Christian life and bring the dominion of sin
to an end.

VII. CONCLUSION

When we review the course of our argument, one thing stands out as the heart of the Gospel : Christ has removed the last obstacle to salvation by his victory over sin. This creates a new world-situation. The distinguishing feature of the message of the New Testament, that which gives it its decisive quality, is its eschatological sense of history, its conviction that the final stage of the fulfilment of God's purpose for this world has been inaugurated : a new world is breaking in because Christ has conquered sin.[1] The important·point is the stress on his victory, and there is good reason for this in the fact that the special character of Christianity is to be found in its attitude to sin. This has been pointed out, on the historical side, by R. Reitzenstein and K. Latte, and on the theological side by K. Holl and G. Kittel, and we shall quote their words.

R. Reitzenstein, Poimandres 180 A 1 : " What is new seems to me to be that this redemption is not merely getting rid of evil passions and burdens, escaping from death and securing eternal life, but

[1] This point of view has been brought to the fore by Bultmann's criticism of Holl in Theol. Rundsch., 1932, 1 ff., and is proving fruitful in the discussion of the relation of early Christianity to the history of religion. But cf. also Kittel, Probleme, 130 f. ; Rel. gesch. u. Urchr. 151 f., n. 315, where Bultmann's generalisation is applied to Jesus and the Synoptists. There is really no need to follow Bultmann in his radical disagreement with Holl, since the eschatological point of view necessarily involves the proclamation of a conviction about God, man and the world, that is quite unique, and justifies its sense of history by an appeal to truth.

above all the forgiveness of sins. Hellenism, so far as I can see, lacks the tremendous earnestness of the preaching of guilt and atonement. . . . When the early Christians brought together the death of Jesus and this deep feeling of guilt and belief in the forgiveness of the worst guilt, then, for the first time, the Christian Saviour-doctrine found its unique, world-conquering strength ; its Hellenistic rivals could do no more than prepare the way for it in a world that had recovered the consciousness of sin."

K. Latte, Schuld und Sünde in der griechischen Religion, 298 : " When Paul separates sin from all other forms of evil, taking an exclusively moral view of it, and gives prominence to the gracious act of God, whereby man's sin and weakness are covered, redemption comes to mean primarily the forgiveness of sins. . . . In spite of all its efforts, the heathen world had failed to reach a clear formulation of this idea. The new religion owed to Paul a very real part of its growing strength." By way of criticism it should be pointed out that " an exclusively moral view " is not true to the N.T., which takes a theological view, and is only moral in so far as the claim of God covers social behaviour. The rest of the terminology may be accepted with the same proviso.

K. Holl, Urchristentum und Religionsgeschichte, Zeitschr. Syst. Theol., 1924, 399 ff., esp. 425 : " A mystery which offered the remission of sins would have been a monstrosity to the Greeks." [See p. 89.]

G. Kittel, Die Lebenskräfte der ersten christlichen Gemeinden (1926), 19 ff. : " An entirely different problem dominates Christian thinking. Christianity is the sinner's religion. The sinner stands before God." (See also Kittel's Urchristentum, Spätjudentum, Hellenismus, 1926, 27, and his reply, in Th. Lit. Bl., 1929, 373 f., to the objections of J. Leipoldt in

Das Gotteserlebnis Jesu, 1927, 35. (See p. 62 n. 5 for Leipoldt's later agreement ; as a historian of ideas he has no use for eschatology, and so does not get beyond relativity.) Kittel has further developed his theme in Die Religionsgeschichte und das Urchristentum, 1932, 118 ff. : " This religion, while never for a single moment ceasing to be a moral religion, calls a halt at the fact of non-fulfilment (of God's commandment). This is the religion, at the centre of which stands the consciousness of having failed to do what ought to have been done, the consciousness of sin (120). . . . " The first place is given to victory over guilt, over sin, and after that, over death, the wages of sin (122). . . . The announcement of forgiveness is always for the early Church the announcement of Christ. In Christ the holiness of God is the judging of sin ; and in Christ the love of God is the saving of the sinner (124)."

This is the view which our argument has established. It may be stated finally in three propositions : (i) sin is as fundamental a characteristic of this world as the fact that it has been created ; (ii) sin is man's rebellious self-assertion over against the claim of God, not only on the part of certain Promethean individuals, but universally, as an essential of all human existence ; and (iii) the whole meaning of redemption is concentrated in the forgiveness of sins. This is what distinguishes Christianity from Hellenism and from Judaism. To understand this is to understand the fact of Christ.

[*Note.* There is a good presentation of Holl's views in O. S. Rankin, Israel's Wisdom Literature (1936), 40-44.]

INDEX

(Scripture references are to the English Bible; where Hebrew and/or Greek enumeration differs, this is shown throughout the book.)

APOCRYPHA, ETC.

RABBINIC

IV

RIGHTEOUSNESS

BY

GOTTFRIED QUELL &
GOTTLOB SCHRENK

Translated from the German
first edition, Stuttgart, 1935
and with additional notes
by J. R. Coates

PREFACE

THE quarrel of the world to-day is not so much between right and wrong as between rival ways of defining and doing right, and this points to the underlying unity of mankind. The concept of righteousness is a vital part of the ultimate mystery of man as a social and individual being, and also a clear mark of his capacity for pure worship. But every man experiences frustration and failure, a sense, however faint and fitful, of fundamental guilt and unrighteousness.

That is why the Bible is our Gospel. Matthew Arnold wrote truly in the preface to a cheaper edition of *Literature and Dogma* : " The subject of the Old Testament, Salvation by righteousness, the subject of the New, Righteousness by Jesus Christ, are, in positive strict truth, man's most momentous matters of concern ". But he failed to appreciate the root of the matter, as understood by Paul. This was stated with much warmth and simplicity by an unknown apologist of the second century : " When our iniquity had been fully accomplished, and it had been made perfectly manifest that punishment and death were expected as its recompense, and the season came which God had ordained, when henceforth he should manifest his goodness and power (O the exceeding great kindness and love of God), he hated us not, neither rejected us, nor bore us malice, but was longsuffering and patient, and in pity for us took upon himself our sins, and himself parted with his own son as a ransom for us, the holy for the lawless, the guileless for the evil, the just for the unjust, the incorruptible for the corruptible,

v

the immortal for the mortal. For what else but his righteousness would have covered our sins ? In whom was it possible for us lawless and ungodly men to have been justified, save only in the son of God ? O the sweet exchange, O the inscrutable creation, O the unexpected benefits ; that the iniquity of many should be concealed in one righteous man, and the righteousness of one should justify many that are iniquitous ! Having then in the former time demonstrated the inability of our nature to obtain life, and having now revealed a saviour able to save even creatures which have no ability, he willed that for both reasons we should believe in his goodness and should regard him as nurse, father, teacher, counsellor, physician, mind, light, honour, glory, strength and life." (Epistle to Diognetus ix, trans. Lightfoot.)

It was the rediscovery of this Gospel which gave new life to the Church in the sixteenth century, and there are signs that the same thing is happening in our time. Professor Otto Piper, writing in 1934,* says : " Progressive theology emphasises that there is no really Christian experience as long as we do not believe in the justification of our whole existence through God's mercy ".

Gerhard Kittel's famous Wörterbuch is playing a leading part in this revival, bringing all the relevant resources of modern knowledge to the interpretation of Scripture. In the present volume a brief but penetrating study of Justice in the Old Testament, by Dr. Quell, and a short contribution from Dr. Kleinknecht on Greek ideas, lead to a full presentation and interpretation of Jewish and early Christian material in Dr. Schrenk's discussion of the great words of the New Testament. We are fortunate in having already in English two exceptionally good

* Recent Developments in German Protestantism, p. 117.

articles on Righteousness, one (O.T.) by John Skinner *
and the other (N.T.) by James Moffatt.† The present
work serves to confirm and supplement these, Dr.
Schrenk's exposition of the doctrine of Justification
being of special value. The linguistic material
has been abbreviated in this translation, but nothing
has been omitted which bears directly on the exegesis
of the New Testament.

The Greek words under consideration present
difficulties to the German translator, and further it is not
always easy to be sure of the precise English equivalents
for the terms which he uses. It is the old problem
of ben Sira's grandson, and I can only say with him that
some diligence and travail have been applied to the
matter, in the knowledge that "things originally
spoken in one language have not the same force when
they are translated into another ".‡ The best introduction to the pages which follow is that part of
The Bible and the Greeks (pp. 42-59), in which C. H.
Dodd treats of " righteousness ", reminding us that
" the apostle [Paul] wrote Greek, and read the LXX,
but he was also familiar with the Hebrew original.
Thus while his language largely follows that of the
LXX, the Greek words are for him always coloured
by their Hebrew association."

Gottlob Schrenk was born at Frankfurt am Main
on 10th February, 1879, his father being the founder of
the " Deutsche kirkliche freie Evangelisation ". He
studied theology at Erlangen, Tübingen, Halle, Bonn
and Geneva, and was specially influenced by Martin
Kähler and Adolf Schlatter. After working as a
Rhineland pastor, as Missions-inspektor in the Ostafrika-
mission at Bielefeld, and as a lecturer at the Theological

---

* *Hastings, D. B.* IV, 272-281.
† *Hastings Dict. Apost. Ch.* II, 370-392.   ‡ *Ecclus. Prologue.*

School in Bethel bei Bielefeld, he was appointed in 1923 to the Chair of New Testament at Zürich, occupying it until 1949.

A list of Dr. Schrenk's other writings is given below; * but his main literary work since 1932 has been for the " Kittel " N.T. Dictionary, and this has continued since his retirement. Among his numerous contributions are the articles on βούλομαι, γράφω, ἐντολή, εὐδοκία θέλω, ἱερός, ἐκλεκτός, λεῖμμα, and soon we are to have the longest of all, on πατήρ.

J. R. COATES.

* Gottesreich und Bund im älteren Protestantismus, vornehmlich bei Johannes Coccejus. Zugleich ein Beitrag zur Geschichte des Pietismus und der heilsgeschichtlichen Theologie, 1923.

Grundmotive des Glaubens, 1928.

Die Geschichtsanschauung des Paulus auf dem Hintergrund seines Zeitalters, 1932. (Jahrbuch der theologischen Schule Bethel.)

Der Römerbrief . als Missionsdokument, 1933. (Festgabe für E. F. K. Müller.)

Urchristliche Missionspredigt im ersten Jahrhundert, 1948. (Festgabe für Th. Wurm.)

Rabbinische Charakterköpfe im urchristlichen Zeitalter, 1945. (Judaica I, ii.)

Sabbat oder Sonntag, 1946. (Judaica II, iii.)

Was bedeutet " Israel Gottes " Gal. vi, 16 ? 1949. (Judaica V, ii.)

Der Segensspruch nach der Kampfesepistel : Erwiderung auf Prof. Dahl, Oslo, 1950. (Judaica VI, iii.)

CONTENTS

BIBLIOGRAPHY

W. BAUDISSIN : Kyrios III, 379-428, 1929.
H. BECK : Neue Jahrb. f. deutsche Theol. IV, 249 ff., 1895.
J. A. BEET : Expositor V, vii., 275 ff., 1898.
BOUSSET-GRESSMANN : Rel. d. Jud., 379 ff., 393.
H. BRAUN : Gerichtsged. u. Rechtfert. bei Paul, 1890.
K. BRUGMANN : Indogerm. Forsch. xxxix, 144-149, 1921.
R. BULTMANN : R.G.G., 2nd edn., IV, 1037 f.
H. CREMER : Die paul. Rechtf. Lehre, 2nd edn., 1900.
CREMER-KÖGEL : Wörterbuch d. N.T. Gr., 1923.
J. DENNEY : Expositor IV, 4, 1901.
L. DIESTEL : Jahrb. f. deutsche Theol. V, 173 ff., 1860.
E. VON DOBSCHÜTZ : Th.St.Kr. LXXV, 38 ff., 1912.
V. EHRENBERG : Die Rechtsidee in frühen Griechentum, 1921.
K. H. FALGREN : Uppsala Dissertation on * çedhaqah*, 1932.
F. V. FILSON : St. Paul's Conception of Recompense, 1931.
E. FRAENKEL : Gr. Denominativa, 68 f., 73, 124, 1906.
G. A. FRICKE : Der paul. Grundbegr. d. Δικαιοσύνη θεοῦ, 1888.
H. FUCHS : Christentum und Wissenschaft III, 101-118, 1927.
W. GRUNDMANN : Z.N.W. XXXII, 52-65, 1933.
J. H. GERRETSEN : Rechtvaardigmaking bij Paulus, 1905.
J. GONDA : Utrecht Dissertation on Δείκνυμι etc. 224-232, 1929.
Th. HAERING : Th.St.Kr. LXIX, 139 ff., 1896.
J. HEMPEL : Z.S.Th. X, 377-395, 1930.
H. W. HERTZBERG : Z.A.W. XL, 256-287, 1922.
R. HIRZEL : Themis, Dike, etc. 56-227, 1907.
W. JAEGER : Paideia, 1934.
E. KAUTZSCH : Über die Derivate d. Stammes *çedheq*, 1881.
G. KITTEL : Th.St.Kr. LXXX, 217 ff.
P. KÖLBING : Th.St.Kr. LXVIII, 7 ff., 1895.
P. KRETSCHMER : Glotta I, 381, 1907.
E. KÜHL : Rechtfertigung, etc. bei Paulus, 1904.
K. G. KUHN : Z.N.W. XXX, 305-310, 1931.
R. A. LIPSIUS : Die paul. Rechtf. Lehre, 1853.
E. LOHMEYER : Grundlagen paulin. Theol., 1929.
W. MACHOLZ : Th.St.Kr. LXXX, 29 ff., 1915.
W. MICHAELIS : Festgabe f. A. Deissmann, 1927.
A. MICHELSEN : Z.W.L. V, 133 ff., 1884.
K. MITTRING : Heilswirklichkeit bei Paulus, 1929.
C. G. MONTEFIORE : Judaism and St. Paul, 1914.
MOULTON-MILLIGAN : Vocabulary of the Gk. Test.
E. F. K. MÜLLER : Beobachtungen z. paul. Rechtf. Lehre, 1905.

W. Mundle : Der Glaubensbegriff des Paulus, 1932.

K. Oltmanns : Th.Bl., VIII, 110-116, 1929.

C. von Orelli : Z.W.L. V, 73 ff., 1864.

R. Reitzenstein : Hell. Myst., 257 ff.

A. Ritschl : Die christl. Lehre v. d. Rechtf., etc. II, 4th edn., 1900.

A. Robertson : Expositor V, 9, 187 ff., 1899.

J. H. Ropes : J.B.L. XXII, 211 ff., 1903.

A. Schlatter : Der Glaube im N.T., 4th edn., 1927, etc.

A. Schmitt : Natalicium f. J. Geffcken, 111-131, 1931.

H. Schultz : Th.St.Kr. LXIII, 1890.

A. Schweitzer : The Mysticism of Paul the Apostle, Trans. 1931.

C. A. A. Scott : Christianity According to St. Paul, 1927.

H. St. J. Thackeray : The Relation of St. P. to cont. Jew. Thought, 1900.

Th. Thalheim : Pauly-Wissowa V, s.v. Δίκη, 1905.

E. Tobac : Le Probléme de la Justification dans St. Paul, 1908.

E. Vischer : R.G.G., 2nd edn., IV, 1745 ff.

H. E. Weber : Eschatol. u. Myst. im N.T. 90 ff., 109 ff., 1930.

G. P. Wetter : Der Vergeltungsged. bei Paulus, 161 ff., 1912.

E. Wissmann : D. Verhältnis v. πίστις u. Chr. Frömmigkeit, 1926.

O. Zänker : Z.S.Th. IX, 398-420, 1931.

[S. A. Cook : (See p. 8).

C. H. Dodd : The Bible and the Greeks, 42-59, 1935.

J. Denney, P. Shorey, and others : E.R.E. X, 777-811, 1918.

E. G. Hirsch : J.E. X, 420-424.

R. H. Kennett, Mrs. Adam, H. M. Gwatkin : Early Ideals of Righteousness 1910.

T. W. Manson : Law and Religion, ed. Rosenthal, 127 ff., 1938.

J. Moffatt : (See Preface, p. vii).

A. D. Nock : St. Paul VI, VIII and Bibliography 1938.; Conversion, 1933.

N. L. Robinson : Christian Justice, 1922.

E. Schürer : Gesch. d. Jüd. Volkes, 4th edn., II, 545-579, 1907. Cf. Eng. Tr., 92 f., 1885.

J. Skinner : (See Preface, p. vii).

C. Ryder Smith : The Bible Doctrine of Society, 125-159, 1920.]

For Paul see Commentaries on Rom. and Gal., esp. Excursus in Lietzmann, Sanday and Headlam, Zahn ; and for O.T. Theology esp. Eichrodt, [Davidson], Sellin.

Note.—Square brackets indicate additions by the translator.

ABBREVIATIONS

A.G.G. Abhandlungen d. Kgl. Gesellschaft d. Wissensch. zu Göttingen.

A.P.F. Archiv f. Papyrusforschung.

Bill. Strack u. Billerbeck, Komm. z. N.T. aus Talmud u. Midrasch, 1922-8.

C.A.H. Cambridge Ancient History.

C.B. Cambridge Bible.

D.A.C. Hastings Dictionary of the Apostolic Church.

E.R.E. Hastings Encyclopædia of Religion and Ethics.

H.D.B. Hastings Dictionary of the Bible (5 vols.).

J.B.L. Journal of Biblical Literature (Philadelphia).

J.E. Jewish Encyclopedia.

J.T.S. Journal of Theological Studies.

R.G.G. Die Religion in Geschichte und Gegenwart, 2nd edn., 1927 ff.

S.A.B. Sitzungsberichte . . . Akademie . . . Berlin.

Th.Bl. Theologische Blätter.

Th.St.Kr. Theologische Studien und Kritiken.

W.A. Weimar edition of Luther.

Z.A.W. Zeitschr. f. A.T. Wissenschaft.

Z.S.Th. Zeitschrift f. systematische Theologie.

Z.W.L. Zeitschrift f. kirkliche Wissenschaft u. kirkl. Leben.

I. JUSTICE IN THE OLD TESTAMENT

ALL mutual relationships in Israel were viewed in the light of the idea of justice, and this inevitably determined theological apprehension of the relation established between God and man. The Old Testament doctrine of God is based on the idea of justice, which in turn receives ethical reinforcement through its association with religion. Linguistic usage makes this clear, a variety of expressions being used to indicate, not only the true nature of the mutual relations of God and man, but also divine and human behaviour under these conditions. The supreme importance of justice as a norm in religion gives it validity in ethics.

1. LINGUISTIC

The wealth of the Hebrew vocabulary is shown by the variety of terms for which LXX uses δίκη, δικαιοσύνη, δίκαιος, δικαιοῦν, while an examination of the different terms used throughout LXX for the principal Hebrew words shows how carefully the Greek translators tried to reproduce the sense of the original—even where their rendering is not quite happy.

Δίκη is used 9 times for *ribh* (verb and noun), but only once for *din* (Ps. ix, 5), once for *mishpaṭ* (Ps. cxl, 12 [Heb. 13] LXX cxxxix, 13) and once for the obscure *ḥaruç* (Joel iii, 14–Heb. and LXX iv, 14, " decision " ?). As a rendering of *naqam* (Exod. xxi, 20 ; Lev. xxvi, 25 ; Deut. xxxii, 41, 43), it weakens the idea of vengeance. Its use at Hos. xiii, 14, seems to be a mistake due to the confusion

1

of *debher* with *dabhar*. It is surprising that LXX is so sparing in the use of δίκη ; one would have expected it frequently as an accurate rendering of *mishpaṭ* or even *çedheq*.

Δικαιοσύνη occurs relevantly for *çedheq* 81 times, for *çᵉdhaqah* 134 times, and in periphrasis for *çaddiq* 6 times (Ps. lxxii, 7–LXX lxxi, 7 ; Prov. ii, 20 ; xi, 21, 30 ; xv, 6 ; xx, 7) ; cf. also Is. xxvi, 2. Its equivalent is *ḥeṣedh* only 8 times (Gen. xix, 19 ; xx, 13 ; xxi, 23 ; xxxii, 10 ; Exod. xv, 13 ; xxxiv, 7 ; Prov. xx, 28–LXX 22 ; Is. lxiii, 7), and *'ᵉmeth* 6 times (Gen. xxiv, 49 ; Josh. xxiv, 14 ; Is. xxxviii, 19 ; xxxix, 8 ; Dan. viii, 12 ; ix, 13). It is also used for *mesharim* (I Chron. xxix, 17) ; *ṭobh* (Ps. xxxviii, 21–LXX xxxvii, 21) ; *madhon* (Prov. xvii, 14) ; *niqqayon* (Gen. xx, 5) ; even for *pethi*, "simplicity" (Prov. i, 22) and *zakhu* (Aram.), "innocence" (Dan. vi, 23, [but cf. Heb. *zakhah*, Micah vi, 11 ; Ps. li, 6]). Through carelessness it stands for *haskel* at Prov. xxi, 16.

Δίκαιος occurs 189 times for *çaddiq* ; in free rendering 24 times for *çedheq* ; 5 times for *çᵉdhaqah* ; at Dan. xii, 3 for *hiçdiq*. It is also found for *yashar* (Job i, 1, 8 ; ii, 3 ; Prov. iii, 32 ; xi, 4 ; xiv, 9 ; xxi, 2, 18) ; *naqi* (Job. ix, 23 ; xvii, 8, etc.) ; *tamim* (Prov. xxviii, 18). Elsewhere it is used loosely for *'ᵉmeth*, *din*, *ḥeṣedh*, *ṭahor*, *mishpaṭ*, *nadhibh* and *naqam*.

Δικαιοῦν comes relevantly 21 times for various parts of the verb *çadhaq*, and once for the noun *çedheq* (Is. xlii, 21) ; twice for *ribh* (Mic. vii, 9 and Is. i, 17) ; once for *shaphaṭ* (Niph. at I Sam. xii, 7) ; and a few times for parts of *zakhah* and *baḥan*.

Δικαίωμα stands for *ḥoq* (48 times), *ḥuqqah* (22), *mishpaṭ* (38), *miçwah* (Deut. xxx, 16 ; I Kings ii, 3), *çᵉdhaqah* (II Sam. xix, 28 ; Prov. viii, 20), *ribh* (Jer. xi, 20 ; xviii, 19) and, with less appropriateness, a few other terms.

The one Hebrew expression which is generally represented by δίκη and its derivatives (esp. δικαιοσύνη) is *çedheq* and its derivatives, other synonymous terms being very rarely thus indicated. Of the latter, *mishpaṭ* stands out as a word not sufficiently appreciated by LXX; its connotation in Hebrew is only partly conveyed by LXX κρίμα (182 times) and κρίσις (142), which emphasise the act of judgment. Another word for which δικαιοσύνη is an excellent equivalent is *ḥesedh* : but LXX prefers to use ἔλεος (172 times), emphasising the emotional element without due regard to Hebrew usage. The Greek translators also failed to appreciate the value of *tamam* and its derivatives in the sphere of *çᵉdhaqah* and *mishpaṭ*.

Our key words are thus *mishpaṭ*,[1] *çedheq* (*çᵉdhaqah*),[2] *ḥesedh*,[3] and *ḥoq*.[4] These terms, like *bᵉrith*, have both

---

[1] *Mishpaṭ* exemplifies almost all the types of meaning which belong to nouns with the prefix *M*. The primary sense of "judgment", concrete (I Kings xx, 40 : Ps. xvii, 2) or more abstract (Lev. xix, 15), gives rise to its common use for legal norm, legal claim, legal custom.

[2] There seems to be no difference in meaning between the masculine and feminine forms. The shorter form is preferred for the *genetivus epexegeticus*, and means "correctness".

[3] *Ḥesedh* is the natural sense of justice which regulates non-legal relationships, e.g. among members of the same tribe or group. "Love" is a misleading translation because it is always a matter of intention, having regard to what is just, and not a spontaneous, personal feeling, like '*ahebh*, etc. Love may, or may not, find expression in *ḥesedh*, which is always governed by objective considerations. A better translation, though not quite adequate, is "loyalty". (It has the late Hebrew meaning, "charm" or "grace", in Is. xl, 6, but is a scribal error, cf. I Pet. i, 24.) The etymology is obscure ; cf. Nöldeke, Neue Beiträge zur sem. Sprachwiss. (1910) 93. It belongs to the covenant circle of ideas : cf. I Sam. xx, 8, etc.

[4] *Ḥoq* means something engraved or inscribed on a hard substance, and so denotes statute or law in a narrower sense.

a juristic and a theological use, and the obvious presumption that the latter grew out of the former, though not directly demonstrable, may be allowed to pass, since we are mainly concerned here with theology, i.e. with the application of the words to God or to a specifically religious attitude on the part of man.

2. THE RIGHTEOUSNESS OF GOD

God is the author of justice, and, as a just God, is bound to act justly ; this is the immovable ground of Old Testament faith in all its varieties, the common denominator which gives religious unity to Israel : prophets, priests, lawgivers, the common people—all are convinced of the justice of God as the disposer of all things and the ground of hope. It cannot be denied that there is a causal connexion between this association of justice with religion and the historical development of the Yahwe religion out of a tribal religion in which the Godhead was not only over his people but also in fellowship with them. Yahwe is the fountain of justice from which all O.T. codes of law are derived ; [1] his decisions on matters of civil law and on political questions in the nomadic period are made known through the sacred lot (Exod. xxviii, 30) ; these judgments (*mishpaṭim*) form his *torah* (instruction, guidance, *weisung* : Deut. xxxiii, 10). Because he is the supreme judge, his divine authority is involved in the details of Israel's historical situation. " Shall not the judge of all the earth do right ? " (Gen. xviii, 25 J). Abraham's trustful question may sound like an example of man's audacious

---

[1] " The judgment is God's " (Deut. i, 17). This is fundamental in other Semitic religions ; cf. Baudissin, Kyrios III (1929), 382 ff.

effort to drag God into the service of his moral convictions; but it is really an expression of absolute assurance that whatever God does must have the force of a *mishpaṭ*, and testifies to the submission that always characterises the worshippers of Yahwe. Yahwe's law is indisputable and unchangeable; to disregard it is contrary to nature (Jer. viii, 7). "His work is perfect" (Deut. xxxii, 4)—a faultless whole, inherently permanent; "for all his ways are judgment"—awarding to every man that which belongs to him and giving him security. Yahwe's judgment is righteous because he is righteous—"a God of faithfulness and without iniquity, just and right is he"—and as such he can be trusted; there is nothing crooked or deceptive in his ordinance, for his thoughts are straight and true.[1]

Utterances like the one just quoted picture Yahwe as a ruler and judge discharging the duties of his office, "a righteous judge" (Ps. vii, 12; cf. Jer. xii, 1). This view appeared early in Israel, even when it had nothing in common with the just administration of civil law. The Song of Deborah calls the victory of the tribes of Israel "the righteous acts of Yahwe" (Judg. v, 11). It is easy to see how confidence in the judicial qualities of Yahwe leads to progress in the idea of God: if his favour is felt to be a righteous judgment in the case of a victory over nations with other gods, that must involve some sort of belief in the extension of his sovereignty over those nations. At all events it was from legal proceedings that Israel drew its picture of the world order. The danger of this view lies obviously in the fact that it postulates a splitting up of mankind into hostile groups, and leads only too easily to the forestalling

[1] Cf. Ps. xi, 7, where "righteousness" may mean either right verdicts or right actions.

of the divine judgment. Those who pray are apt to
make a claim upon Yahwe's righteousness, and to
ask him to pronounce their enemies guilty (e.g.
Ps. v, 10, 12–Heb. 9, 11).[1] The idea of righteousness
loses its objective power when the suppliant urges his
own sense of justice upon the judge. God's righteousness may even come to be thought of as concerned
only with the affairs of the upright and the pure
(Ps. xviii, 25 f.–Heb. 26 f.). It is, however, hardly
fair to such utterances, simply to track down the
consequences of their theory of justice. They show,
rather, how strong religious motifs can come to life
out of a theologically coloured way of regarding the
justice of God, so that it is hardly possible any longer
to base an adequate interpretation of the application
of the idea of righteousness to God upon its formal
outlines alone. This belongs to the sphere of faith,
for it is the expression of unconditional trust in the
moral will of God, by the force of which goodness is
rewarded with preservation while wickedness is condemned to destruction. Out of *çᵉdhaqah* as the norm
for perfect *shalom* there develops *çᵉdhaqah* as action
which achieves, renews and secures it.

3. THE RIGHTEOUSNESS OF MAN

What has just been said applies not only to divine
activities, but also to human behaviour towards both
God and man. Old Testament writers show a
marked preference for a juristic view of ethical and
religious practice. They constantly see the " righteous " pleading his cause before the judge, defending
himself against malevolence and falsehood, and

---

[1] Habakkuk adapts the individual lamentation motif to the
contrast between Israel and the Chaldeans, e.g. i, 13 ; cf. ii, 4.

winning his case. In this way the good man's misery and anxiety disappears before the mighty power of faith in the unchangeable grace and favour of the covenant God. The "righteous" (*çaddiq*) is the man whom God's verdict has justified (*hiçdiq*), and the "wicked" (*rasha'*) is the man whom God has condemned; the background being the picture of a judicial process (*ribh*).[1] So *çaddiq* comes to mean "godly", and *çedhaqah* "godliness"—as that which earns the divine acquittal.[2] Another term for the latter is *'emunah*, fidelity in the fulfilment of God's commandments in the midst of uncertainty and opposition. "The righteous lives by his fidelity" (Hab. ii, 4): i.e. he escapes the death penalty, planned for him by his enemies, through his unflinching faithfulness to God's commandment.[3] The word *'emunah* aptly expresses that which is demanded by faith in God's righteousness and hope of his approval.

Personal or national misfortune often enough suggests that Yahwe's verdict is unfavourable. In such a case *çedheq*, in the sense of success,[4] is not in view; the idea of "righteousness" gives place to other motifs. Yahwe is a rock, the last refuge of the godly in distress: Ps. lxii, 7 (8), etc. Yet even then faith can cry, "Unto thee, O Lord, belongeth the love of justice (*hesedh*): for thou renderest to every man according to his work": Ps. lxii, 12 (13). Job's

---

[1] Cf. Deut. xxv, 1.

[2] Cf. I Sam. xxvi, 23; I Kings viii, 32; Deut. vi, 25 (here righteousness almost means acquittal, cf. Gen. xv, 1).

[3] Paul is not mistaken in his use of the quotation in Rom. i, 17; Gal. iii, 11, though he certainly reads more into the word *'emunah* than was intended by Habakkuk. LXX ἐκ πίστεώς μου is most simply explained as a mistake; but it might be that the translator was theologising—like Paul.

[4] As of Cyrus, in Is. xli, 2 [see Skinner, C. B. (1929) *ad loc.*].

torment is the agony of doubting the righteousness of God. Is Justice between God and man really valid as a self-evident axiom? This is the question which the poet is asking in his dialogue. He knows that the traditional dogma will become a merely fantastic assertion, unless it is projected into a higher sphere.

[*Note.*—There is an important discussion, with useful references, bearing on the questions raised in chapters I and II, by S. A. Cook in W. R. Smith, *The Religion of the Semites*, 3rd ed. (1927), pp. 655-671. Cf. W. R. Smith, *The Prophets of Israel*, 2nd ed. (1902), pp. 70 ff., and S. A. Cook, *Cambridge Ancient History*, vol. II (1931), pp. 397 ff., 669 f.]

II. THE GREEK IDEA OF JUSTICE

1. GREEK society from the eighth to the beginning of the fifth century B.C. was based on the idea of justice—religious, political and ethical—and the political philosophy of the fourth century was built on the same foundation.[1] It is significant that for the Greeks it was not the rational and logical conception which came first, but the mythical figure of the goddess: "There is virgin Justice, the daughter of Zeus, who is honoured and reverenced among the gods who dwell on Olympus" (Hesiod, Works and Days, 256 f., trans. H. G. Evelyn–White).[2] Hesiod's incipient rationalism turned the sturdy figure of the goddess, sitting beside the judgment-seat of Zeus, into the reign of law, no less divine, prevailing in the world and in the life of the city, as understood by Solon.[3] Justice is for the latter still divine, although his more modern conception of divinity differs from that of Hesiod ; it is not a human device, but a law, independent of man, which he cannot evade, however he may twist and turn. The recognition of justice in politics now leads to its discovery, by analogy, as the law of the universe : the only remaining fragment

---

[1] See pp. 26 f.

[2] ἡ δέ τε παρθένος ἐστὶ Δίκη, Διὸς ἐκγεγαυῖα κυδρή τ' αἰδοίη τε θεοῖς, οἳ Ὄλυμπον ἔχουσιν. [P. Shorey, in E.R.E. (1918) X, 801, regards this as "conscious allegory" ; and it may be noted that δίκη occurs 9 times in lines 248-273, and has to be translated into 4 different English words.]

[3] Frag. i, 8 (i, 17 Diehl) ; Frag. iii, 14 ff. (i, 23 Diehl). Cf. W. Jaeger, Solons Eunomie, S.A.B. (1926), 69-85.

of Anaximander speaks of its immanence.[1] The advance from punishment by an external deity to immanent punitive justice thus leads to the conception of a divine world-order : [2] as Heraclitus has it, " For the sun will not pass his bounds, else will the avenging deities, helpers of justice, find him out " (Frag. 94, Diels I, 96).

2. Next to Solon, the greatest exponent of the idea of justice is Theognis, among whose sayings the famous verse occurs : " In justice all virtue is comprehended." [3] Justice is here, in this early period, not an inner quality, but the legally prescribed behaviour of the citizen towards society. This explains how all virtues came to be included in the later conception of δικαιοσύνη. [4] When Plato makes this the guiding principle, both for the State and for the individual (Rep. IV, 443c ff.), he is harking back to the primitive religious aspect of justice. Aristotle devotes a whole book of his treatise on ethics to δικαιοσύνη, and gives it the place of honour among the virtues (Eth. Nic. V, iii, 1129b, 27) ; it means the performance of all one's social duties (ib. v, 1130b, 11 f.). The comprehensive connotation is primary, and is to be distinguished from the narrower, juristic

[1] Frag. ix (i, 15 Diels) : the elements " make reparation and satisfaction to one another for their injustice " (δίκην καὶ τίσιν ἀλλήλοις τῆς ἀδικίας). The time-process itself continually redresses the balance. Parmenides also presents δίκη as a principle universally at work, identical with necessity or fate (Frag. viii, 12 f. ; cf. the same in Euripides—see W. Nestle, Gr. Religiosität II, 1933, 124).

[2] Cf. Jaeger, Paideia 217 ff. ; " The recognition of this law or norm in nature has a direct religious significance. It is not simply a description of fact ; it is a justification of the universe " (219).

[3] ἐν δὲ δικαιοσύνῃ συλλήβδην πᾶσ' ἀρετή ἐστιν (147, i, 124 Diehl). [Quoted from Phocylides, Frag. 15 ; see P. Shorey in E.R.E. X, 802.] [4] See pp. 26 f.

use, which makes it one among other virtues (ib. iv, 1130*a*, 14 ; 1130*b*, 3 ff., 30 ff.). The double reference is also indicated by etymological research.[1]

3. Many views have been held concerning the original connotation of the word δίκη [which we have translated as " justice "]. It used to be thought, from its connexion with δείκνυμι, " indicate ", that it meant " way " or " custom ", as that which is indicated, and that it thus came to mean " right " or " justice ".[2] Another view was that the legal reference came first, connecting it with δικεῖν, as if this meant " to strike ", the reference being to the stroke of the judge's staff ; [3] but this will not do, because δικεῖν means " to throw " ; nor is it satisfactory to make it refer to the " throw " which determined the divine judgment.[4] Even if we connect δικεῖν with δεικνύναι [5] or take it to mean the stretching out of the hand by Justice when she makes her award,[6] this recognises as primitive only the ideas of right and justice. The fact is that from the beginning, as far as our observation extends, δίκη is used to express both sets of ideas, viz. custom, etc. as well as right, etc. The question therefore arises whether both meanings may not have been developed simultaneously from the same root ; and this has now been shown to have been the case.[7]

The fundamental meaning of the root " deik " is " showing the way ", " determining ". It is represented figuratively by the outstretched hand. Δίκη

---

[1] Paragraphs 1 and 2 are contributed by Hermann Kleinknecht.

[2] G. Curtius, Grundzüge der Gr. Etymol., 5th ed. (1879), 134 ; Cremer-Kögel, 296. Gonda (see Bibl.), 216 f. Aristotle's derivation from δίχα is only valuable for the appended comment (Eth. Nic. V, vii, 1132*a*, 28).

[3] Hirzel, 60 ff., 94. [Cf. E.R.E. X, 801.]

[4] Ehrenberg, 76 ff.   [5] Brugmann, 144 ff.

[6] Kretschmer, 268.   [7] Gonda, 228, 230 f.

thus means directing, determining, and that which is directed or determined (cf. statuere, statutum, etc.). This is the starting-point for both lines of development, which may be traced as follows.

General. (*a*) What is usual : Homer, Od. iv, 691 ; what is right : Pindar, Ol. ii, 18 ; manner : Pindar, Pyth. ii, 84 ; traditional custom : II Macc. viii, 26 (A), and frequently in the Papyri. (*b*) Due : Hesiod, Shield of H., 85 ; fair dealing : Homer, Od. xiv, 84 ; reciprocity (cf. Aristot. Eth. Nic. V, vii, 1131*b*). (*c*) Fate, natural necessity,[1] lot : Homer, Od. xi, 218 ; the corresponding Sanskrit root means " lot ".

Juristic. (*a*) Justice : Homer, Il. xvi, 388 ; in Hesiod (see p. 9) it means the right of the oppressed, recognised by the community ;[2] Josephus, War, V, 2. (*b*) Legal action, judgment : Homer and Hesiod ; LXX for *ribh*, Job xxix, 16 ; *din*, Ps. ix, 4 (5) ; *mishpaṭ*, Ps. cxl, 12 (13) ; *ḥaruç*, Joel iii, 14 ; also Josephus, Philo, Epictetus. (*c*) Punishment, commonly personified[3] (cf. Wis. xi, 20), but also impersonally, esp. in LXX, e.g. Exod. xxi, 20.[4]

4. The New Testament has δίκη only 3 times, viz., Acts xxviii, 4 ; II Thess. i, 9 ; Jude 7 ; always in the sense of punishment or penal justice. (The true reading in Acts xxv, 15, is καταδίκην, condemnation.)

---

[1] Ehrenberg, 60.   [2] Ehrenberg, 65 f.

[3] Schlatter (Theol. Jud., 40 ff.) rightly emphasises the personification of δίκη by Josephus : e.g. Bell. vii, 34. At IV Macc. viii, 14, 22 δίκη is merciful.

[4] On δίκη in Corp. Herm. cf. J. Kroll, Die Lehren des Herm. Trismeg. (1914) 219 f.

III. RIGHTEOUS

1. GREEK AND HELLENISTIC

(*a*) Δίκαιος denotes one who is correct according to the traditions of polite society, observing δίκη as opposed to ὕβρις (Homer, Od. vi, 119 ff.).

(*b*) It also covers duty towards man and towards God. Usually the latter is expressed by ὅσιος, εὐσεβής, θεοφιλής, θεοσεβής; δίκαιος being frequently used with one of these to indicate one who does both his moral and his religious duty, e.g. Jos. Ant., x, 215.¹ An example of the purely religious reference is Aesch. Seven ag. Th., 594, where it is contrasted with δυσσεβής.

(*c*) A specially common use of δίκαιος is for one who observes legal norms; as Aristotle says, " Clearly the righteous man will be he who is both law-abiding and impartial " (Eth. Nic. V, ii, 1129*a*, 33).

(*d*) Moral philosophy extends the reference of the term so as to embrace the whole of life, with all its social virtues, making what is righteous equivalent to what is beautiful, good, fitting (Epict. Diss., I, xxii, 1; II, xvii, 6). The quality indicated by δίκαιος thus takes its place as one of the four cardinal virtues, wisdom, temperance, justice, courage.² The Stoic

¹ Schlatter op. cit. 37, points out that Josephus here expresses a Pharisaic idea, similar to Jesus' summary of the Law as love to God and man. As a Hellenistic Jew, he is debtor both to Greece and to the O.T.; but though his idiom is Greek, he knows well that for the Jew religion is everything (Ap. ii, 171, 181).

² The fourfold summary of virtues is considerably older than Plato, being found first in Aeschylus (Sept. c. Theb. 610). Wilamowitz wrongly regarded the line as an interpolation from a Platonic source. Aeschylus was no doubt using an early Greek idea.

interpretation makes it specially clear that man is here always considered theoretically and never empirically. And indeed Plato himself, though expressly treating of justice as a political virtue, finds the root of the matter in the human soul, where the individual is truly himself, with all his powers in order and harmony (Rep. iv, 433c ff.). Δίκαιος thus comes to signify an innate quality of human nature, of which man avails himself in his activities.[1] Josephus not only regards it as belonging to the sphere of virtue, but goes the length of speaking of his heroes as men who are " naturally " (τὴν φύσιν) righteous, e.g. Ant. vii, 110 ; ix, 216, etc., and calls the opposite of righteousness a deviation from virtue (Ant. vi, 93) ; his δίκαιος may refer either to virtue or to faithfulness to the Law, but his lists of virtues always include righteousness along with goodness, etc., and differ in no way from those of his non-Jewish contemporaries, e.g. Ant. ix, 260.[2]

Philo is still more pronounced in his emphasis on righteousness as one of the cardinal virtues. His excessive praise of the righteous is suggestive of the Hellenistic glorification of man. As the mainstay of the human race, the righteous man stands over against the unrighteous multitude, exercising the healing influence of the justice which has made him whole (Migr. Abr. 61, 121, 124 ; Det. Pot. Ins. 123) ; he seeks the essential nature of things (Leg. All. III, 78). Faith is a δίκαιον, i.e. a meritorious virtue (Rer. Div.

---

[1] [" This cheerful acceptance of man's nature as being disposed to walk aright, provided that his powers and instincts are duly guided, and not warped by hardships or excessive prosperity, runs throughout the whole course of Greek thought " (Mrs. Adam in Early Ideals of Righteousness, 1910, p. 35).]

[2] Josephus is fond of associating δίκαιος with words for goodness, such as εὔνοια (Ant. i, 318), ἀγαθός (vii, 389 ; viii, 248) or χρηστός (ix, 133).

Her. 94), displayed in the patriarchs—specially in Noah, on the ground of a mistaken etymology—who are called righteous on this account (Leg. All. III, 228; Det. Pot. Ins. 121). This is, of course, a blending of Hellenistic ethics with the Old Testament description of the godly man as " the righteous " (çaddiq). Apart from the points mentioned, Josephus and Philo keep close to Hebrew and Jewish tradition. Josephus is familiar with the Pharisaic conception of righteousness as obedience to God's commandments (Ap. ii, 293, etc.), uses δίκαιος in the sense of " punctilious " (Ant. xv, 106), and holds the conviction that righteousness can be gained through repentance (Ant. vi, 21). Philo applies δίκαιος to God much more frequently than Josephus, e.g. Somn. II, 194.

(e) A quantitative view of morality is indicated by the frequent appearance of the comparative and superlative of δίκαιος in Greek writers of all ages, but these are not found in the New Testament.

(f) The application of δίκαιος to things is also absent from the N.T., though it is used with "judgment " (John v, 30; [cf. Rev. xvi, 7; xix, 2]); "ways " (Rev. xv, 3); ["commandment " (Rom. vii, 12)]. "Righteous blood " (Matt. xxiii, 35) means "innocent ", cf. xxvii, 4, and Jonah i, 14, LXX.

(g) Tὸ δίκαιον is defined by Aristotle as "that which is legal and fair " (Eth. Nic. V, ii, 1129a, 34 : τὸ μὲν δίκαιον ἄρα τὸ νόμιμον καὶ τὸ ἴσον, τὸ δ' ἄ δικον τὸ παράνομον καὶ τὸ ἄνισον) ; cf. Col. iv, 1. Other definitions reflect different ideals of justice,[1] the Pythagoreans equating it with retaliation, Plato with the virtue of the citizen who obeys the law of his own nature.[2] The Plural (τά δίκαια) is used in a juristic sense, esp. in the Papyri, meaning rights, orders, claims, etc. LXX has both Sing. and Plur. in this

[1] Hirzel 186 ff.   [2] See p. 14.

sense,[1] but it is not found in the N.T. Josephus applies the term δίκαιον to all law, Jewish and Gentile, and can speak of " natural right " (War I, 507 : τὸ τῆς φύσεως δίκαιον).

(*h*) Josephus also uses δίκαιος with verbs of thinking (cf. II Pet. i, 13), speaking, doing, etc., as the N.T. uses δικαιοσύνη (Matt. vi, 1 ; Rom. ix, 30). The latter word with him refers to the practice of right, the former to its content.

(*i*) The simple conventional formula, " it is right ", occurs in Josephus, sometimes meaning " according to the Law ".

(*j*) The adverb means " with full right " or " deservedly " or " justly ", and is used with the verb " judge " (Deut. i, 16 ; Prov. xxxi, 9 (LXX xxiv, 77) ; Ecclus. xxxii, 22), and with " suffer " (Wis. xix, 13 ; Test. Sim. iv, 3).

2. SEPTUAGINT

A decisive change in the use of δίκαιος took place in the LXX, in spite of what has been said about its conformity with ordinary Greek and Hellenistic usage, under the influence of O.T. faith, which had the effect of linking it closely with the thought of the judgment of God. The idea of virtue gave place to the fundamental question of man's standing in the light of that judgment, as made known in the Law. The rest of Greek literature means by δίκαιος one who does what is commonly thought to be right, fulfilling his duty as a citizen ; here it means one who obeys God as a member of the theocratic community. This comes out very clearly in the words used to indicate the opposite of δίκαιος, viz. ἄδικος, Prov. xii, 17 ; xxix, 27 ; ἁμαρτωλός, Ps. cxxv, 3 (LXX

[1] E.g. Job viii, 3 ; xxxiv, 12, A ; Prov. xvi, 33 ; xviii, 5.

cxxiv, 3) ; Tob. iv, 17 ; ἀσεβής, Gen. xviii, 23 ; Prov. x, 28 ; Wis. iii, 10 ; παράνομος, Job. xvii, 8.

The background of this is the conviction that God himself is δίκαιος. Hellenistic Judaism thus prepares the way for the central religious value of the term in the New Testament, by maintaining that God always observes the self-imposed law of his own being, and never fails to fulfil his promises, in loyalty to his covenant : e.g. I Sam. ii, 2 [not in Heb.] ; Ezra ix, 15 ; Tob. iii, 2. God is said to be just and holy (δίκαιος καὶ ὅσιος) : Deut. xxxii, 4 ; Ps. cxlv (cxliv), 17. It is not only as the righteous judge, inflicting just punishment, that God is called δίκαιος, but also as the bestower of salvation : Ps. cxvi (cxiv), 5 (see p. 30).

3. RABBINICAL JUDAISM

(a) The doctrine of rewards and punishments led the Rabbis to draw a hard and fast line between the righteous and the godless, and to take an optimistic view of man's ability to achieve righteousness before God. Corresponding to δίκαιος are the Hebrew çaddiq, yashar, kasher, and their Aramaic equivalents,[1] which mean that a man has observed the Law generally,[2] and that his merits outweigh his transgressions. The godless man is he whose balance is on the other side. Two further types are also recognised, viz. the mediocre (benoni) [3] and the penitent (ba'al t͏ᵉshubhah).[4] Hillel and Shammai differed in their views of the former,[5] and there was keen debate

---

[1] çaddiqa', koshra', kashshira', zakka'ah, zakka'y. See Billerbeck III, 222 f.

[2] Bab. Ab. Z. 4a ; Shir Rabb. ii, 1 (62a), etc. ; see Bill. I, 816.

[3] Jer. R. ha Sh. 57a, 49, Bill. III, 230 f.

[4] Bab. Sukkah 53a Bar., Bill. II, 211.

[5] Bill. II, 361 f.

as to whether the penitent or the perfectly righteous should be given the highest place.[1]   The patriarchs were accounted perfectly righteous, partly because they perfectly repressed the evil inclination.[2]   The striking prominence of Abel in the N.T. has no parallel in Rabbinical literature, which never tires of pointing to Abraham, Isaac, Jacob[3] and others,[4] while Philo refers to Noah.[5]   (On the merit of the Fathers, cf. p. 32 [and see M. Joseph in E.R.E. xi, 144 f.]).

Many teachers are specially commended as being righteous, and the prophet and the righteous often go together.[6]   The prayer of a righteous man, towards whom God's heart goes out,[7] changes severity into mercy.[8]

(b) The Messiah is called righteous, because he is altogether conformed to the divine will.   Both Rabbis and apocalyptic writers frequently use the predicate in this connexion.[9]   The synagogue loves the expression, " Messiah our righteousness ",[10] with special

[1] Bab. Ber. 34b, Bill. I, 603.

[2] Bab. B.B. 16b-17a Bar., Bill. III, 187 ; IV, 479.

[3] Cf. Prayer Man. 8.

[4] Cf. Schlatter, Matt. 688.

[5] Cf. Ecclus. xliv, 17.

[6] Pesiqta Rab. 40 (167b), Bill. III, 124.

[7] Bab. Yeb. 64a, Bab. Ḥull. 60b, Bill. I, 453.

[8] Bab. Sukkah 14a, Bill. I, 454.   On the prayer of the righteous, see Enoch xlvii, 1, 4 ; xcvii, 3, 4 ; Jos. Bell. v, 403. [Cf. Prov. xv, 8, 29 ; James v, 16.]

[9] H. Dechent, Der " Gerechte "—eine Bezeichnung für den Messias, Theol. Stud. Krit. 100 (1927-1928), 439 ff. Cf. as parallels the $\delta\iota\kappa\alpha\iota o\nu$ $\pi\nu\epsilon\hat{\upsilon}\mu\alpha$ of Apollo (Anc. Gr. Inscr. Brit. Mus. IV, 1062) and $\delta\iota\kappa\alpha\iota o\varsigma$ as epithet of Isis, P. Roussel, Les Cultes Egyptiens à Delos (1925 f.), 171, 276.

[10] Pesiqta Rab. 36 (162a) ; 37 (162b, 163a), Billerbeck II, 289 f. Cf. Shemoneh 'Esreh 14 (Palest. Rec.) : Meshiaḥ çidhqekha, thy righteous Messiah, Bill. IV, 213 [text in Dalman, Die Worte Jesu (1898), 300].

reference to Jer. xxiii, 5 [1] and 6 [2] ; xxxiii, 15 [3] ; Zech. ix, 9.[4] On the other hand Is. liii, 11*b* and Dan. xii, 3, are taken to mean Israel and those who are righteous.[5] Only since the third century A.D. has Is. liii, 11 been interpreted Messianically.[6] The book of Wisdom abounds in the use of the title "the Righteous" for the Messiah, e.g. at ii, 18.[7] The Psalms of Solomon also associate righteousness with the Messiah : xvii, 25, 28, 31, 35, 42 ; xviii, 8 f. It is fundamental in Enoch (xxxviii, 2 ; liii, 6) that righteousness is the characteristic of the Messianic age, and the righteous will obtain the greatest promises in the day of salvation, because of their good works.[8] At Habakkuk ii, 4 faithfulness is the summing-up of a life of meritorious obedience to the Law.[9]

4. NEW TESTAMENT

A deep gulf separates the N.T. δίκαιος from the world of Greek idealism, in which every man is the captain of his own soul. Echoes of the latter are heard in the Gospels, e.g. when Romans apply the conventional epithet to Jesus ; and the word is also

[1] Targ., Bill. II, 113.

[2] Bab. Bab. B. 75*b* ; Shir Rabb. on i, 16, Bill. I, 66 ; Midr. Ps. xxi, § 2, ib. II, 352 ; Midr. Prov. xix, 21, ib. IV, 784.

[3] Targ., Bill. II, 113.

[4] Pes. Rab. 34 (159*b*), Bill. I, 844.

[5] Bill. I, 481-485.   [6] Bab. Sanh. 98*b*, ib. 481 f.

[7] [But cf. R. H. Charles, Eschatology 2nd ed. (1913) 309 : "Our author makes no reference to the Messiah " ; J. A. F. Gregg, C.B. (1909) xlviii : "Strictly speaking, there is no Messianic hope in Wisdom " ; E. Schürer, Gesch. Jüd. Volk., 4th ed. (1907) II, 593 : "The former Messianic interpretation of Wis. ii, 12-20 is totally unfounded."]

[8] Bill. IV, 799 ff.

[9] Targ., Hab. ii, 4, Bill. III, 542 ; cf. ib. I, 907.

found in some common phrases which are not bound up with the Greek view of life. Otherwise this term provides a specially good example of the influence of the Old Testament and of the change brought about by the Gospel.

(a) When Pilate's wife calls Jesus righteous (Matt. xxvii, 19), she may mean both that he is innocent and that he is a good man from the ethical point of view, unless she—or the narrator—is "judaising".[1] The same can be said of the use of the word by Pilate himself (Matt. xxvii, 24).[2] The centurion at the Cross (Luke xxiii, 47), and Herod, speaking of John the Baptist (Mark vi, 20), are to be understood as meaning what is commonly meant when a man is called a saint, the former indicating innocence as well. Paul includes "whatsoever things are just" in the list of social virtues which he borrows from Hellenism (Phil. iv, 8), but it is inconceivable that he should mean anything other than doing God's will. Another clear echo of Greek ethics is heard in the language of Titus ii, 12, but there is nothing Greek in the thought of the passage.

We need not dwell on the use of δίκαιον, etc., in common phrases, e.g. II Pet. i, 13 ; Luke xii, 57 ; Col. iv, 1 ; Matt. xx, 4 ; Phil. i, 7 ; but in some cases it has been found necessary to deepen the meaning by adding an explicit reference to God : e.g. Acts iv, 19 ; II Thess. i, 6 ; and of course this reference is implied in Eph. vi, 1 (cf. Josephus Ant. ix, 58).

(b) The connotation of δίκαιος in the New Testament is largely determined by the Old Testament ;

---

[1] Acta Pilati, 2nd ed. 1876 (Tischendorf), 223.

[2] τοῦ δικαίου is not in B D Syr. Sin. On the other hand, the apostles are called οἱ δίκαιοι in the Harkleian margin at Acts xiv, 2.

but a new feature comes into view, which may be illustrated as follows.

(i) In line with the O.T. are passages which speak of God as Judge, e.g. Rev. xv, 3 ; xvi, 5, 7 ; xix, 2 ; I Pet. ii, 23 ; John xvii, 25. As these confirm and deepen the idea of the divine justice, so Rom. vii, 12 emphasises the truth that the Law is invested with the glory of its Author.

On the other hand, it is something new, when absolute justice is said to be shown in the atonement through the sacrificial death of Jesus (Rom. iii, 26) and when God is called "faithful and just to forgive our sins" (I John i, 9), δίκαιος combining the ideas of judgment and salvation. In both these examples the influence of Is. xl-lv and Psalms can be recognised ; what is new is the linking of righteousness with the atoning death of Christ, in which God is proved to be δίκαιος.

(ii) As applied to the Messiah, δίκαιος has its O.T. meaning at Acts iii, 13 f. and vii, 52, and refers to the perfect obedience of Jesus to the will of God, the context also suggesting his innocence in contrast to those who put him to death, in line with the preaching of the Cross in Acts (cf. Matt. xxvii, 4, where some MSS have δίκαιον). The attestation of the innocent victim in the resurrection is meant at Acts xxii, 14. Those who belong to the righteous Jesus must do righteousness, in opposition to licentiousness (I John ii, 29 ; iii, 7).[1] Christ's vicarious death is presented in I Pet. iii, 18 as the suffering of the righteous for the unrighteous. According to I John ii, 1 he continues his vicarious work in the sphere of glory.

---

[1] Both passages are in amplification of what Bultmann calls "Homileten" (Analyse des I Joh., Festg. f. A. Jülicher, 1927, 138-158).

In all these cases the righteous Christ does the will of God to perfection.

On the other hand, John v, 30 represents Christ as sharing in the righteous judgment of God at the end of the world, for the (typically Johannine) reason that he is completely devoted to the will of God, and this is contrasted with judging according to appearance (vii, 24). Cf. II Tim. iv, 8.

(iii) Men who do God's will are called righteous, as in the O.T. : e.g. Abel (Matt. xxiii, 35 ; Heb. i, 14 ; cf. I John iii, 12) and Lot (II Pet. ii, 7 f.), in contrast with their lawless neighbours. With such examples are coupled the prophet and the martyr (Matt. xiii, 17 ; xxiii, 29, 35 ; cf. [v, 10-12 ;] x, 41). See also Luke i, 6 ; ii, 25 ; Acts x, 22 ; Matt. i, 19.[1]

It is very striking that, according to the Synoptists, Jesus adopted quite seriously the traditional Jewish contrast between the righteous and the sinner : Mark ii, 17 and par., cf. Matt. v, 45 ; Luke v, 32 ; xv, 7. Although in fact all are called to repentance, it is clear that the ordinary standards are recognised and the zeal of the " righteous " is acknowledged.[2] The same is true of Paul (Rom. v, 7, cf. ver. 6)—without prejudice to his doctrine of justification. Jewish distinctions are not abandoned ; what the Gospels do is to put a question mark after the word, " righteous ", as applied to themselves by men who were hypocritical, complacent and scornful of others (Luke xviii, 14 ; xvi, 15 ; cf. p. 60 (c) (d)). The retention of the Pharisaic belief in the resurrection of the righteous (Luke xiv, 14 ; cf. Acts xxiv, 15) shows the persistence of this fundamental distinction, which is

---

[1] Joseph's behaviour is fundamentally that of a righteous man. Cf. Schlatter, Matt. p. 13, differing from Billerbeck I, 50 f., where the reference is limited to fulfilment of the Law.

[2] Schlatter, Matt. 194, 309 ; Zahn, Matt. *ad loc.*

valid even at the Last Judgment, as it is for Paul. The context of Luke xiv, 14 shows that love is the ultimate test.[1]

(iv) The Christian is δίκαιος in the sense that he fulfils the Law, doing God's will. The righteous man (Matt. x, 41) has God's approval, and he who receives him because he is righteous, shares in his reward.[2] " Righteous " means " Christian " at Matt. xiii, 43, 49,[3] as contrasted with " them that do iniquity (ἀνομίαν) ", ver. 41. See also Matt. xxv, 37, 46. The O.T. colouring of Luke i, 17 should not blind us to the Messianic promise that the disobedient will receive the mind of the righteous who obey God. The righteous in James v, 6, 16 are poor Christians suffering violence at the hands of rich enemies.[4] Like the godly of the O.T., Christians are contrasted with the ungodly and with sinners : I Pet. iii, 12 ; iv, 18 ; Heb. xii, 23 ; Rev. xxii, 11. What makes them righteous, it remains for Paul to say.

(v) Paul, as we have noted (p. 22), occasionally retains the ordinary contrast of righteous with unrighteous, quite apart from his new doctrine of justification, which itself starts from the self-evident demand to do the will of God (see Rom. ii, 13), as

[1] On the question of general or partial resurrection, see Bill. IV, 1167 ff. ; Bousset-Gressmann 272 (1st ed. 256 ff.) ; E. Klostermann, Luke 151. Josephus knows only the resurrection of the righteous, but does not represent the full Pharisaic position (Bill. IV, 1188 f.). The Lucan tradition can hardly be said to be inconsistent, since Luke xiv, 14 only mentions the righteous because they gain the reward.

[2] Schlatter, Matt. 352 ; Zahn, ad loc. ; Meyer, Ursprung I, 143.

[3] [LXX and] Theod. read συνιέντες for δίκαιοι. For Jewish parallels to this use of Dan. xii, 3, see Schlatter, Matt. 446 ; Bill. I, 673 f. Cf. Bevan, Driver, Montgomery ad loc.

[4] Parallels from LXX and Apocr. in the comm. of Dibelius and Hauck.

presented in the Law. In this connexion, δίκαιος means one whom God pronounces righteous because he has kept the Law. But now another axiom has to be stated, viz. that "there is none righteous, no, not one", this being the first of a series of verses quoted at Rom. iii, 10 from Ps. xiv and Eccles. vii, 20, expressing universal sinfulness. Not being righteous means not fulfilling the Law because we are under sin. To become righteous now means receiving in faith the revealed righteousness of God as the power of God and salvation. When Paul quotes Hab. ii, 4 at Rom. i, 17 ; Gal. iii, 11, he omits LXX μου after πίστεως, and thus agrees substantially with the Hebrew, "his fidelity", but he reads a new meaning into the old words, using "righteous" in the sense of "justified by faith".[1] The Last Judgment is indicated at Rom. v, 19 : "shall be placed in the class and condition of *righteous*" [Sanday and Headlam] ;[2] the antithetical structure of this passage enables Paul here to contrast the righteous with sinners, but he does not go the length of saying, "we are now righteous". It should be noted, however, that he uses the word at I Thess. ii, 10 to characterise the Christian life as one of obedience to the divine law.[3]

[1] Lietzmann and Kühl *ad loc.* connect ἐκ πίστεως with δίκαιος instead of with ζήσεται. But this goes against both Heb. and LXX, and is rejected by Zahn and Preuschen-Bauer. Heb. x, 38, quoting LXX A, connects ἐκ πίστεως, in the O.T. sense of constancy, with ζήσεται, which ver. 39 makes eschatological (see E. Riggenbach, Heb., 2nd ed., 337 f.). For Rabbinic treatment of Hab. ii, 4 see Schlatter, Der Glaube im N.T., 4th ed. (1927), 609 f., Bill. III, 542 ff.

[2] E. F. K. Müller, Beobachtungen zur paulin. Rechtfertigungslehre (1905), 15. Zahn finds here a logical Future. See J de. Zwaan, Th. St. 31 (1913), 85 ff.

[3] E. von Dobschütz, Thess. 99 ; R. C. Trench, Synonyms (1865), 313 f.

In the wider field of Paulinism, the Christian is contrasted with the antinomians, whose weak point is their attitude to the Law,[1] as being δίκαιος (I Tim. i, 9) : no law is prescribed for him, because he judges himself according to the divine norm.[2] Among the qualifications of a bishop it is required that he should be δίκαιος (Tit. i, 8) : this means that his life must conform to the will of God, or possibly that he must be able to make right decisions.

[1] H. von Soden, Past. 2nd ed. (1893), 160 ; W. Lütgert, Die Irrlehrer der Past. (1909), 16.

[2] Cf. Rom. x, 4 ; vi, 14 f.

IV. RIGHTEOUSNESS IN THE NEW TESTAMENT

1. INTRODUCTION

In order to understand the meaning of the word δικαιοσύνη in the New Testament, it is necessary to know something of its use in the non-Christian world.

(a) Greek and Hellenistic

Δικαιοσύνη belongs to the third stage in word-formation, following δίκη and δίκαιος. Words with the termination -σύνη begin to appear in the age of abstract thought, and this explains the frequent use of the concept after the time of Homer and Hesiod, while they do not have it.[1] The linguistic development is closely connected with the growth of the Greek feeling for justice. The juridical, the ethical and the religious are vitally related to one another in the development of ideas, as the result of the domination of early Greek thought by δίκη, justice, not only in the sphere of law, but also in politics and ethics, and above all, religion (see p. 9). Four uses of δικαιοσύνη should be noted.

(i) Already in the fifth century B.C. it indicates the virtue of the citizen who behaves uprightly and does his duty. Plato adopts this : " To mind one's own business, and not be meddlesome, is justice " (Rep. iv, 433). He founds his ideal state on this, and names it with temperance as a popular and social virtue (Phaedo 82).

---

[1] R. Hirzel (169) thinks this due to their aristocratic tone. But that would not apply to Hesiod.

(ii) Justice is the compendium of all virtues, according to Theognis, as quoted by Aristotle (see p. 10).

(iii) Plato also mentions justice with piety, along with knowledge, courage and temperance, as a part of perfection (Prot. 330*b*) (see p. 13).

(iv) The mystical hymn in Corp. Herm. xiii, 18 calls upon Justice with Temperance to offer praise. The virtue is here transformed into a moral force, which is communicated to the re-born. (See p. 57 and note.)

The fundamental idea among the Greeks is that δικαιοσύνη, like all other virtues, is natural to man. Cf. Aristotle, Eth. Nic. VI, xiii, 1144*b*, 27, and see p. 14.

Aristotle shows the close connexion between the idea of justice and general ethics in his definition of δικαιοσύνη as the virtue through which every man possesses that which belongs to him according to the law (Rhet. I, ix, 1366*b*, 9 ff.). He is here harking back to the thought of the judge, who awards to each his due. Solon played an important part in the development of the idea by his insistence on distributive justice.[1] A forensic reference thus continued to belong to the word, though it did not colour all its uses, after moral philosophy had generalised the idea. Thus δικαιοσύνη is not only the virtue of the good citizen, but also legislative and judicial justice (Plato Gorg. 464*c*; Aristot. Pol. IV, iv, 1291*a*, 27). Aristotle discusses its relation to ἐπιείκεια (equity) in Eth. Nic. V, xiv, 1137*a*, 31 ff.

In a few instances δικαιοσύνη means "correctness": Clem. Al. Strom. VI, iv, 36, 2 (cubit of *c*.); Deut. xxxiii, 19, Ps. iv, 5, (6), li, 19 (l, 21) (sacrifice of *c*.); Ps. xxiii (xxii), 3 (paths of *c*.). These all represent the Hebrew çedheq.

Josephus does not use δικαιοσύνη very often, and

[1] Cf. W. Jaeger, Solons Eunomie, S.A.B. 1926, 69-85.

when he does, it is usually in the Hellenistic sense
meaning virtuous human behaviour, or even one of
the virtues, though he retains the Jewish attitude to
the Law as divine : " The reason why the constitution of this legislation was ever better directed
to the utility of all than other legislations were is this,
that Moses did not make religion a part of virtue,
but he saw and he ordained other virtues to be a
part of religion—I mean justice and fortitude and
temperance and a universal agreement of the members
of the community with one another ; for all our
actions and studies, and all our words, have a reference to piety towards God " (Apion II, 170 f.,
Whiston II, xvii). The Greek point of view is clearly
implied when Josephus says that Samuel was opposed
to monarchy " because of his innate justice " (διὰ τὴν
σύμφυτον δικαιοσύνην : Ant. VI, 36, Whiston VI, iii).

Philo's only treatment of the righteousness of God
is in Deus Imm. 79, where he speaks of it as one among
other virtues in Stoic fashion. He has a striking
parallel to Rom. iii, 25 f. in Vit. Mos. II, 237 : πρὸς
ἐπίδειξιν ἀληθείας καὶ δικαιοσύνης, though the words
have not their Pauline meaning, but refer to revelation
in answer to prayer. In general, Philo's usage corresponds to the teaching of the Law, δικαιοσύνη being
the Lawgiver's main concern : Spec. Leg. IV, 143.
He takes over from the Pythagoreans the idea that
equality (ἰσότης) is the " mother " of justice : Spec.
Leg. IV, 231. Philo's exposition of δικαιοσύνη as a
virtue is more elaborate than that of Josephus ; he
calls it the queen (ἡγεμονίς) of the cardinal virtues
(see p. 13). His warmest religious interest is evident
when he is pursuing the psychological and the mystical within the limits of Platonic and Stoic tradition.
This is the case when the rise of δικαιοσύνη in the
· soul is under investigation : it can be said to be there

when the three parts of the soul are in harmony, when reason guides spirit and appetite, like a man driving two horses. Clement of Alexandria (Strom. IV, xxvi, 163, 4) copies this figure—which comes originally from Plato (Phaedr. 253d and Rep. IV, 443d) and Posidonius. The effect of δικαιοσύνη in the soul is healing (Det. Pot. Ins. 123), peace (ib. 122), joy (Leg. All. III, 247), reason and asceticism playing the chief part (Det. Pot. Ins. 121 f.). In spite of the assertion that virtue is a gift from God (Sacr. A.C. 56 f.), ideas of merit still prevail (Leg. All. III, 77), and faith is the product of righteousness (Rer. Div. Mer. 93-95).[1]

(b) Septuagint

(i) The righteousness of God, as expressed by the words ṣedheq and ṣᵉdhaqah, as we have seen, has in the Old Testament an extraordinary wealth of meaning (see pp. 4-6). This certainly includes the thought of consistent, normal behaviour on the part of God—though the norm never stands over him, he is himself the norm—as is urged by Diestel and Kautzsch on etymological grounds, but this is far from exhausting the meaning of the term. The first point to be established is that ṣᵉdhaqah belongs to the terminology of relationship. He is just who does justice to claims made upon him in the name of a relationship. Thus God's righteousness is manifested first in that he rules according to the covenant in fellowship with his people.[2] This concrete, rather than abstract, way of conceiving it, means that it

---

[1] In one place only (Spec. Leg. IV, 181) δικαιοσύναι means righteous acts ; cf. LXX Ezek. iii, 20 ; Dan. ix, 18 ; Ecclus. xliv, 10 ; Tob. ii, 14 ; II Clem. vi, 9.

[2] Cf. W. Eichrodt, Theol. des A.T. (1933), 121 ff. It was H. Cremer, above all, who explained ṣᵉdhaqah as a term of relationship.

includes both a forensic and a soteriological element. The former was unduly minimised by Diestel and Ritschl in their reaction against the older orthodoxy, both Catholic and Protestant. But the thought of judicial righteousness, with retribution, rewards and punishments, cannot be separated from the rule of him who is both King and Judge. This is specially characteristic of Is. xl-lv, where the argument again and again is couched in the language of a lawsuit (cf. "justified" in xliii, 9, 26) : Yahwe's judicial righteousness secures justice for his oppressed people in the proceedings against their conquerors ; "he that justifieth" (Is. l, 8 f.) makes justice to triumph. Cf. Is. lviii, 2, where *mishpaṭ* is a synonym for *çᵉdhaqah*.

This leads directly to the thought of God's judgment and righteousness as bringing help and salvation— e.g. Deut. xxxii, 4, 35 f. ; Hos. ii, 19 (21) ; Mic. vii, 9. Kindness, truth, loyalty, salvation are coupled with righteousness, specially in Is. xl-lv and Psalms. God's saving act, and loyalty to the Covenant, are represented as righteousness : Jer. l, 7 ; Is. xli, 2, 10 ; xlii, 6 ; xlv, 8 ; li, 5. Yahwe reveals to his people the way of salvation prescribed by his righteousness. LXX corresponds exactly to the Heb. when it explains δικαιοσύνη by σωτηρία, etc. : Ps. lxv, 5 (lxiv, 6) ; lxxi (lxx), 15 f. ; xcviii (xcvii), 2 f. ; Is. xlvi, 12 f. ; li, 5 ; lix, 17 ; lxi, 10 f. The same idea is conveyed negatively in Ps. lxix, 27 (lxviii, 28) ; cf. Is. xlv, 23-25. The root of this coupling of justice with salvation is to be found in the idea of the covenant.

The equation of righteousness with the gift of salvation becomes even more explicit when LXX employs δικαιοσύνη as the translation of *ḥeṣedh* (Gen. xix, 19 ; xx, 13 ; xxi, 23 ; xxiv, 27 ; xxxii, 10 ; Exod. xv, 13 ; xxxiv, 7 ; Prov. xx, 28–LXX 22), the

usual rendering being ἔλεος[1] (Ps. xxxvi, 10–LXX xxxv,
11 ; etc.). Δικαιοσύνη also stands for '*emeth*, loyalty
to the covenant : Gen. xxiv, 49 ; Is. xxxviii, 19 ;
xxxix, 8 ; Dan. viii, 12. But the forensic reference
is often found in LXX, as when it stands beside
κρίσις and κρίμα, and can even, occasionally, itself
represent *mishpaṭ* (Is. lxi, 8 ; Mal. ii, 17) ; apart
from those cases in which the emphasis is soteriological,
it represents the purely judicial righteousness of God :
Ps. ix, 5 ; xxxv (xxxiv), 24 ; xcvi (xcv), 13.

(ii) Human righteousness consists in doing God's
will. Its opposite is lawlessness (ἀνομία) : Is. v, 7.
It is often coupled with truth (I Kings iii, 6), as it is
when used of God (Zech. viii, 8). Cf. Test. Gad.
iii, 1 and Eph. v, 9, where it means good behaviour.

(c) *Synagogue*

(i) The righteousness of God in the sense of Rom.
iii, 21 is not known in the Synagogue.[2] A typical
specimen of the Rabbinical interpretation is seen in
the case of Deut. xxxiii, 21, where *çidhqath Yahwe* is
said to be executed by Moses, as bestowing benefits
like Yahwe,[3] or earning merit in the eyes of Yahwe,[4]
or giving righteous judgment.[5] (LXX misunder-
stands the passage, and makes Yahwe the subject.)
On the other hand, the Messiah is often spoken of
as the righteous one, or as righteousness (see pp. 18 f.).

[1] *Ḥeṣedh* is generally rendered ἔλεος ; but this is not satisfactory, since, like *çᵉdhaqah*, it denotes a mutual relation of rights
and duties, and particularly the obligation of loving service
which springs from some form of fellowship, e.g. tribe, friendship, league. See N. Glueck, Das Wort *ḥeṣedh* im A.T. Sprach-
gebrauch, Beih. Z.A.W. 47 (1927) ; [W. F. Lofthouse, *Ḥen* and
Ḥeṣedh in the Old Testament, Z.A.W. 1933, 31-35 ; C. H. Dodd,
The Bible and the Greeks (1935), 59-65).]
[2] Billerbeck III, 163.
[3] Sifre, Deut. 355 on xxxiii, 21, Billerbeck III, 163.
[4] Targ. Onq. *ad loc.*   [5] Sifre, Deut. *loc. cit.*

Occasionally, in eschatological passages referring to the Messiah, righteousness means mercy.[1]

(ii) Righteousness as human activity. Rabbinical usage significantly narrowed down the meaning of çᵉdhaqah (Aram. çidhqah) to the giving of alms, as the most important way of fulfilling the law.[2] Private benevolence (çᵉdhaqah or miçwah) is one of the most meritorious of good works.[3] This limitation frequently appears in Rabbinical exposition of the O.T.[4] The Rabbinic parallel to ποιεῖν ἐλεημοσύνην (Matt. vi, 2) is çidhqah ʿasah or miçwah ʿasah.[5] LXX again and again has ἐλεημοσύνη for çᵉdhaqah : Deut. vi, 25 ; xxiv, 13 ; Ps. xxiv (xxiii), 5 ; xxxiii (xxxii), 5 ; ciii (cii), 6 : Is. i, 27 ; xxviii, 17 ; lix, 16 ; Dan. iv, 24 ; ix, 16 Theod. ; cf. Ecclus. iii, 30 ; vii, 10 ; xvi, 14. Almsgiving must be meant by çᵉdhaqah in Prov. x, 2, though LXX has δικαιοσύνη : cf. Tob. iv, 10 ; xii, 9 ; xiv, 11.

(iii) The background of the Rabbinic and LXX doctrine is the theory of merit : every act of obedience (miçwah) earns merit (zakhuth) for the Israelite in the sight of God.[6] The latter term means originally " righteousness ", and the verb, zakhah, means to be righteous, worthy, deserving.[7] The piling up of good works becomes an end in itself.[8] Almsgiving, works of charity, the merit of the fathers—all supplement

[1] Jer. Shebi. 35c, 31 ; Midr. Ps. xxii, § 32 (99a), Billerbeck II, 575. [2] Billerbeck I, 387 f.

[3] Ib. IV, 12, 536 ff.

[4] E.g. II Sam. viii, 15 (T. Sanh. i, 2 ff., Bill. III, 210) ; Prov. xxi, 3, 21 (Bab. Sukk. 49b, Bill. I, 500 ; Bab. Bab. B. 9b, 10b, Bill. III, 525 ; Gen. Rabb. 58 on xxiv, 19, Bill. IV, 561c) ; Is. xxxii, 17 (Ab. ii, 7, Bill. I, 387) ; Is. lix, 17 (Bab. Bab. B. 9b, Bill. III, 618) ; Hos. x, 12 (Bab. Sukk. 49b, Bill. III, 451).

[5] Bab. Gitt. 7a ; Lev. Rabb. 34 on xxv, 39, Bill. I, 388.

[6] Bill. I, 251.

[7] Ib. IV, 10. Cf. Bab. Ber. 28b ; Bab. Bab. B, 10b Bar., Bill. II, 254. [8] Ib. IV, 6.

the keeping of the commandments.[1] A man's standing before God is settled by striking a balance between his good deeds and his transgressions.[2] If the former outweigh the latter, he is acquitted at the Last Judgment.[3] Everything depends on which way he scales turn.[4] (See p. 58 (d).)

(iv) The divine judgment and mercy stand immediately side by side in Ps. Sol., where God's righteousness is his just judgment (ii, 16; iii, 5; iv, 28; viii, 29-31; ix, 3, 7; cf. ii, 12, 19, 36; iii, 3; v, 1; viii, 27; x, 6; xvii, 3).[5] Along with this appears kindness, mercy, grace, without any indication of the relation between the two (ii, 40; v, 2, 17; vii, 4 f., 8, 9; viii, 33 f.; ix, 15 f.; x, 8; xi, 2, 9). The thought of salvation is expressed by ἔλεος and χάρις, but not by δικαιοσύνη (see p. 58 (f)).

Jubilees similarly combines God's kindness and mercy (x, 3) with his righteousness, which is predominantly judicial (xxi, 4).[6] But Jub. differs from Ps. Sol. in that it can speak of "salvation in righteousness" (i, 15), and joins mercy and judgment more closely together (xxxi, 25).[7] But here also no attempt is made to explain the connexion between the two ideas.

II Esdras viii, 36, on the other hand, comes very near to the language of Paul: "In this, O Lord, thy righteousness and thy goodness shall be declared, if thou be merciful unto them which have no store of good works". Such a statement is unthinkable in Ps. Sol., and represents a very late type of Judaism.

[1] Bill. IV, 6.   [2] Ib. I, 251.   [3] Ib. IV, 5.
[4] Jer. Qidd., 61d, 47, Bill. IV, 11.
[5] God's chastening (παιδεύειν) of Israel is frequently coupled with his mercy: vii, 3-5; viii, 32-35, etc. The righteousness in which the Messiah is to rule (xvii, 28) is his spotlessness in the sight of God.
[6] At Jub. xxv, 1, and xxx, 20, δικαιοσύνη means good human behaviour.   [7] So also En. xxxix, 5; lxxi, 3.

The Rabbinical word for legal right is not *ç⁰dhaqah*
but *din*. There was much discussion in the Synagogue about the relationship between God's judgment
and his mercy. The two were sharply contrasted as
middath haddin and *middath haraḥᵃmin*.[1] It is frequently
stated that kindness exceeds severity.[2] When pardon
is granted, mercy restrains wrath and displaces punitive
justice.[3] Thus in Gen. xviii, 19, *ç⁰dhaqah* is interpreted as mercy, and *mishpaṭ* as justice (cf. *din* above).[4]
The problem is also reflected in the contrast between
shurath haddin and *liphnim mishshurath haddin* (judicial
strictness and indulgence).[5] Kindliness ranks higher
among men than mere legality,[6] and God himself is
said to be indulgent.[7] But it always remains uncertain among the Rabbis, a matter of *pro* and *con*,
whether God will be just or merciful.

2. NEW TESTAMENT : NON-PAULINE

(*a*) Δικαιοσύνη as just judgment and government.
A few passages use the word for God's righteous
judgment through the returning Christ : Acts xvii,
31 ; Rev. xix, 11 ; cf. the revelation of retributive
justice through Christ in the Freer logion at Mark
xvi, 14 ; it means God's just government of the

[1] Mek. on Exod. xv, 2, Bill. I, 1042 ; Gen. Rab. 12 on ii, 4
(end), Bill. III, 292 ; Midr. Shir i, 14, Bill. II, 279 ; Gen.
Rab. 65 on xxvii, 1, Bill. III, 694.

[2] Bab. Sanh. 100*a* Bar., Bill. I, 444 ; Sifra Lev. on v, 17,
Bill. III, 230 ; T. Sotah iv, 1. On the appeal to severity see
Gen. Rab. 45 on xvi, 5, Bill. III, 301.

[3] Bab. Ber. 7*a* Bar., Bill. II, 79.

[4] E.g., Gen. Rab. 49 on xviii, 19, Bill. III, 196.

[5] Bill. I, 341 ; IV, 18.

[6] Bab. Bab. Q. 99*b*, Bill. iv, 19, cf. 15 ; Mek. on Exod.
xviii, 20, Bill. I, 345.

[7] Bab. Ber. 7*a* Bar., Bill. II, 79 ; Deut. Rab. 4 on x, 1, Bill.
IV, 18.

Christian community [giving equal privileges to all] at II Pet. i, 1 ; and the justice of judges and kings at Heb. xi, 33. " The word of righteousness " (Heb. v, 13) means " regular, normal speech ".[1]

(b) Δικαιοσύνη as doing right in the sight of God. Apart from the passages just mentioned, and the Pauline usage, with its special formula, " the righteousness of God ", it may be stated generally that in the New Testament righteousness means almost always human behaviour in harmony with God's will, and well-pleasing to him—uprightness of life, doing what is right in God's sight. This is differentiated from Greek and Hellenistic moral ideas, and closely related to the Old Testament, by its constant reference to God and its vital connexion with his mighty acts.

(i) Matthew always uses the word in this sense. The baptism of Jesus (iii, 15) is to fulfil all duty to God,[2] not " every ordinance " (δικαίωμα).[3] There is no need to take the fourth beatitude (v, 6) as referring to the judging and saving righteousness of God, in a forensic, eschatological sense.[4] On the other hand, it is quite clear that righteousness is here not a matter of merit, as with the Jews, but a free gift of God to those who earnestly desire it.[5] " His Kingdom and righteousness " (vi, 33) means that which will bring the disciples into perfect harmony with God's will. Again it is a gift, like everything connected with the Kingdom.

[1] Riggenbach, Hab. 144 f. Cf. δικαιοσύνη as substantive of δίκαιος, " correct " (see pp. 15 and 27).

[2] Schlatter, Matt. 89 ff. Cf. on Matt. iii, 15, A. Friedrichsen in Revue d'histoire et de Philos. Relig. VII (1927), 245 ff.

[3] Zahn, Matt. 140, cf. Zahn, Einleitung, 3rd ed., II, 318, n. 10. So also Klostermann ad. loc., Preuschen-Bauer, 306.

[4] Cremer, Paul. Rechtfertigungslehre 190.

[5] Schlatter, Matt. 136 f. ; Bill. I, 201 f.

The parallelism with Paul's gospel of justification is here as obvious as it is in all the other passages in which Matthew emphasises the merciful saving of sinners.[1] Doing right before God leads to persecution (v, 10). It must exceed the righteousness of the Pharisees.[2] Matt. vi, 1 uses "righteousness" as a general heading for a number of pious observances.[3] These do not exhaust the meaning of the term, but they provide characteristic examples of righteousness as that which is done in the sight of God and for his sake. John the Baptist came in the way of righteousness (xxi, 32), and therefore called for conduct in harmony with God's will. (For "way", cf. Job xxiv, 13 ; Prov. viii, 20 ; xii, 28 ; xvi, 31 ; xvii, 23 ; xxi, 16, 21.)

(ii) Luke agrees with Matthew. The Benedictus, in the emotional language of liturgy, speaks of serving God in holiness and righteousness before him (i, 75). The association of the two words is suggestive of Greece (cf. Wis. ix, 3 ; Josh. xxiv, 14, LXX), but "righteousness before him" is something bigger than a Greek virtue. The distinction between "moral" and "religious" does not hold. This means the fulfilment of God's will by doing what pleases him. Acts brings out the point that God seeks this in the Gentile world (xiii, 10 ; xxiv, 25), and recognises it wherever it is found (x, 35)—though it should be

[1] Cf. R. Bultmann, Die Bedeutung des geschichtl. Jesus für die Theologie des Paulus, Th. Bl. VIII (1929), 143.

[2] Schlatter takes Matt. v, 20 to mean going further beyond the letter of the Law than the Pharisees (Matt. 159 ff.). It is simpler to regard $\dot{\epsilon}\grave{\alpha}\nu$ $\mu\grave{\eta}$ $\pi\epsilon\rho\iota\sigma\sigma\epsilon\acute{\upsilon}\sigma\eta$ $\pi\lambda\epsilon\hat{\iota}o\nu$ as an emphatic comparative. Cf. Dalman, Jesus-Jeshua (1922, Eng. trans. 1929), 67 ff.

[3] The reading $\delta\iota\kappa\alpha\iota\sigma\sigma\acute{\upsilon}\nu\eta\nu$ (Sin B D Syr Sin) is preferable to $\dot{\epsilon}\lambda\epsilon\eta\mu\sigma\sigma\acute{\upsilon}\nu\eta\nu$.

noted that something more is needed for salvation, viz. forgiveness of sins (x, 43).

(iii) Similarly, in I and II Peter, righteousness is always doing right so as to please God. It is made possible by deliverance from sin through the Cross (I Pet. ii, 24)—as Paul also says (Rom. vi ; see p. 53). As in Matt. v, 10, it will involve suffering (iii, 14). Noah, as a herald of righteousness (II Pet. ii, 5), represents the life of obedience to God over against the world of the ungodly. The way of righteousness is shown by the holy commandment (ii, 21). The new world will be the home of righteousness (iii, 13 ; cf. p. 19).

(iv) Hebrews also presents the same picture, apart from the two Hellenistic phrases noted above (p. 35). The quotation from Ps. xlv (xliv), 8 is used (Heb. i, 9) to show Christ's exaltation as the reward for his life of righteousness. Melchizedek means " king to whom righteousness belongs " (vii, 2) ; it is as such that he is a type of Christ. The righteousness of which Noah became heir (xi, 7) has not a forensic meaning, but refers to the godly life which corresponds to faith.[1] Hebrews here—like Matthew—agrees with Paul that righteousness is a gift. As a fruit of chastening (xii, 11), righteousness means a life fully conformed to God's will.

(v) The only difference between John and the foregoing is that he shows, more clearly than Matt. iii, 15 and Hebrews, the vital bearing of Christ's righteous life on the whole conception of righteousness. He does this by means of his Christology, so that righteousness is inseparable from the Christ as the righteous one. Jesus is set forth as having this character in his resurrection and exaltation (John xvi, 8, 10).

---

[1] $Κατά$ is a periphrasis for the Genitive. Cf. Riggenbach, 352 f.

Accordingly, the doing of righteousness is the practice
and confirmation of that which is embodied in him,
and therefore evidence of being begotten of God
(I John ii, 29).[1] Those who are antinomian on the
ground that he is righteous are exhorted to imitate
him, avoiding sin (iii. 7 f.) ; and this means brotherly
love (iii, 10). See also Rev. xxii, 11.

Do the passages so far adduced show the way to
righteousness in the sight of God? Matthew says
clearly that it is a gift of the Kingdom of God, and
I Peter (ii, 24) connects it impressively with deliverance from sin through the Cross. This points definitely, though not dogmatically, in the direction of
Pauline doctrine. John also connects true righteousness exclusively with the revelation in Christ, by
making it the result of union with him as the righteous
one. But Israel's old problem of justification before
God was only really settled by James and Paul.

(c) Δικαιοσύνη in James. The "righteousness of
God" of James i, 20, cannot be identified with Paul's
watchword, which conveys the essence of his doctrine
of salvation through the Cross. The reference must
be to works of righteousness, which is said to be of
God because its definition and demand are from him
alone. Such works cannot be wrought by human
wrath, which is irreconcilably opposed to the righteousness of God. What is remarkable is that this
saying puts good works under the heading of divine,
and not of human, righteousness. This is well on
the way towards Paul's concern for subjection to the
righteousness of God (Rom. x, 3).[2] "The fruit of
righteousness" (iii, 18 ; cf. Prov. iii, 9 ; xi, 30, etc.;
Am. vi, 12) means the righteousness which is the

---

[1] Cf. II Sam. viii, 15 ; Ps. cvi (cv), 3 ; Is. lvi, 1 ; lviii, 2 ;
Ps. Sol. ix, 5.
[2] Cf. Schlatter, Jak. 51, 142.

harvest of a life devoted to the will of God. (Genitive of apposition or content.)

While James thus shares the prevailing view of those parts of the N.T. so far considered, he goes beyond them when he says of Abraham, "it was reckoned unto him for righteousness" (ii, 23),[1] providing an answer to the question concerning the way to righteousness before God—the way of salvation. This hotly disputed passage brings us close to Paul's great subject of justification. (For the word ἐλογίσθη, "was reckoned", see Gen. xv, 6; Ps. cvi (cv), 31; I Macc. ii, 52; Jub. xiv, 6; xxxi, 23; xxx, 17; xxxv, 2; Philo Rer. Div. Her. xc, 94; Abr. 262.)

The subject is treated polemically, and an attack made upon the dead orthodoxy, which certainly talks about "faith", but is not interested in work. A strong point is therefore made of the marriage of faith with work. The reference is not to carrying out the details of the Law in a Rabbinical sense, but to practical love and obedience, the sort of thing that Paul describes as the fruit of the Spirit, the hall-mark of a Christian. The whole epistle teaches the same lesson, which is as far removed from the Jewish idea of earning merit as from Greek ethics. James simply demands, in a direct, untheological way, that faith shall not be distorted into a substitute for work. Abraham is righteous in God's sight because he is credited with the faith that is accompanied and perfected by work (ii, 23). It is perfectly true that this way of putting it is more like the Jewish view than Paul's way, lacking, as it does, the contrast between grace and works; and it cannot be denied that James here presents a conception of faith which

[1] Cf. comm. of Dibelius 168, Windisch 20 f., Hauck 124 ff., Schlatter 51-60, 202 f.; A. Meyer, Rätsel des Jak. (1930), 86 ff.; [J. Moffatt in D.A.C. II, 373*b*].

differs "theologically" from that of Paul. But it must be remembered that this is a popular piece of practical polemics, directed against the attempt to set up a doctrine of faith without work, and has nothing to do with what Paul says about faith "apart from the works of the Law". The remark about demons believing (ii, 19) is not the only thing James has to say about faith. An examination of the whole collection of his sayings in this epistle shows that fundamentally faith means more to him than that bit of orthodoxy. At the same time it must be granted that Paul could never have stood for the contention that Abraham was justified on the ground of the work which accompanied and authenticated his faith. James is not here concerned with the judgment through which all works must pass, whether enjoined by the Law or not ; nor does he touch on the aspects of the subject presented at Matt. vi, 33 and I Pet. ii, 24 (see pp. 35 and 38). But his exhortation, in spite of the disputable theology of ii, 23, is at one with the general doctrine of the early Church in its plea for a faith which produces the right kind of behaviour.[1]

3. PAUL

(a) Origin and basis of the Pauline gospel of justification. In order to understand what Paul means by "the righteousness of God", we must go back to the Law, which he calls a law of righteousness because it demands righteousness (Rom. ix, 30). " Moses writeth that the man that doeth the righteous-

---

[1] Schlatter (Jak. 51 ff.) suggests that " apart from works " is a development from the earlier Pauline " apart from works of the Law ", comparable with Corinthian libertinism. This is illuminating, but does not relieve the tension due to the fact that James includes works in the reckoning.

ness which is of the Law shall live thereby " (Rom.
x, 5 ; cf. Test. Dan vi, 10, where the first Slavonic
version adds " cf the Law " ; Apoc. Bar. li, 3 ;
lxiii, 3 ; lxvii, 6) : i.e. it is a condition of life. But
that stage in the plan of salvation is past ; there is
now actually no " righteousness which is of the Law ".
It is true that a relative perfection may be attained
(Phil. iii, 6), but Paul has come to understand that
the Law cannot produce true righteousness before
God (Gal. iii, 21). The self-righteousness which it
does produce (Rom. x, 3 ; Phil. iii, 9) is only " loss "
and " refuse " (Phil. iii, 8). See further Gal. ii, 21 ;
Titus iii, 5.[1]

Paul reaches the new truth of the " righteousness
of God " in the effort to define his position in relation
to the Law. But it cannot be said [2] that his gospel
of justification [3] owes more to that effort than to his
personal spiritual experience. No doubt this is the
crucial point in his discussion with Judaism. He
speaks in a different way to the Corinthians. But he
is under the necessity of clarifying his position to
himself, and the question of the Law is fundamental
for his whole theology. What is commonly called the
" mysticism " of Paul cannot be separated from the
new relationship to God, brought about apart from
the Law. Justification became the battle-cry of his
mission because it expressed a new understanding of
the relation of Christ to the Law. Paul uses the
sacred word of Judaism—righteousness—in the service
of his polemic against the Jewish conception of the
Law.

[1] On works of the Law cf. E. Lohmeyer, Probl. paulin. Theol.
II, Z.N.W., 28 (1929), 177 ff.

[2] As by A. Meyer, op. cit. 99 f., following Wrede, Paulus
(1904), 72 ff.

[3] Cf. H. E. Weber, " Eschatologie " und " Mystik " im N.T.,
100 f.

The presupposition of Paul's message is the O.T. idea of God, as the Judge, who demands obedience and distributes rewards and punishments. It is also fundamental with him that man is the slave of sin, and guilty before God. But he goes right away from Judaism in his radical rejection of the optimism which believes it possible to fulfil the Law. This is bound up with the complete collapse of Rabbinical piety in his own life. He still believes that only the righteous can have true fellowship with God ; but according to the Gospel no effort on man's part can qualify him for this fellowship ; God's sovereign grace alone can do that, taking action in Christ on behalf of mankind.

(b) The full formula, "righteousness of God", is used by Paul in his most solemn and striking utterances on the subject of salvation ; elsewhere he speaks simply of righteousness. In the former, there can be no doubt that θεοῦ is to be understood as a subjective Genitive. God's righteousness is exclusively his own, and man is brought into it and given a place within it.[1] The righteousness of God is judgment and mercy in one ; it belongs to him, and he

---

[1] So rightly O. Zanker 399, 418. In the discussion of "the righteousness of God" A. Ritschl and L. Diestel lay proper emphasis on salvation, but neglect the forensic element, which is recognised by A. Schmitt 129. Zahn identifies it with Christ ; but the exceptional statement of I Cor. i, 30 should not be generalised. Kühl takes it, too formally, to mean the objective norm set forth in the Gospel. Lietzmann leaves the question open : either God's own righteousness or that which he imputes. [But see his " The Beginnings of the Christian Church ", 2nd ed. (trans. B. L. Woolf, 1949), 115 f. : " God *is* righteous and *makes* righteous ".] The most important contributions to the discussion are those of Kölbing and Haering, who apprehend the twofold nature of the idea, combining the redemptive and the judicial, though they limit the former to the atoning death, under the influence of Ritschl.

manifests it in what he does when he imparts it in absolving the sinner ; but it also inaugurates a new life of duty in the service of the King ; its perfect demonstration is at the Last Judgment. (Cf. Deut. xxxiii, 21 ; Od. Sol. xxv. 10 ; II Esdr. viii, 36.)

The main features of the gospel of justification are as follows.

(i) The whole of mankind forms the setting of the righteousness of God ; it is not simply a matter of individual experience, but primarily an act of God in Christ, affecting the human race as a whole (Rom. i-iii).

(ii) God's righteousness is more than an attribute, in the static sense of Hellenistic ethics, or as in the older Protestant theology. It is dynamic—as active as his wrath (Rom. i, 17 f. ; iii, 5, 21, 25 f.).

(iii) The saving act of propitiation ($\dot{\iota}\lambda\alpha\sigma\tau\acute{\eta}\rho\iota\sigma\nu$, see p. 61 n.) was performed at a particular place (Rom. iii, 25 f. ; v, 9 f. ; cf. II Cor. v, 18 ; Gal. iii, 13), at a particular time (Rom. iii, 21, 26), viz. at the Cross of Christ, which marks the end of the way of the Law (iii, 21). But the Resurrection always goes along with the Cross ; for this is more than a formal declaration in the unseen world. The Cross as the mighty act of God in history forms the keystone of Paul's closely-knit argument. Hence it is possible to use the formula, found only at 1 Cor. i, 30 (see p. 42, n. 1)—" Christ was made righteousness and sanctification and redemption ". There is no need to give $\delta\iota\kappa\alpha\iota\sigma\sigma\acute{\nu}\eta$, which is unmistakably regarded here as the foundation, a meaning different from that which it has in Galatians and Romans.[1] A similar personification, so to speak, is involved in Rom. x, 4.

(iv) God both is and imparts righteousness. Paul's formula means that God is just, righteousness belongs

[1] With Schmiedel, I Cor. 77, but not J. Weiss, I Cor. 41.

to him ; not, however, in the sense of a mere attribute, but as something actually put forth in the showing of his judgment (Rom. iii, 25 f.). This is certainly a manifestation of God's mercy, but at the same time it is an uncompromising putting forth of his righteousness as judge. It is attested in an act of atonement, and makes it impossible to misunderstand the " passing over of the sins done aforetime ".[1] Cf. the linking of the idea of judgment with what God did at the Cross in Gal. iii, 13 ; II Cor. v, 21 ; Rom. viii, 3. At the same time, ἔνδειξις is the granting of the absolution that saves the sinner.[2] It says two things, has two sides—is, in fact, the marrying of judgment and mercy. Judaism had wrestled in vain with the problem of adjusting these to each other (see p. 34), with only an occasional glimpse of the hope that God's sympathy might get the better of his severity. When Paul sees God's act in the Cross, he is convinced, with the absolute certainty of faith, that this is the final and effectual revelation of justice and mercy in one. This rules out unconditionally the antinomian misunderstanding of moral laxity and feeble compromise. Forgiveness as a genuine act of judgment, maintaining God's justice, is a form of redemption which knows no compromise with evil. The legalistic Pharisee speaks of the Law as disclosing the demand of God's righteousness ; Paul the Pharisee, apprehended by Christ, goes on to speak of the Cross as making known its work of judgment and mercy.

(v) Justification in the forensic sense is included in " the righteousness of God ". The believer is pronounced righteous and is given a new character in the sight of God. The divine judgment produces

---

[1] This cannot refer to pre-baptismal sins (Mundle, Der Glaubensbegriff des Paulus 88) ; its context is the history of salvation. [2] N.B. Rom. iii, 19 : " under judgment ".

righteousness in the believer through absolution (see pp. 61 and 70, and note the contrast with condemnation in Rom. viii, 34 and II Cor. iii, 9, cf. xi, 15). " Forensic " does not mean that the sinner is treated as if he were righteous, for God's sovereign judicial declaration produces an actual effect. Nor does it mean the setting up of a moral ideal to be striven after. What is indicated is that he who has righteousness is right with God. Law court language is really only used parabolically for being what one ought to be before God, and legal corollaries ought not to be pressed. This is not a case of human judicial proceedings, for the divine Judge is at the same time the omnipotent King. We certainly have to do with a picture, just as when words like " reconciliation " are used, but its glorious meaning is not to be apprehended by working out the logical implications of the legal metaphor. We must pass at once from the law court into the presence of God. The *justificatio injusti* is contrary to all the rules of human justice. The illustration is inadequate for the reality. This act of mercy goes far beyond all ordinary legal procedure. As a judicial pronouncement, it is incomparable of its kind. But what chiefly claims our attention is the underlying motif : the sole purpose of the use of legal terminology is to make it clear that the grace of God is not something arbitrary and capricious, but that it operates according to the principles of the holy Covenant, and is in perfect harmony with his justice. Objection could only be taken to the legal metaphor if it implied the Pharisaic doctrine of merit in such a way as to prejudice the holiness of God. The picture of the judge is admissible, because, in spite of its shortcomings, the Law does express abiding divine principles ; it can be applied to God just as well as the picture of father or king, in spite of human associations. The danger is minimised by the fact that logically the Pauline gospel of justification is a complete paradox.

(vi) Paul means much more than forgiveness and reconciliation, though he occasionally uses these expressions (Rom. iv, 7 ; v, 9 f. ; II Cor. v, 18-20). Whereas Judaism looked for a favourable verdict at the Last Judgment, on the ground of good works, Paul believed in the present possession of righteousness as a free gift of God (Rom. iii, 24-26 ; v, 1, 9, 17 ; viii, 30 ; ix, 30 ; I Cor. vi, 11 ; cf. viii, 10 ; x, 6), meaning not only the forgiveness of sins, but also the effectual working of the grace of God, a radical salvation (cf. *çedhaqah* in Ps. and Is.). This is something new, and makes it possible to speak of " a state of justification " [Westminster Confession]. Phil. iii, 9 refers to the continual renewal of this experience of receiving righteousness through faith, emphasising the point that it comes from God, and not from the Law (cf. Is. liv, 17 ; Bar. v, 2, 9) : but it must not be taken as the key to all that Paul meant by the righteousness of God ; [1] for that we must turn to Rom. i, 17 ; iii, 21 ff. The essential point is that δικαιοσύνη θεοῦ means both the righteousness which God has, manifesting it in the act of salvation, and that which, as Saviour, he continually communicates ; however the wording may vary, the fact remains that it is always ultimately his righteousness alone. The state of justification is in no sense a human achievement ; it is the free gift of God, who draws man into his own righteousness.

(vii) Faith is the means whereby the individual is drawn into participation in the consequences of the saving event. Although Paul does not exactly try to localise personal justification, since he is not particu-

[1] So rightly Haering, p. 6.

larly interested in isolated experiences, he nevertheless has in mind always God's action in justifying the individual, and not only the community.[1] Actually, he does not think of the individual as existing by himself ; when a man is justified, he becomes forthwith a member of the Body of Christ, as formerly he belonged to Israel, or the Gentiles, or the human race. The gift of justification does not diminish personal obligation ; it defines it. But, over against all exaggeration of the importance of the personal experience of justification, it is essential to insist that what is said in this connexion is all orientated to the completely objective fact of what God has done. This is shown in the belief that Paul's converts were justified when they were baptised and received the Spirit (I Cor. vi, 11 ; Gal. iii, 6, cf. iii, 1-5).[2] But the sacrament must not be regarded as working by magic. That is excluded by I Cor. i, 17, and indeed by the whole Pauline conception of faith. Abraham's circumcision is similarly " a seal of the righteousness of faith which he had while he was in uncircumcision ". He also received the gift of righteousness before the sacrament. Sacramental magic is ruled out (see p. 63, n. 3).

The relation of the subjective attitude to the objective act of redemption needs special explanation. Rom. x, 3 shows that the historical manifestation of pardoning righteousness is the very power of God, who rules over all, and it is man's business to submit to it. We cannot dismiss this, on the strength of Phil. iii, 9, as meaning merely the righteousness which is granted to the believer. This means being directly challenged and arrested by God, brought under his

[1] Ritschl, Rechtf. u. Versöhn. III (1888), 545 f.
[2] Mundle (84 ff., 135 ff.) goes far beyond Paul when he identifies justification with transplanting into the sacramental process of salvation.

authority, made partaker at once in the mighty act
of salvation through faith, and set within the sphere
of God's righteousness (cf. Rom. iii, 22).[1] All who
believe share in that righteousness. The demand for
faith always accompanies the most objective utterances concerning the righteousness of God (Rom.
i, 17 ; iii, 22-28 ; iv, 5, 1). The achievement and
proclamation of salvation are never separated from
the appropriation of it, and the revelation under discussion can never be taken out of the sphere of the
I–and–Thou relation. From the very beginning,
faith is an indispensable condition of the new experience. See Rom. iii, 21 ; 25 f. (διὰ πίστεως goes with
δικαιοσύνη θεοῦ) ; Phil. iii, 9.

Thus the divine objectivity in the work of salvation
is throughout relative to those who are being saved.
But the same may be said, from the opposite point
of view, concerning faith. Whereas to Philo faith is
a separable and definable property (σχέσις) of the
soul, it means for Paul man's total surrender to God's
saving act. The faith which is reckoned for righteousness is not a psychic force, or an achievement of
almighty reason, or the perfection of religious virtue
(Philo) ; it is the realisation of God alone as saviour,
the one and only way of opening the door to the
revelation of the one and only true object of faith.
The fact that different prepositions are used to link
the words δικαιοσύνη and πίστις shows that faith is
not a special kind of meritorious work (with the simple
genitives of Rom. iv, 11, 13, cf. the prepositions in
ix, 30 ; x, 6 ;[2] Phil. iii, 9) ; it is significant that
δικαιοσύνη διὰ τὴν πίστιν never occurs.[3] This con-

---

[1] The Alex. text is to be preferred [with R.V.], omitting " and
upon all ". So Lietzmann (46), but not Zahn (176).

[2] Cf. Bultmann, Der Stil der paulin. Predigt (1910), 87 f.

[3] Cf. W. Michaelis, Rechtf. aus Glauben bei Paulus (1927), 136.

clusion is confirmed by the use of the term λογίζεσθαι
(see p. 39). It is true that it indicates reckoning,
and by itself might well lead to misunderstanding,
as if righteousness could be earned (Gal. iii, 9 ; Rom.
iv, 3, 5 f., 9, 11, 22) ; but it is just by means of this
sharp antithesis that the doctrine of merit is overthrown. Faith comes of God ; no merit attaches to
it ; to say that it was reckoned is to exhibit the sheer
grace of the divine generosity. That which is reckoned is the creation of sovereign grace. God himself
acknowledges that in the faith he has found the full
satisfaction of justice.

(viii) Hope is an outstanding characteristic of
righteousness. The experience of salvation in the
present is a pledge of salvation in the future, for
justification is grace bridging the gap and inaugurat-
ing the world to come ; Paul's " But now " (Rom.
iii, 21) has the force of fulfilment ; what remains of
earthly life is an *interim*. Therein lies the great
revolution. Judaism put justification at the end of
the world, and was not sure of it ; the Christian
actually has it now. History offers it, and faith takes
hold of it. Imputed righteousness foreshortens time
and points to fulfilment, thus producing hope that
is beyond comparison with the vague uncertainty of
the Jew. The believer, who has found immediate
absolution at the Cross, looks forward to the Last
Judgment with confidence. This is not quietism ; it
is the dynamic of a new way of life. " The righteousness we hope for " (Gal. v, 5 [Moffatt]) is acquittal
at the Last Judgment (cf. Gal. ii, 16 ; Rom. ii, 13 ; [1]
iii, 20, 30 ; v, 19 ; viii, 33—referring to the Last
Judgment ; x, 4-10—eschatological, cf. v, 17).[2]

---

[1] But see p. 64.
[2] Cf. Mark xvi, Freer Logion, 22-24 : " the glory to be inherited, which consists of righteousness ".

Present and future are united in the association of righteousness with salvation (Rom. x, 10, etc.), the latter, like "life" (v, 17, cf. x, 10), being an eschatological term.[1] It is not that the Last Judgment is anticipated by faith,[2] but rather that it is both present and future at the same time, like redemption and adoption, as Paul understands them. The future form of expression indicates that what is given is not a static condition, but a movement towards a goal; like all Christ's gifts, it involves the tension of hope.

Paul saw no contradiction between justification by the mercy of God and the Last Judgment according to works, which he constantly took for granted in his preaching. This was not a mere relic of Judaism,[3] like a fossil, but an organic and radical part of his doctrine,[4] enabling him to show how the present and the future are one to the believer in justification. His treatment of the subject sets the divine standard over all, and is a radical summons to the fear of God. We have already seen that the idea of God as judge is the indispensable premise to the gospel of justification. It is quite true that Paul does not devote a theological discussion to the relation between justification and the Last Judgment. But it is the judgment motif which gives its seriousness both to the new confidence and to the tireless pursuit of the goal, and guards against a false sense of security. The assurance of salvation is not thereby shaken. The thought of judgment acts as a powerful stimulant to obedience. The new faith demands repeated encounters with the relentless severity of God, as seen at the Cross. It is only the absolute standard, associated with the idea of the

[1] Cf. Haering, p. 61.
[2] Cf. Kölbing, p. 8 ff. ; Haering, pp. 58 f.
[3] The antinomy has often been thus explained, cf. Braun, 24 f.
[4] Cf. Braun, 48, 76, 94.

Last Judgment, that can preserve the understanding of the Cross from degenerating into the antinomian view that justification does away with the duty of doing the will of God. Paul does not work this out logically ; his task is to get people to press on. He has broken away completely from the pretentious eschatological calculations of Judaism. As for Luther's [1] view that when God justifies a man, he starts a process of complete renewal, assuring him of eventual perfection—this certainly is to be found in Rom. viii, 30, but not as a piece of logic or mathematics, for when God saves a man, he performs an act of creation, and that is a miracle.

(ix) Justification is closely related to Paul's so-called " mysticism ". He connects it with the Spirit (I Cor. vi, 11 ; Rom. x, 8 f.), and says that both are received apart from works (Rom. iii, 28 ; Gal. iii, 2, 5). Saving faith and union with Christ in his death go together (Gal. ii, 16-21 ; iii, 26-29). The close connexion between the two appears in the unusual wording of II Cor. v, 21, where identification is substituted for imputation (cf. Jer. xxiii, 6 ; xxxiii, 16– LXX xl, 16) ; righteousness still belongs to God, but identification is very strongly expressed.[2] The juridical is combined with the mystical in Phil. iii, 7-11. In Romans generally it is impossible to separate the state of justification from being " in Christ ". If we were to interpret the latter as meaning mystical union in the technical sense, we should have to accuse Paul of living a double life theologically, because justification and faith necessarily involve the idea of separation between God and man ; in fact they may

[1] W. A. II, 108, 3 ff. ; cf. Holl, Ges. Auf. zur Kirchengesch. I, Luther, 2nd and 3rd eds. (1923), 123 ff. ; H. J. Holtzmann, Lehrb. der N.T. Theol. 2nd ed. II (1911), 226 ff. ; Braun, 31.

[2] Windisch, II Cor. 199, sees here mystical perfectionism.

be said to be intended to guard against just such a misunderstanding. What happens is that the gift of righteousness transfers a man into fellowship with Christ. Paul's mystical terminology is used by way of illustration, and must not be pressed to its logical conclusions, any more than the illustrations from the law-court. The justification formula is one among others. The linking of the juridical with the mystical shows that the work of justification is brought to completion by the Spirit.[1]

(x) Righteousness is the power of the new life. Justification does not mean quietism at any stage ; it is always teleological, and leads to the royal rule of grace (Rom. v, 12-21), which is the sure way to eternal life. This is a rule of righteousness (ver. 21), which is not only the starting-point, but also the secret of progress, for it brings the believer within the movement of the rule of God. Statements about justification should not be separated from the life-giving Lordship of Christ (ver. 21) or from the gift of life to the community. Righteousness and life are intertwined (vv. 17, 21), and lead to life eternal, whereas sin leads to death. " Righteousness " in Rom. viii, 10 does not mean the good life, but the state of justification : the Spirit is the power of the new life.

It is a complete mistake to ascribe to Paul the idea of salvation as a process that is ended.[2] When a man is declared righteous, he enters the service of

---

[1] See W. Grundmann, in Z.N.W., 32 (1933), 52 ff., for argument against the view of Pfleiderer, Wrede and Schweitzer [The Mysticism of Paul the Apostle, tr. by W. Montgomery, 1931, 205-226] that the doctrine of justification is a subsidiary crater within the main doctrine of redemption through mystical union with Christ.

[2] Windisch in R.G.G., 2nd ed., II, 1204.

righteousness, becoming, so to speak, its property ;
his faith in God's righteousness is obedience, and
leads to obedience ; and thus there is a close parallelism between his experience and the inseparable Cross
and resurrection which form the starting-point of
justification. See Rom. vi, 12-23. There is no
difficulty or contradiction in passing from the forensic
idea of righteousness to thinking of it as the power of
life which conquers sin. The gift of righteousness
brings the believer into the custody of this power.
Again, it is righteousness which gives admission to the
state of sanctification. It takes command of the
whole of life as the victor over unrighteousness and
sin. Thus Paul uses δικαιοσύνη to mean both the
righteousness which acquits the sinner and the life-
force which breaks the bondage of sin. It is impossible
to charge him with lack of interest in the good life,
as if δικαιοσύνη referred only to the beginning of the
Christian life, and so what we are here discussing
ought to come under the heading of missionary theory.
Of course Paul does not think of righteousness as
actually belonging to the believer ; it is an objective
norm which exercises divine authority over him ;
and at the same time the word can be applied to right
action (Rom. vi, 16), just as to the state of justification
(see p. 46). " The armour of righteousness " (II Cor.
vi, 7 : subjective Genitive) is that which is provided
by the divine righteousness.[1] The Christian life bears
the stamp of righteousness as opposed to iniquity
(II Cor. vi, 14 [in ver. 15 Christ is the personification
of righteousness]), and its ethical aspect, in the sense
of Rom. vi, is emphasised at Rom. xiv, 17. " Almsgiving " might be suggested as the meaning of
δικαιοσύνη in the quotations from Ps. cxii (cxi), 9,

[1] There is no analogy in Paul for Bachmann's interpretation :
weapons for righteous use.

and Hos. x, 12 at II Cor. ix, 9 f., because the context deals with the collection : but since ver. 8 speaks of "every good work", it is more likely to mean the goodness which expresses itself in charity. "The fruit of righteousness " (Phil. i, 11)—whether the Genitive is of apposition, origin or quality—is to be understood in the sense of Rom. vi. That righteousness, as "fruit", is the gift of God, and not just natural goodness, is also indicated at Eph. v, 9. The same idea is implied in " the breastplate of righteousness " (Eph. vi, 14, cf. Is. lix, 17), which means the power regulating the life of the Christian, without special reference to justification by faith. "Godly behaviour " is the meaning at II Tim. iii, 16 (cf. Bar. iv, 13), and " the crown of a good life " (II Tim. iv, 8 [Moffatt]) is more likely to be what Paul meant than complete acquittal at the Last Judgment. A general review of Paul's usage shows that the formula, "the righteousness of God", carries with it the conviction that at the very moment of justification the believer is admitted into the status of righteousness in the new life : justification is the means whereby he is brought under the creative power of the righteousness of God.

(xi) Hellenistic moral philosophy plays no part in the Pauline or deutero-Pauline doctrine of righteousness. The word ἀρετή (virtue) is never used in this connexion [N.T. only has it at Phil. iv, 8 ; I Pet. ii, 9 ; II Pet. i, 3, 5]. One might perhaps say that in the Pastoral Epistles the idea of truth was taken from Hellenistic ethics and given a higher, Christian meaning. Righteousness receives special attention in the Pastorals because of their emphasis on the ethical over against the gnostic. Ephesians has a liturgical phrase (iv, 24) which describes the Christian as a new man, " created in righteousness and holiness of truth " (cf. Luke i, 75). The two clearest reminders of the Greek lists of virtues are at I Tim. vi, 11 and II Tim. ii, 22, where righteousness is one among other marks of Christian behaviour ; but the contents of these Christian lists differentiate them fundamentally from those of Philo, etc.

V. JUSTIFICATION

1. Δικαιόω IN GREEK AND HELLENISTIC

THE verb δικαιόω comes from the adjective δίκαιος, and means " to set right " or " make valid " (as ἀκυροῦν means " to cancel ", etc.).

(a) Pindar, in the famous fragment quoted by Plato (Gorg. 484b), says that convention, king of men and gods, pronounces right what otherwise would be called an act of violence.[1] Plato here sees natural right coming to its own ;[2] according to nature, might is right.[3] Philo often uses the word for the divine ordinance in the Law ; Josephus does so once (Ant. iv, 278) ; and the Passive Participles mean " prescribed " in Dion. Hal. Ant. Rom. X, i, 2 and Pap. Tebt. II, 444.

(b) From the legal sphere δικαιοῦν comes into general use to denote holding a thing to be right, reasonable, suitable. This is its commonest meaning, being found in Philo and Josephus as well as in classical authors. (For Paul's δικαιοῦν Josephus has ἀγαπῆσαι with the Genitive.[4]) Epictetus does not use the word at all.

(c) Applied to persons, δικαιοῦν is widely used for doing justice, and so comes to mean passing sentence (Thuc. III, 40), punishing (Herodot. I, 100),

[1] δικαιῶν τὸ βιαιότατον. U. von Wilamowitz, Platon II (1920), 93, 99, adopts the reading βιαιῶν τὸ δικαιότατον, " doing violence to what is most just ". Cf. J. Geffcken, Studien zu Plat. Gorg. in Herm. 65 (1930), 19. A. Busse, in Herm. 66 (1931), 126 ff., argues convincingly for the old reading.   [2] Cf. Laws III, 690c ; IV, 715a.
[3] Cf. A. Busse, 127 f. [and R. W. Wenley, E.R.E. III, 242].
[4] Cf. Schlatter, Wie sprach Jos. von Gott ? (1910), 63.

executing (Jos. Ant. xvii, 206), defending (Polyb. III, 31). The last comes nearest to Paul's usage, but it is only in LXX and N.T. that it means justifying a person.

(d) The mystical use of the word in the Hermetic tractate on Regeneration (Corp. Herm. xiii, 9) claims special attention : χωρὶς γὰρ κρίσεως ἰδὲ πῶς τὴν ἀδικίαν ἐξήλασεν. ἐδικαιώθημεν, ὦ τέκνον, ἀδικίας ἀπούσης.¹ The formula means " we have become sinless ", and may be intended to recall Christian teaching. Righteousness is imparted to the initiate, ἀδικία being banished by the annihilation of all evil bodily desires (see p. 27). The absence of the idea of judicial acquittal may be intended to counter the Jewish-Christian view of justification. Perhaps it is a presentation on the mystical plane of the Egyptian idea of justification by means of the judgment of the dead,² according to which the [heart of the] dead man is weighed in the scales in the presence of Osiris, and absolution depends on good works and knowledge, faults being cleared away by magic.³

2. Δικαιόω IN THE SEPTUAGINT, ETC.

Δικαιοῦν in LXX, like its Hebrew equivalents hiṣdiq and ṣaddeq, is a forensic term, always favourable

¹ Reitzenstein, Poim, 343 ; Scott, I, 244. Cf. Reitzenstein, Hell. Myst. 258 ff. ; C. F. G. Heinrici, Die Herm.-Myst. u. d. N.T. (1918), 37. [But C. H. Dodd, The Bible and the Greeks, 1935, pp. 58 f., urges that the reference is to " an ethical change ".]

² Reitzenstein, Hell. Myst. 258, also recalls the Persian Judgment of the Dead, and the rather different Mandaic ideas.

³ The Egyptian equivalent for " he is justified " is " his voice is true ", this being decided by weighing the heart against a feather, after forty-two questions have been answered, concerning behaviour during life. Cf. Erman-Grapow, Wörterb. d. äg. Spr. (1926-31), II, 2 f., 22, 15 ; III, 324 ; J. H. Breasted, Hist. Anc. Eg. (1908), 149.

in meaning (absolve, justify, vindicate). Its object is always personal. Sometimes it is more explicitly forensic than the Hebrew (e.g. Is. xlv, 25). The following uses should be noted.

Active. (*a*) For *hiçdiq* : acquit, pronounce righteous, secure justice—always for those who are righteous (I Kings viii, 32), never for the wicked (Exod. xxiii, 7).

(*b*) For *çaddeq* : show to be righteous (Jer. iii, 11).

(*c*) For *ribh* : get justice done for (Is. i, 17).

(*d*) Rarely for *zikkah* : cleanse (Ps. lxxiii, 13, LXX lxxii, 13). This word is very common in Rabbinic, meaning " pronounce righteous " : God does so on the Day of Atonement, making a man " a new creature " (Pesiqta Rabbati [9th cent.], 40, 169*a*) ; at death (Bab. Erub. 19*a*) ; or at the Last Judgment, on the ground of a preponderance of good works (see pp. 32 f., and cf. Midr. Ps. cxliii, 1, 266*b* ; Targ. Ps. li, 4, Heb. 6).[1] Justification is for the righteous, but evidently there is much uncertainty about it.[2]

(*e*) Rarely also for *shaphaṭ* : judge (I Sam. xii, 7, A ; B has δικάσω).

(*f*) Ps. Sol. never uses the word for justifying man, but only for recognising the justice, etc. of God (ii, 16, etc.). Cf. Luke vii, 29 (see p. 59). The same idea is often expressed in Rabbinic by *hiçdiq* or *çiddaq* (Bab. Ber. 19*a* ; Sifre Deut. 307 on xxxii, 4 ; Sifra Lev. on x, 3).

Passive. (*a*) To be shown to be righteous, to be justified—of God (Ps. li, 4 LXX l, 6 ; cf. Od. Sol. xxxi, 5—of the face of the Christ)[3] or of man (Ps. cxliii, LXX cxlii, 2). In the last example LXX is more

---

[1] Cf. Bill. III, 134 f. ; I, 640 f. ; Schlatter, Matt. 375.
[2] Cf. Bill. III, 134, 186 ff. [3] [See D.A.C., II, 374*b*.]

sweeping than the Hebrew, and influences Paul in
his doctrine of justification (Gal. ii, 16 ; Rom. iii, 20),
though he always adds "by works of the Law".
In Ecclus. the Passive means "to be guiltless", being
in one place the equivalent of *niqqah* Niph. (xxxi,
LXX xxxiv, 5). This usage is frequent in the Greek
translations of Job other than LXX.[1]

(*b*) LXX changes Heb. Active into Passive in Job
xxxiii, 32. [This might be on theological grounds,
because God alone can justify.]

(*c*) The Perfect Passive means "to be righteous"
(Gen. xxxviii, 26 ; Ps. xix, 9 LXX xviii, 10). Cf.
Protevang. Jac. v, 1, where the Part. means "justi-
fied " after the offering of sacrifice.

(*d*) For *zakhah* : to be legally innocent (Mic.
vi, 11).

(*e*) For *çdhq* Hithpa. : to justify oneself (Gen.
xliv, 16 ; cf. Ecclus. vii, 5 and Luke xvi, 15—see
p. 22).

3. Δικαιόω IN THE NEW TESTAMENT

Δικαιοῦν in the N.T. almost always implies the forensic metaphor, as it does in the LXX. It never
has the ordinary Greek sense of holding right and
reasonable.

(*a*) Δικαιωθήτω (Rev. xxii, 11) [2] means "practise
righteousness ". This is exceptional. [Cf. Gen. xliv,
16.]

(*b*) The justification of God (Luke vii, 29), Wisdom

---

[1] At. Tob. vi, 12 f. Sin. the reference is to civil right.

[2] This is the reading of 38, 79, 2020, Vulg. Cl., Ep. Lugd.
(Eus. Hist. Eccl. v, 1, 58), [accepted by Zahn, in Nestle's Einf.,
264 f., and Bebb, Studia Biblica ii, 209 f., but] rejected by
Nestle [and Moffatt ; Charles thinks the ver. an interpolation];
Cyprian, Test. III, 23, has *justiora faciat*.

(Matt. xi, 19 ; Luke vii, 35),[1] Christ (I Tim. iii, 16), means recognition of the divine justice.[2] (The last example says this took place in the sphere of the Spirit, i.e. his Messiahship was confirmed through the resurrection.) The juridical reference is more marked in Rom. iii, 4 (Ps. li, 4).

(c) The self-justification of the lawyer (Luke x, 29) is on a lower plane, though it still echoes the forensic. That of the Pharisees (Luke xvi, 15) comes nearer to the ordinary N.T. usage, suggesting, as it does, the usurping of the divine prerogative of judgment.

(d) Justification in the sense of being saved, with a definitely forensic reference, is found in the Synoptic Gospels, as well as in Paul. The publican (Luke xviii, 14) is judicially absolved on the spot,[3] the only difference from Paul being that there is no reference to the Cross.[4] Matt. xii, 37 speaks only of the Last Judgment (see p. 64).[5]

---

[1] P. de Lagarde, Agathangelos, A.G.G., 35 (1888), 128, suggested that the original Aramaic word, '*bdyh*' or '*bdy*', could be pointed so as to mean either " servants " or " works ". But Luke would hardly have used τέκνα for " servants ". If Schlatter, Matt. 374 f., were right in giving the verb its Hellenistic sense (condemn), we should have to regard this as pre-Lucan, since elsewhere in Luke the verb always has the positive meaning. The preposition ἀπό with " works " means " because of " ; with " children " it means " by " (for ὑπό, cf. Matt. xvi, 21 ; James i, 13) ; it is unnecessary to translate it " far from " (Dibelius, Joh. d. Täufer (1911), 19), or " in the presence of " (Wellhausen, Matt. (1904), 55, for Aram. *min qᵒdham*). The " works " denote not only the asceticism of the messengers, but the whole of their life.

[2] Cf. Bill. I, 604. See p. 58 for Ps. Sol. and Rabbinic. Euthymius ad loc. (M.P.G. cxxix, 357c) : δικαία καὶ ἀνέγκλητος ἐλογίσθη. Similarly, Jos. (Schlatter, Matt. 375 f.).

[3] Bill. II, 247 f.

[4] For the text, see Nestle. Παρ' ἐκεῖνον is exclusive and not comparative. Cf. II Esdr. xii, 7 : *prae multis*.

[5] Rabbinic par. in Schlatter, Matt. 412.

(e) Paul's doctrine of justification requires fuller treatment.

(i) The forensic idea is here clear and indisputable ; the opposite of δικαιοῦν is κατακρίνειν (Rom. viii, 34). What Paul has in mind is not the infusion of a moral quality, *justum efficere* in the sense of creating a life of righteousness, but the absolution and acquittal of the wicked, when he becomes a believer, on the ground of God's justifying action in the death and resurrection of Christ. This is certainly an act of mercy, not a judicial award according to works ; but it can still be called forensic, because on the Cross as ἱλαστήριον [Rom. iii, 25] all sin is finally judged in our representative.[1] Paul's originality lies in his use of δικαιοῦσθαι to denote that which God does as saviour now—leaving open the question of the relation of this to the Last Judgment, in which he still believes (see pp. 50 f.). The most thorough-going presentation of the matter is at Rom. iv, 5 ff., where Abraham is said to believe on "him that justifieth the ungodly" —in plain contradiction of the civil justice which justifies the righteous (cf. p. 58) ; the contrast is obviously intentional between an incomprehensible act of grace and conventional legality. Paul's "justification" is the effectual pronouncement of absolution now by the judge as saviour. It is neither absolutely objective in the Cross nor absolutely subjective in the experience of the believer ; its objectivity is relative—effectual in the Cross and realised in faith (see pp. 47-49). It is sometimes denied that the

[1] J. T. Beck, Rom. (1884), 217-223, limits the forensic references to the Last Judgment, as in O.T. and Rom. ii, 13, rejecting the judicial aspect of the Cross (222), where God is Father but not Judge. But this is contradicted by Paul's usage ; he loves to clothe God's act of forgiveness in forensic imagery. [On ἱλαστήριον see C. H. Dodd, Romans (1932), 54 f. and J.T.S. XXXII, 352-360.]

judicial act belongs to the present course of the religious life and can only mean the Last Judgment. This would mean translating δικαιωθῆναι (Gal. ii, 16 f.) " become righteous in the sight of God " ; justification would mean that the sinner receives from God the status of a righteous man.[1] This is a legitimate interpretation, but it should be added that the new status is the result of a judicial pronouncement.

It may be admitted that the forensic reference is not always made explicit by stressing the judicial act. Thus οἵτινες ἐν νόμῳ δικαιοῦσθε (Gal. v, 4) means simply " ye who fundamentally want to be righteous through the Law ". But the whole argument is haunted by the judicial idea, which again and again receives impressive formulation : e.g. Gal. iii, 11 ; cf. Rom. iii, 20 (from Ps. cxliii, LXX cxlii, 2). All becomes obscure unless the main point is firmly held, viz., that the forensic act is effectual in the act of salvation, and is bound up with it. Only so can the value of the new doctrine be seen, in comparison with the Rabbinical view of justification, which postpones the judicial act until the Last Judgment. On the other hand, the forensic objectivity of the saving act is endangered when supreme importance is attached to the experience of the believer.

(ii) Paul's use of the verb δικαιοῦσθαι throws light on the problem of experience, to which reference has just been made. The present immediacy of justification is typically represented by a verbal " Present " at Gal. iii, 8, 11, cf. ii, 16 and iii, 24 ; Rom. iii, 24, 26, 28, cf. Acts xiii, 39. " Past " forms are just as important for our purpose (see p. 63, n. 3), because they treat being justified as something which happens at a given time, as an event. But to concentrate

---

[1] Zahn, Gal., 124 f. He agrees with Beck (see preceding note).

exclusively on the experiential aspect, in opposition
to the view that δικαιοῦσθαι means the act of universal
salvation perfected in the death of Christ,[1] is to
overlook the fact that this is the very event which
makes salvation continually present in actuality, and
thereby makes the personal attitude possible. The
latter is of course indispensable. Wherever justification is being discussed, faith must be included.[2]
It is impossible to separate justification once for all in
the Cross from personal justification in faith (see p. 48).
The locale of justification is the saving act (Rom. v, 9).
The historic Cross is the ground of salvation now.
"Being justified by faith" (Rom. v, 1) is the consequence of "our justification" (iv, 25). What this
means cannot be truly or adequately stated in a formula
which is limited to the experiential aspect of the
matter ; the Cross and its work in the soul are too
closely bound up together ; it is impossible to con-
template the one without the other. The Past form
of the verb certainly expresses the completion of the
act of granting pardon.[3] But the addition of the
word "faith" (ἐκ πίστεως : Gal. iii, 8, 11, 24 ; Rom.
iii, 30 ; v, 1 ; or διὰ πίστεως : Gal. ii, 16) should
correct any tendency towards isolating the mere experience, since it necessarily implies a connexion with

[1] Zahn, Rom. 179 f., 209 n.17, 258.

[2] Gal. ii, 16 (twice) ; iii, 8, 11, 24 ; Rom. iii, 28, 30 ; iv, 5 ;
v, 1.

[3] See I Cor. vi, 11 ; Rom. iv, 2 ; v, 1, 9 ; Tit. iii, 7. The
genuine Paulinism of the last is questioned by Dibelius *ad loc.*,
but justification is associated with baptism here as at 1 Cor.
vi, 11 (see p. 47), and the connexion with inheritance and the
Spirit is thoroughly Pauline. Joh. Weiss's reference to Corp.
Herm. XIII, 9 (see p. 57) in explanation of I Cor. vi, 11 is
misleading, and is expressly disputed by Reitzenstein (Hell.
Myst. 259) ; he overlooks both Paul's dependence on the O.T.
and his view of the Christian's continual warfare with the flesh.
Cf. Gal. ii, 17 ; Phil. iii, 9.

the saving event. The tense of the verb in Rom. viii, 30 does not mean that justification is past and gone ; [1] the string of Aorists signifies that God's eternal purpose has now been fulfilled. This leads to the decisive point in connexion with the time-process : the division between past and present is brought to an end, so to speak, by the eternal quality of the event which justifies and saves. That event remains a continuing present.

(iii) The idea of justification according to works at the Last Judgment finds expression at I Cor. iv, 4 (cf. Matt. xii, 37) : judicial approval and absolution in the full sense can only be given when a man's whole life is under review. That is evidently a different use of the term from the one which we have been considering. It shows that Paul continued to associate justification with the Last Judgment. The question whether he expresses this idea elsewhere cannot be settled by reference to cases in which he employs Future forms of the verb δικαιόω. The example in Gal. ii, 16 ; Rom. iii, 20 (see pp. 49-51) is not decisive, because the word occurs in a quotation (see p. 62), but it may be presumed that Jews would take it as pointing to the Last Judgment (see pp. 32 f.). The context of Rom. ii, 13 shows that it cannot be regarded as a complete statement of Christian belief, though it maintains an abiding principle of divine judgment ; it is one of a series of premises in an extended argument. The time-process is implied in Rom. iii, 30 ; v, 19 ; viii, 33 ; the words are both logical [2] and eschatological : the divine absolution of sins, made effectual in the Cross and accepted by faith here and now, is expected to reach its final consummation in acquittal at the Last Judgment (see pp. 49-51).

---

[1] Zahn, Rom. 209 (" vergangener ").
[2] Lipsius, Zahn, Kühl, on Rom. v, 19.

Elsewhere Paul speaks of hope as the guarantee of present redemption (Rom. viii, 24).

(iv) The note of redemption is struck when the preposition ἀπό is used with the verb δικαιωθῆναι (cf. Ecclus. xxvi, 29 ; Test. Sim. vi, 1). This appears in the speech attributed to Paul in Acts xiii, where vv. 38 f. refer to forensic acquittal. (To say that the words imply the admission of a partial justification through the Law is an example of *Tendenz* criticism.[1]) What looks like an erratic boulder is found at Rom. vi, 7 : " He that hath died is justified from sin ". But this is a Rabbinical cliché, found, e.g., at Sifre Numb. 112 on xv, 31 (*kol hammethim bammithah mithkappᵉrim*) and implied in the doctrine of atonement through martyrdom.[2] Paul applies the saying to the Christian who has died with Christ, and is thus freed from his bondage to sin. The real point of his argument is conformity, through faith, with Christ's death, which holds the secret of justification. Comparison with the Rabbinic parallel is valuable as showing how Paul brought justification and atonement together ; it adds confirmation to the doctrine that justification rests on " propitiation " (ἱλαστήριον).[3]

[1] As in F. Overbeck, Kurze Erkl. der Ap. gesch. (1870), following Baur, and Preuschen, Ap. gesch. (1912). [" Critics advocate two interpretations : (i) the ὧν οὐκ ἠδυνήθητε, etc. means that by the Law of Moses acquittal of some things was possible, but not of others, and Paul was announcing this possible method of going beyond what the Law could do ; (ii) ὧν, etc., merely qualify πάντων, ' forgiveness for everything—which the Law never offered '. The former view is possible, but the latter seems more natural " (K. Lake and H. J. Cadbury, The Beginnings of Christianity, 1933, I, iv, 157).]

[2] First proved by K. G. Kuhn, Rom. vi, 7, Z.N.W., 30 (1931), 305 ff., to have been current in the first century A.D. See Horovitz (1917), 121, 13.

[3] It also makes it unnecessary to refer to the magical and mystical ideas of Corp. Herm. XIII, 9 (Reitzenstein, 259 f.). [For ἱλαστήριον see p. 61 n.]

(*f*) James uses the formula, "justified by works", three times [ii, 14 ff.], meaning justification here and now, and supports the doctrine with the examples of Abraham and Rahab. Paul denies this in the case of Abraham (Rom. iv, 2), but James is fighting against a form of orthodox monotheism that is ethically lifeless, and insists that faith without works cannot achieve justification (see p. 39). The problem of faith and works, and the terminology of the discussion, remind us of Paul, but there is no need to think that they come from him, or that this is a polemic against pseudo-paulinism or a misunderstanding of Paul. The similarity is due to the fact that both writers were familiar with the Rabbinical tradition. What is noteworthy is their agreement with the general view of the early Church that true faith is not an excuse for idleness, but a stimulus to work (see p. 40).

4. Δικαίωμα [1]

(*a*) Outside the New Testament this verbal noun, with the termination signifying result, has five meanings.

(i) Legal argument, plea, claim (Thuc. I, xli, 1 ; II Sam. xix, 28 LXX ; Jer. xi, 20 ; Jos. Ant. xix, 285 ; Jos. Ap. ii, 37 ; and often in Papyri).

(ii) Written evidence, deeds, minutes, etc., specially those in favour of the defence (Aristot., Fragm. p. 427

---

[1] See Cremer-Kögel ; Moulton-Milligan ; Zahn Rom., 278 f. ; Sickenberger Rom., 4th ed., 216 ; Rohr Heb., 4th ed., 40. Definitions : Aristot., Rhet. I, xiii, 1373*b*, 20 ff. ; Eth. Nic. V, x, 1135*a*, 9-14 ; Pseudo-Justin, Quaest. et Resp. ad Orth., III, ii, 138*c* (Otto) ; Origen Selecta in Ps. xviii (M.P.G. xii, 1244*c*).

Rose ; [1] Jos. Ant. xvii, 228 ; specially frequent in Papyri).[2]

(iii) Legal statute, ordinance, demand (often in LXX for *ḥoq*, *ḥuqqah*, Gen. xxvi, 5, etc. ; *mishpaṭ*, Exod. xxi, 1, etc. ; rarely for *miçwah*, Deut. xxx, 16 ; also in Philo, Josephus and Apostolic Fathers, the latter sometimes applying it to the Gospel, under the influence of the O.T. use of *çᵉdhaqah* (see p. 30)).

(iv) Judgment, sentence, condemnation (Plato Leg. IX, 864*e* ; I Kings iii, 28 ; viii, 45, 59 LXX). In Biblical usage it begins to mean a favourable verdict —like the verb.

(v) Right action, setting right, making good—the opposite of ἀδίκημα (Aristot. Rhet. I, iii, 1359*a*, 24 f. ; Eth. Nic. V, x, 1135 a 9-14 ; Theodoret on Ps. cxix (cxviii), 2 : νόμον καλεῖ . . . δικαιώματα, ὡς δικαιοῦν τὸν κατορθοῦντα δυνάμενον [3] ; Bar. ii, 29 : τὰ δικαιώματα τῶν πατέρων ἡμῶν).

(*b*) Three meanings of δικαίωμα are found in N.T.

(i) Most commonly it stands for " ordinance ", illustrating the close adherence of N.T. to LXX, as in Luke i, 6 (see iii above). Paul, however, uses the word in the Singular, in a way which shows that he has gone deeper than LXX, and has the underlying principle in mind. Apart from Prov. viii, 20 and xix, 28 (25), LXX only means a particular ordinance by δικαίωμα, and usually has the Plural. Paul is concerned to show that the heathen also recognise a uniform moral order, according to which, by God's

---

[1] Cf. op. cit. 386 f. and ref. in Harpocration, Lexicon in Decem Oratores Atticos (Dindorf, 1853), s.v. δρυμός.

[2] Cf. A.P.F. VI, 1 (1913), 36 ; Moulton-Milligan and Preisigke s.v.—Dikaiomata, Auszüge aus alexandrin. Gesetzen u. Verordnungen, herausg. von der Graeca Halensis (1913), 26.

[3] Suidas, s.v., δικαιώματα.

decree, death is the penalty for perversion of worship and social corruption (Rom. i, 32, where the word may have the force of " condemnation "—see p. 67, iv). There is a significant difference when the Plural occurs at Rom. ii, 26. Then again, it is not accidental that the Singular is found at Rom. viii, 4 [A.V. righteousness ; R.V. ordinance ; R.V.m. require-ment ; Tyndale, the rightewesnes requyred of the law ; Moffatt misses the point with " requirements "], where Paul is speaking of the fulfilment of the Law as a whole by walking according to the Spirit. There is no reference to the underlying principle at Heb. ix, 1, 10, where the Plural has the same force as in LXX.

(ii) Another meaning of δικαίωμα in the N.T. is " righteous act ". In this sense it is attributed to God (Rev. xv, 4, referring to his judgments, cf. Rom. i, 32 and see iv and v above, p. 67) ; to the saints, the members of the Church (Rev. xix, 8) ; and to Christ. The last requires fuller discussion.

Whereas in Rom. v, 16 (see p. 70) it is contrasted with κατάκριμα, condemnation, in ver. 18 its op-posite is παράπτωμα, trespass (ruin as result), and this is explained by the paraphrase in ver. 19, where the contrast is between obedience and disobedience. " One " in ver. 18 must be read as masculine, as it is in the other ten cases of its occurrence in vv. 12-19, referring to Adam and Christ respectively : " As one man's trespass issued in doom for all, so one man's act of redress issued in acquittal and life for all " [Moffatt].[1] This harmonises with what Paul says elsewhere, viz., that the Christ, put under the Law (Gal. iv, 4), not only knew no sin (II Cor. v, 21) in the sense of per-

---

[1] So e.g., Hofmann, Zahn, Lietzmann. It is taken as neuter by Althaus, N.T. Deutsch [and by Sanday and Headlam].

sonal wrong-doing, but also, positively, was obedient even unto death (Phil. ii, 8). All that is included in the single formula which sums up the whole of his life as δικαίωμα, perfect realisation of the righteous will of God (cf. Matt. iii, 15 ; see p. 35).[1]

The other interpretation, which renders δικαίωμα "pronouncement of justification",[2] though consistent with the rendering of the word in the rest of this passage, breaks down on the fact that it presents no true parallel to παράπτωμα, and this is absolutely necessary. It also involves taking ἑνός as neuter [agreeing with δικαιώματος], for the pronouncement of justification is nowhere else by Paul ascribed to Christ.[3] But the most serious difficulty lies in the last three words of the verse : εἰς δικαίωσιν ζωῆς. If δικαίωμα means the sentence of justification, we are compelled to think that Paul here distinguishes between the objective sentence and the individual justification.[4] But there is no support for this in any of the apostle's other utterances on the subject (see pp. 47 and 62 ff.) ; God's justifying action (which on this view would have to be the meaning of δικαίωμα in ver. 18) is always represented as being actualised in the faith of the believer.

[1] Cf. Zahn on Rom. v, 18. The parallels given above preclude limitation to the Cross, though its centrality is thoroughly Pauline ; cf. Phil. ii, 8, where, however, obedience is " even unto ", not " only in " death.

[2] B. Weiss, Godet, Schlatter, Kühl, the last preferring " legal arrangement " (Rechtsordnung)—but this is too formal.

[3] Consequently K. Barth suggests " the absolution made known in the one ", but this is not a precise rendering.

[4] Godet and Lipsius (δικαίωσις, the actual pronouncement, δικαίωμα, its content). But Rom. v, 16, the only place where Paul unquestionably uses δικαίωμα for the pronouncement, shows, by the contrast with κατάκριμα, that it is immediately realised in the fullness of its working power.

(iii) The pronouncement of justification[1] is what δικαίωμα means in Rom. v, 16, where it is called a free gift and contrasted with condemnation. This is practically the same as δικαίωσις, the act of justification. A comparison of the use of the two words shows how easily the meaning fluctuates between punishment, claim, demand, ordinance, and when δικαίωμα means "righteous act" it includes elements of redress and reparation, which bring it very close to vindication (δικαίωσις ; see p. 71, ii). No doubt the exceptional use of δικαίωμα in Rom. v, 16 is partly to be explained on the ground of style, as being due to the presence in the same verse of 5 (6) other words ending in -μα.[2] Paul thus agrees here with the LXX usage (see p. 67, iv and cf. pp. 29 and 57).

The fact that δικαίωμα has so many different shades of meaning explains what is at first sight surprising—the use of the word in two senses in neighbouring verses (Rom. v, 16, 18) ; there is no reason to object to this, insisting on uniformity, since in each case the contrasted word makes the sense perfectly clear, and Paul elsewhere uses other connotations of this comprehensive term (Rom. i, 32 ; ii, 26 ; viii, 4).

5. Δικαίωσις

(a) General Greek literature employs this word to indicate five different aspects of putting into action that which is δίκαιον (right). It only occurs rarely, and is not found in Polybius, Philo,[3] Epictetus, or in any Papyrus or Inscription.

---

[1] Fritzsche, Meyer, Philippi, Godet, Barth, etc. Beck's "righteous standing" is impossible.

[2] Lietzmann, Rom. 60 ; Preuschen-Bauer, 308.

[3] The reading δικαίωσις for δεξίωσις (Deus. Imm. 79) makes no sense.

(i) The commonest meaning is condemnation, punishment (Thuc. VIII, lxvi, 2 ; [1] Jos. Ant. xviii, 14).

(ii) Judicial vindication and justification (Lysias ix, 8).[2] Paul uses the word in this sense. It also means self-vindication, justification of action taken in daily life (Plut., De Virt. Mor. 9 (II, 449b)).

(iii) Claim to real or apparent right (Thuc. I, cxli, 1).

(iv) Arbitrary decision (Thuc. III, lxxxii, 4). See p. 56 (b).

(v) Right (Plut., De Fort. 5 (ii, 99c) ; Lev. iv, 22 LXX for mishpaṭ).

Comparable expressions in Rabbinic are "pronouncement of judgment unto life" and "sentence of death" ('eyppophṣiṣ shel ḥayyim and 'eyppophṣiṣ shellahem leʿmithah—Greek ἀπόφασις).[3] These are opposed to each other in Jer. Rosh Hash. 57a, 49.[4] Cf. beshalom (in peace), ib. 59c, 51,[5] and bedhimmuṣ (in acquittal [Latin dimissus]), Pesiqt. 155b,[6] both as the result of the divine judgment.

(b) Δικαίωσις is only found twice in N.T., Rom. iv, 25 ; v, 18, and means the act of justification through God's absolving judgment, which affects the whole of man's religious existence.

---

[1] Not equivalent to δικαιολογία, ἀπολογία (Cremer-Kögel, 332), but to κόλασις, as the scholiast has it (Hirzel, 138 ; cf. Liddell and Scott, s.v. ; Harpocration, s.v.).

[2] Harpocration, s.v.

[3] Cf. S. Krauss, Gr. u. lat. Lehnwörter in Talm. u. Midr. II (1899), 101 f.   [4] Bill. III, 230 f.   [5] Ib. 217 f.

[6] Ib. 218. [Cf. L. N. Dembitz, Acquittal in Talmudic Law, in J.E. : "Death-sentences were rare " ; Makkoth i, 10 : "A Sanhedrin that puts one man to death in a week of years is called bloody. Rabbi Eliezer ben Azariah says, Or one in even seventy years. Rabbi Tarfon and Rabbi Aqiba say, Had we been in the Sanhedrin none would ever have been put to death. Rabban Simeon ben Gamaliel says, They would even have multiplied the shedders of blood in Israel."]

Rom. iv, 25 says Christ " was delivered up for our trespasses, and was raised for our justification ", the preposition indicating cause in the first clause and purpose in the second. To take the second διά also as causal,[1] and translate, " because we have been justified ", leaves out of account the Abraham parallel, in which justification is the result of faith in God who quickeneth the dead [ver. 17]. It is rather that justification is brought about through the resurrection, which is so impressively connected with the faith of Abraham. It has been suggested [2] that the clause means that the resurrection is necessary for the realisation of justification, since it first produces faith, which needs as its object more than one who has merely died. In reply to this it may be said that Paul does not construct his arguments in this fashion ; he prefers to say " much more " (Rom. v, 9) or " rather " (viii, 34). Christ's death and resurrection are inseparable in the N.T. ; the Crucified is what he is, only because he rose again ; and so Paul can say both that we are justified through his death, and that he was raised for our justification. Both the matter itself and the form in which it is stated are properly defined as synthetic parallelism.[3] One single idea is presented here in parallel expressions, while the reference to Abraham lays special emphasis on " was raised ".

Rom. v, 18 ends with the words, " to justification of life ", reiterating that God's pronouncement of justification is realised through the absolution of the believer. Justification and life are correlative, the former having perfect life as its content and making a present of it to the believer, so that it goes on working

[1] Lipsius, Rom., 2nd ed. (1892), 120.
[2] Zahn, Rom. 241 ; Kühl, Rom. 155 ff.
[3] J. Weiss, Beitr. zu paul. Rhet. (1897), 171.

in him eternally and is his final goal, just as condemnation is the end and outcome of transgression.
It is clear, from vv. 17 and 21, that " life " must be
understood eschatologically. But that it begins here
and now in him who is absolved, is proved, apart
from other arguments, by the use which Paul makes
of the term, " life ", in other places (Rom. vi, 4 ;
viii, 2, 6, 10). The phrase, "justification of life ",
therefore, like " be made righteous " in ver. 19,
confirms the observation that for Paul justification
looks forward to the perfecting through which alone
it receives its ideal (τέλος) and its final manifestation
(see pp. 49 ff. and 64).

6. Δικαιοκρισία only occurs once, in the eschatological setting of Rom. ii, 5. God's righteousness as
judge is contrasted with the moralising judgment of
those who condemn evil and yet do it themselves ;
" the judgment of God is according to truth " (ver. 2).
Cf. II Thess. i, 5, where the words " righteous " and
" judgment " are written separately, and the reference
is to the justice of the divine awards to persecutor and
persecuted respectively.

INDEX OF WORDS AND REFERENCES

(Scripture references are to the English Bible)